THE FIRST 25 YEARS

Written by
Jake Black, Jon Hill, and Dean Miller

CONTENTS

1993... 6

1994... 12

1995... 18

1996... 24

1997... 30

1998... 36

1999... 44

2000... 52

2001... 58

2002... 66

2003... 74

2004... 84

2005... 90

2006... 98

2007... 106

2008... 112

2009... 122

2010... 130

2011... 138

2012... 146

2013... 154

2014... 164

2015... 170

2016... 176

2017... 184

2018... 192

Glossary.................................... 196

Index... 198

Acknowledgements.................... 200

January 4, 1999: Mankind celebrates his
first WWE Championship win against
The Rock with D-Generation X members
Billy Gunn, Shawn Michaels, and X-Pac.

February 1, 1993: The Manhattan Center in New York hosts an early episode of *RAW*. Its Grand Ballroom held 1,500 excited members of the WWE Universe.

August 21, 2017: The WWE Universe watches the action unfold in a packed Barclays Center in Brooklyn, New York. Today, *RAW* fills a major arena in a different city each week.

FOREWORD

Standing inside the sold-out Manhattan Center on January 11, 1993, it's likely no one—WWE performers, staff, even those in the audience—could have envisioned the depth and luster of the legacy forged by three simple letters. "*RAW*" has given a generation of viewers a reason to look forward to Mondays for a quarter of a century.

Evolving into a live, weekly television juggernaut with nearly 1,300 episodes to date, *Monday Night RAW* represents a milestone not just in WWE history, but truly all of entertainment.

Through many eras and trends in both WWE and media, our top-rated cable mainstay has flourished as an experience that's more than a television program. It's a living, breathing performance that emanates from an arena filled with passionate spectators and resonates with millions watching around the world.

The inaugural *RAW* showcased larger than life characters like Undertaker and Shawn Michaels, and the show became the definitive platform for stars to emerge and ascend. The Rock, Stone Cold Steve Austin, Triple H, Trish Stratus, John Cena, Brock Lesnar, Randy Orton, Roman Reigns, Charlotte Flair, Sasha Banks—the list quite literally goes on, as does the list of unforgettable Monday night moments. Together, these Superstars, with the world's best production team, developed the perfect breed of drama, comedy, occasional romance and—of course—unparalleled action that created the identity of *RAW*.

The only greater satisfaction than reflecting on how far we've come is looking toward what lies ahead for the longest-running, weekly, episodic program in television history.

Vince McMahon

1993

JANUARY 11, 1993 saw WWE debut their new flagship show, *Monday Night RAW*—replacing the iconic *Prime Time Wrestling*. In true WWE fashion, the company wanted to move on from the past, and this show was designed to have an edgier, more stripped-down feel. Filmed at the Manhattan Center in WWE's spiritual home of New York, the show looked different, was different, and proved an instant hit. Now the longest-running episodic show on network television, *RAW* has transcended its humble beginnings to become a genuine TV juggernaut, spanning the country and gracing vast venues each week. WWE *RAW* introduced new stars, in what would prove to be a move toward the Attitude Era. As a result, *RAW* proved compulsive viewing, with a mix of established names, such as "Macho Man" Randy Savage, mixing with a new breed of WWE Superstars, like Razor Ramon and the 1-2-3 Kid.

January 25: With both Superstars' WWE careers on the line, Ric Flair attempts to wear down Mr. Perfect with a strength-sapping sleeper hold. Mr. Perfect would recover and win this Loser Leaves WWE Match.

The loser leaves

January 25: This episode saw legendary "Nature Boy" Ric Flair lose to his former ally Mr. Perfect in a Loser Leaves WWE Match. In an epic, 25-minute encounter, Mr. Perfect pinned Flair, bringing his initial run with WWE to an end. Flair, who returned to WCW following the loss, wouldn't be seen again in WWE programming until the fall of 2001. The double Hall of Famer would later return to *RAW*, not just as a competitor, but also as co-owner in his rivalry with Mr. McMahon.

Hulk Hogan's announcement

February 22: Hulk Hogan wouldn't become a fixture on *RAW* until the early 2000s. However, he made a rare appearance here in a controversial interview with Mr. McMahon, where he announced that he'd be teaming with Brutus "The Barber" Beefcake, alongside Jimmy Hart, to take on Money Inc. at *WrestleMania IX*. Hogan would shockingly go on to win his fifth WWE Championship at the event, following a surprise, totally unscheduled match with the mighty Yokozuna.

Bobby barred

January 11: The first episode of *Monday Night RAW* featured some hilarious cameos from Bobby "The Brain" Heenan. With an announcing team consisting of Mr. McMahon, the Macho Man Randy Savage, and Rob Bartlett in residence, it was left to Heenan to try and gain entry into the Manhattan Centre in a variety of disguises. The Brain even resorted to dressing as an elderly woman in his effort to gain access to the sold-out venue. Elsewhere Shawn Michaels retained his Intercontinental Championship against Max Moon and Undertaker defeated Damien Demento.

Tatanka's winning streak

March 8: Tatanka made short work of his opponent, Phil Apollo, continuing his impressive winning streak. The bout featured his upcoming opponent at *WrestleMania IX*, Shawn Michaels, on the phone with the announcing team lambasting Tatanka, to the annoyance of Mr. McMahon. This victory helped Tatanka maintain his momentum leading up to his Intercontinental Championship Match with Michaels, which he would win via a countout, meaning that Michaels retained the gold. Tatanka's undefeated streak continued until October, when he lost to Ludvig Borga.

Elsewhere in WWE

April 4: For the first—and only—time, *WrestleMania* was held at Las Vegas' world-famous Caesar's Palace. The event had a Roman theme, with both Julius Caesar and Cleopatra adding to the grandeur. The WWE announcers donned togas and Bobby "The Brain" Heenan entered the arena riding backward on a camel.

April 12: Luna Vachon struck fear into the hearts of male and female members of the WWE locker room alike. However, she meets her match when she takes on the equally tough Sensational Sherri.

Luna Vachon's Sensational clash

April 12: On this date, *RAW* went extreme for a segment when a fight broke out between legendary female Superstar Sensational Sherri Martel and Luna Vachon. This was a vicious brawl, with hair, clothing, and fists flying. Fortunately both parties were separated before either got badly hurt.

April 19: Giant Gonzales applies a chokehold to L.A. Gore. Gonzales used his phenomenal size to intimidate and overpower opponents.

Towering over the opposition

April 19: While WWE has seen some notable giants, none have stood as tall as Giant Gonzales. At 8ft (2.43m) tall, the Argentinian behemoth even towered above Undertaker in a gargantuan face-off. Despite his size, Gonzales never got a taste of WWE gold, unlike fellow giants such as Big Show and the legendary Andre the Giant. Ultimately, Gonzales had a short WWE career, leaving the company in the summer of 1993.

The same episode of *RAW* saw Bret "Hit Man" Hart call out Hulk Hogan. This would have been a dream encounter, showcasing the face of the 1980s WWE boom period against the spearhead of the new generation. Unfortunately, fans wouldn't get to see a Hart-Hogan clash until an episode of *WCW Monday Nitro* five years later in 1998, and the two would never meet in a WWE ring.

1993

Parking lot brawl

May 10: "Mr. Perfect" Curt Hennig and Shawn Michaels are perhaps two of the most gifted technical Superstars of all time. All this counted for nothing during this episode when, several years before the word "hardcore" became part of WWE vocabulary, the two brawled in the streets. At one point, Mr. Perfect hurled Michaels on top of a parked car, smashing its windshield. Fortunately, the two combatants were then separated by WWE officials before they could do any more damage.

May 10: Decked in street clothes, Mr. Perfect attempts to gain advantage over Shawn Michaels in their brutal parking lot brawl.

Surprise challengers

May 17: Things didn't get better for Michaels on the following episode of *RAW* when he was shocked by his former tag team partner Marty Jannetty. The cocksure Michaels claimed he would defend his Intercontinental Title against anyone and was aghast when his former Rockers teammate emerged from the crowd, removed his hood, and challenged him to a Championship match. Jannetty, with the help of Mr. Perfect, defeated Michaels to win his first and only Intercontinental Title.

The same episode saw one of the greatest upsets in WWE history when the rookie 1-2-3 Kid defeated Razor "The Bad Guy" Ramon. Ramon had a huge height and weight advantage, but "The Kid's" guile and fighting spirit saw him triumph in a truly memorable *RAW* moment. The embarrassed Ramon offered $10,000 on the result not happening again. Unfortunately for "The Bad Guy", the 1-2-3 Kid swiped his bag of money when they next faced off!

INTRODUCING...

"Big Daddy Cool" Diesel

June 7: Diesel began his WWE career as the bodyguard to Shawn Michaels on *RAW*. He would become a multi-WWE Champion, before departing for WCW in 1996. As part of the legendary New World Order (nWo) stable under his real name, Kevin Nash, he helped to spark the Monday Night Wars, returning to WWE in 2002. In 2015, Diesel was inducted into the WWE Hall of Fame by none other than Shawn Michaels.

Despite being introduced into WWE by Shawn Michaels, it was "Big Daddy Cool" Diesel who would be the first of the pair to be crowned WWE Champion.

May 17: The high-flying 1-2-3 Kid performs a typically spectacular maneuver against Razor Ramon.

July 19: Lex Luger greets fans on his Lex Express bus tour, which helped cement his place as a WWE hero.

August 2: One of the greatest managers of all time, Jim Cornette guided legends such as Owen Hart and Vader, as well as Yokozuna.

"The United States of America truly is the land of opportunity."

Lex Luger on his Lex Express tour (July 19, 1993)

The Lex Express

July 19: When Lex Luger slammed the 589lbs (267kg) Yokozuna on board the USS *Intrepid* on the 4th of July, he became an instant American hero. Fans who once reviled him as "The Narcissist" chanted his name across the country. Luger began his Lex Express tour on *RAW* and used it to connect with fans across the country, traveling from coast to coast in preparation for his bid to win the WWE Championship at *SummerSlam*.

Jim Cornette cracks wise

August 2: The "Louisville Lip," Jim Cornette, made quite a splash in his opening weeks on *RAW*. After Bobby Heenan introduced him as a new manager to the stunned WWE Universe, it only took a week for him to align himself to the mighty WWE Champion, Yokozuna. In his role as Yokozuna's "American spokesman," Cornette added luster to the formidable champion and his ally, manager Mr. Fuji, in their battle against Lex Luger.

Quebec Province Rules

September 13: The team of Jacques and Pierre owed a debt of gratitude to their manager, Johnny Polo, when they claimed the WWE World Tag Team Championships in a surprise victory over the Steiner Brothers. Capitalizing on the match's "Quebec Province Rules," whereby a disqualification would see the Titles change hands, the dastardly Polo lured Rick Steiner into swinging a hockey stick—which cost both Rick and his brother their Titles.

The Bad Guy cometh

October 11: With Intercontinental Champion Shawn Michaels suspended, Razor Ramon seized his chance. After finishing in the final two of an Intercontinental Championship Battle Royal the previous week, Ramon faced fellow survivor Rick Martel for the Title. Martel's experience and technical prowess were more than matched by Ramon's size and power. "The Bad Guy" Ramon duly defeated "The Model" Martel to win his first ever WWE gold.

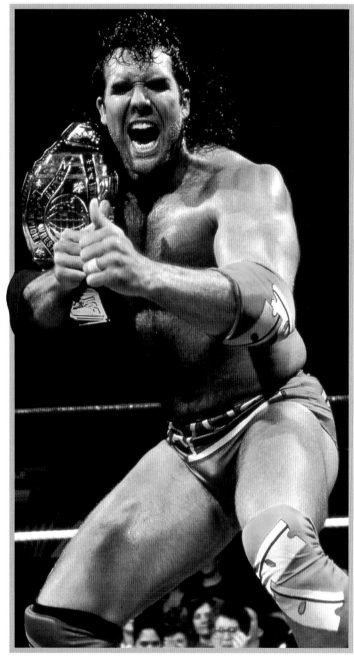

October 11: "The Bad Guy" Razor Ramon celebrates the first of his four WWE Intercontinental Championships following his victory over Rick Martel.

Crush turns on "Macho Man"

October 18: The "Macho Man" Randy Savage watched in horror as his ex-best friend and former mentee, Crush, entered the ring and proceeded to verbally destroy his former mentor. Blaming Savage for not having his back in an encounter with Yokozuna, Crush put this down to Savage being jealous that the apprentice was outshining his master. The big Hawaiian would then brutally attack Savage and align himself with Mr. Fuji and Yokozuna.

Two champions

November 15: Mr. McMahon announced that Shawn Michaels had been reinstated in WWE, sparking an astonishing chain of events. Michaels, who had been stripped of the Intercontinental Title, claimed that he had never lost the Championship. This set him on a collision course with the present champion, Razor Ramon. Differences were settled in an unforgettable Ladder Match at *WrestleMania X* in Madison Square Garden. Ramon defeated Michaels to become the undisputed Champion.

Brotherly hate

November 22: The following week saw the stage set for a brotherly showdown. Owen Hart was so certain that his sibling Bret was about to defeat the defending champion, Yokozuna, and win the title, that he jumped into the ring and started celebrating. When Owen hit Yokozuna's manager, Mr. Fuji, with a bucket, the referee awarded the match to Yokozuna. Owen would eventually turn on his brother at *Royal Rumble 1994*, leading to their historic Brother vs. Brother Match at *WrestleMania X*.

Bobby "The Brain" Heenan fired

December 6: To many, Bobby "The Brain" Heenan is not just the greatest manager in WWE history but also the greatest announcer. Heenan began his WWE career in 1984 and took part in many historic moments, including managing Andre the Giant in his iconic match against Hulk Hogan at *WrestleMania III*. This *RAW* episode saw him fired from WWE and thrown out of the building by his former co-commentator and great friend Gorilla Monsoon.

Pedal to the metal

December 20: Not all WWE Superstars find instant success. Bob Holly is a prime example. Holly made his debut in this *RAW* episode as "Sparky" Plugg— a homage to his love of motor racing. It wouldn't be until the Attitude Era hit that Holly would emerge as a bona fide Superstar and become a multi-time WWE Hardcore and Tag Team Champion. Holly is in good company; both Triple H, formerly a Greenwich snob, and Stone Cold Steve Austin, who debuted as "The Ring Master," shrugged off slow starts to become legendary Superstars.

October 18: Crush uses his freakish strength to gorilla press "Macho Man" Randy Savage. The Hawaiian shocked the crowd by turning on his former friend.

Booger's food fun

November 1: This episode opened with an interview between Bobby Heenan and the rotund Bastion Booger, who was surrounded by plates of raw food. Heenan implored Booger to concentrate on his upcoming match with Razor Ramon. Booger just said that he would eat him, too, and cracked an egg over his own head. In the ensuing hard-fought match, Ramon managed to roll Booger over to secure the pinfall.

December 20: Bob Holly in his "Sparky" Plugg ring wear. He later became Hardcore Holly and won multiple WWE Championships.

1994

1994 SAW THE EMERGENCE of many of WWE's "New Generation," with the likes of Bret "Hit Man" Hart, Shawn Michaels, Diesel, and Razor Ramon rubbing shoulders with established stars, such as Bob Backlund and King Kong Bundy. This was also a year packed with memorable encounters, with younger Superstars, like the 1-2-3 Kid, bringing a new athleticism to the roster. The principal force throughout the year was conspiratorial manager Ted DiBiase and his dastardly Million Dollar Corporation, which was constantly enlisting—or threatening to enlist—perennial fan-favorite Superstars, such as Lex Luger and Undertaker.

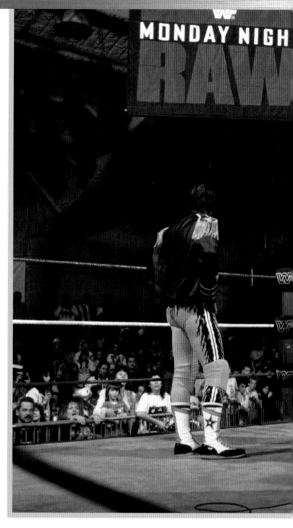

January 31: With their *WrestleMania* fate left to the toss of a coin, Bret Hart and Lex Luger are understandably tense while surrounded by WWE officials.

Underdog victors

January 10: Reigning Champions The Quebecers fell victim to complacency during this first anniversary *RAW* show. The team's manager, Johnny Polo, described this match as a "warm-up" prior to The Quebecers' Title defence at the *Royal Rumble*. It was the underdog duo of the 1-2-3 Kid and Marty Jannetty who had the last laugh when they captured the Titles in a thrilling win.

Elsewhere in WWE

January 22: *Royal Rumble*, from Providence, Rhode Island, saw its first ever co-winners when the last men standing, Bret Hart and Lex Luger, tussled and then fell over the ropes, landing at the exact same time. Both Luger and Hart thus received a WWE Championship shot at *WrestleMania X*. In the same show, Yokozuna inflicted a rare defeat on Undertaker in a Casket Match, resulting in the "Deadman" taking a leave of absence from WWE.

A fifty-fifty chance

January 31: As co-winners of the *Royal Rumble*, both Lex Luger and Bret Hart had a valid claim for a shot at Yokozuna's WWE Championship. WWE President Jack Tunney, along with Mr. McMahon, announced that a coin toss would decide which Superstar would face Yokozuna directly, and which would fight at *WrestleMania X* prior to taking on the Champion. Luger won the toss, meaning Bret was forced to face his brother Owen, before going on to defeat Yokozuna at *WrestleMania* on 20 March.

Outside interference

February 28: "Macho Man" Randy Savage was looking to defeat Yokozuna for the Championship. However, he was deliberately robbed of glory by the sudden arrival in the ring of his former friend Brian "Crush" Adams. Savage appeared to have miraculously overcome exhaustion to defeat Yokozuna and win the Title when he was attacked by Crush. A shocking melee resulted, as first Bret Hart and then Lex Luger invaded the ring to attack Yokozuna and Crush. Yokozuna was disqualified, but thus retained the Championship.

Tatanka honoured

March 7: This episode of *RAW* saw legendary Native American Superstars "Chief" Wahoo McDaniel and "Chief" Jay Strongbow pay tribute to Tatanka by awarding him an honorary headdress. Tatanka, a member of the Lumbee Native American Tribe, was moved to tears by this touching gesture by his fellow Superstars.

April 4: Lounging on the heart-shaped bed on *HeartBreak Hotel*, Shawn Michaels and "Daddy Cool" Diesel, tell Razor Ramon that he can "check out, but never, ever leave."

Lawler dethroned

April 11: Few Superstars have had the legendary career of Jerry "The King" Lawler. He has won multiple championships across the decades, and was inducted into the WWE Hall of Fame in 2007. However, on this episode of *RAW*, The King was unceremoniously tipped from his throne—a moment that Lawler wouldn't want on his Hall of Fame showreel.

April 11: Jerry "The King" Lawler poses prior to being tipped off his portable throne, much to the delight of the crowd.

The Hit Man's vow

March 21: Following his WWE Heavyweight Championship victory at *WrestleMania* against the mighty Yokozuna, Bret "Hit Man" Hart was *RAW*'s returning hero. The Canadian legend declared that he would be a fighting Champion and take on any challengers. The crowd screamed with delight as the Hit Man embarked on his reign as WWE's figurehead. Hart would live up to his promise, defending the Title in a series of epic encounters for 248 days against a host of WWE Superstars.

Enter The Headshrinkers

March 28: When Johnny Polo (later better known as Raven) made an open challenge to any WWE tag team to take on his Quebecers, he wasn't expecting legendary manager "Captain" Lou Albano to emerge and lead out The Headshrinkers. Polo tried to revoke the challenge, but to no avail. The Headshrinkers' imposing team of Fatu and Samu would go on to win the World Tag Team Championships several weeks later.

Heartbreak Hotel

April 4: Influenced by the legendary *Piper's Pit* interviews hosted by "Rowdy" Roddy Piper, Shawn Michaels introduced his new interview segment, entitled *HeartBreak Hotel*. His inaugural guest was his friend "Big Daddy Cool" Diesel. Michaels used the segment as an opportunity to proclaim that Diesel would be bringing the Intercontinental Title home in his upcoming match against "The Bad Guy," Razor Ramon.

1994

First-time Champions

May 2: After weeks of buildup, the moment arrived when The Headshrinkers took on defending World Tag Team Champions, The Quebecers. With The Headshrinkers in control, The Quebecers retreated to the dressing room. They were given an ultimatum: return within a ten count or lose the match and also the Titles. The Quebecers were back in the ring just in time, but they still lost and the Headshrinkers took the Titles for the first—and only—time.

Sumo Match

May 16: The crowd at *RAW* went wild as two of the biggest behemoths in WWE history faced off in a Sumo Match. In this truly spectacular encounter, the former WWE Champion Yokozuna looked to be in total control before he was forced out of the ring, and thus defeated, by former professional sumo wrestler Earthquake. WWE would not feature such an encounter again until Big Show took on Akebono at *WrestleMania 21*.

May 30: Bret "Hit Man" Hart gives Diesel some home truths before being attacked by Jerry Lawler and Shawn Michaels.

May 16: Yokozuna and Earthquake square up in a battle of the giants, competing in *RAW's* first-ever Sumo Match.

Three against one

May 30: Three WWE Superstars are synonymous for their rivalries with "The Hit Man," Bret Hart: Jerry Lawler was a constant thorn in the Hart family's side; Diesel competed against Hart for the WWE Championship in an epic *Survivor Series* match the following year; and Shawn Michaels would, years later, end Bret Hart's active WWE career during the Montreal Screwjob in 1997. On this occasion, all three men attacked The Hit Man simultaneously in a heinous ambush.

The Million Dollar Corporation's new member

June 27: "The Million Dollar Man" Ted DiBiase continued to assemble a formidable group of Superstars—The Million Dollar Corporation. Closing this episode of *RAW*, DiBiase announced to a stunned crowd that he had just acquired the services of "The Beast from the East," Bam Bam Bigelow.

June 27: Ted DiBiase warmly shakes the hand of "The Beast from the East"—and newest Million Dollar Corporation member—Bam Bam Bigelow.

"Everybody has a price for the Million Dollar Man."

Ted DiBiase (June 27, 1994)

High-flying spectacular

July 11: When Bret Hart put the WWE Championship on the line against the 1-2-3 Kid, many fans expected the champion to make short work of his opponent. What followed was a classic encounter full of high-flying moves, near falls, and technically sound mat wrestling in a match that spanned more than 15 minutes. At one point, Hart sportingly declined victory because the 1-2-3 Kid had one foot on the rope—which the referee had failed to notice. The Hit Man eventually won and retained the Title, but the 1-2-3 Kid's display earned the respect of both Hart and the *RAW* audience.

Money talks

July 25: Ted DiBiase continued to splash the cash on *RAW* when he offered Tatanka $10,000 if he could pin his henchman Nikolai Volkoff. Tatanka went on to win the match and was duly paid by DiBiase, with "Macho Man" Randy Savage getting involved to help enforce the payment. In an intriguing twist, some weeks later Tatanka would go on to turn on his tag team partner Lex Luger and join the Million Dollar Corporation.

Getting the boot

August 1: Few Superstars have produced as many classic encounters as Razor Ramon and the "Heartbreak Kid," Shawn Michaels, from their legendary bout at *WrestleMania X* to the memorable rematch at *SummerSlam 1995*. On this occasion, the two men opened *RAW* in an epic match, where both competitors repeatedly swapped offense. The match ended when Michaels whipped Ramon into the boot of Michaels' tag team partner, Diesel, causing the pinfall that gave Michaels the win.

Tracking down Undertaker

August 15: Hollywood star Leslie Nielsen, who was starring as bumbling Police Squad detective Frank Drebin in *The Naked Gun* movie franchise, was tasked with finding the missing Undertaker. With a comedic take on the Undertaker vs. Undertaker storyline that was due to climax at *SummerSlam*, Nielsen delighted *RAW* viewers with his cameo.

In more serious action, Undertaker's long-time manager, Paul Bearer, confronted the fake Undertaker employed by Ted DiBiase, prior to the Undertaker vs. Undertaker match at *SummerSlam*. The bogus Undertaker began choking Bearer in a potentially threatening situation. Bearer was saved when the lights in the arena suddenly went out. When they came on again, Bearer was outside of the ring. Mr. McMahon, on commentary, explained that Bearer must have been saved by "the spirit of Undertaker." In the subsequent match at *SummerSlam*, the real Undertaker won, and Ted DiBiase fled the arena.

August 15: The Million Dollar Man's imposter version of Undertaker attacks the real Undertaker's manager Paul Bearer during the *King's Court* interview segment.

Elsewhere in WWE

August 29: This *SummerSlam* saw Undertaker take on a phony version of himself, managed by Ted DiBiase—an unprecedented main event. Razor Ramon also triumphed against Diesel to win the Intercontinental Championship in a match that was notable for Razor having NFL star Walter Payton in his corner; in the other, Shawn Michaels backed up Diesel.

1994

Send in the clowns

September 12: Following several spats between Jerry "The King" Lawler and clowns Doink and Dink, WWE President Jack Tunney ordered "The King" to apologize. Lawler chose his *King's Court* interview segment to invite the pair out, but it soon became clear that an apology wouldn't be forthcoming. The clowns presented Lawler with a trash can as a peace offering. Offended, "The King" tried to kick it into the crowd, but was left writhing in pain when it refused to budge. The can was loaded with heavy weights.

Backlund's mean streak

September 19: Bob Backlund was a beloved WWE Champion throughout the 1970s and 80s, with a clean-cut image. This image was shattered when, on his return, Backlund proclaimed that both society and the WWE Universe had changed. He then demonstrated the effectiveness of his famed Crossface Chicken Wing finishing hold on his friend Lou Gianfriddo, but refused to release him, even when it became apparent he wasn't responding. It took Mr. McMahon and several referees to pull Backlund away.

September 19: Bob Backlund refuses to release his "long-time friend," *WWE Magazine* writer Lou Gianfriddo, from his famed Crossface Chicken Wing.

September 12: Doink and Dink present "The King" with the gift of a trash can, which was not all it seemed.

Take five

October 10: The returning King Kong Bundy was quite an acquisition for the Million Dollar Corporation. Weighing in at 458lbs (208kg) and 6ft 4in (1.93m) tall, he had previously taken part in the main event of *WrestleMania II*, where he lost to Hulk Hogan inside a steel cage. He also featured at *WrestleMania III*, when he dropped an elbow on his opponent, Little Beaver. Bundy was equally dominant on his return to *RAW*, insisting on pinning his opponent for five seconds, instead of the usual three.

October 10: A Million Dollar Corporation member, the gigantic King Kong Bundy calls for a five-count to show his dominance against his prone opponent.

Outside help

October 31: The main event was a fascinating encounter between one former American hero, Bob Backlund, and a current one, Lex Luger. With Backlund in control, locking Luger in his signature Crossface Chicken Wing, Tatanka entered the ring and added insult to injury by "laying the boots" to the prone Luger. Referees alone couldn't separate Backlund from Luger and it took "Macho Man" Randy Savage to eventually tear them apart.

A family affair

November 7: With two brothers stepping in the ring alongside their brothers-in-law, sparks were sure to fly as Bret Hart and "The British Bulldog" Davey Boy Smith took on Owen Hart and Jim "The Anvil" Neidhart. Bret and the Bulldog claimed victory on this occasion. All four Superstars would join forces in 1997 and become the formidable Hart Foundation, along with Brian Pillman.

INTRODUCING...

The Road Dogg

December 5: Brian James, alias Road Dogg, first appeared in WWE as Jeff Jarrett's sidekick "The Roadie," aiding the "country music Superstar," both in and out of the ring. Road Dogg wouldn't truly find his feet until he began teaming with "Bad Ass" Billy Gunn and formed the New Age Outlaws. The team, who would eventually become part of D-Generation X, won Tag Team Gold on six separate occasions. Road Dogg also saw success as a singles competitor, becoming a multiple Hardcore and Intercontinental Champion.

James' low-key look belied the fact he would often interfere on Jarrett's behalf when things weren't going well.

Brief encounter

December 19: While it won't go down in the list of classic encounters for the ages, festive spirit was clearly evident in this episode of *RAW*. The crowd went wild when two unlikely competitors—renowned ring announcer Howard "The Fink" Finkel and manager Harvey Wippleman—faced off, with Finkel ripping off Wippleman's pants and exposing his snowy white briefs.

December 19: Perhaps the two least intimidating physical specimens in *RAW* history, Harvey Wippleman and Howard Finkel, go nose to nose.

1995

THIS WAS THE YEAR the epic "Monday Night Wars" started, with *RAW* in direct competition with WCW's launch of *Nitro*. This led to the legendary Attitude Era and sparked an unprecedented boom in the sports entertainment business. Rivalry with *Nitro* would see the quality and frequency of *RAW* matches increase, with Superstars like Bret Hart and Undertaker producing memorable matches throughout the year. Diesel was the dominant Superstar, however, holding the WWE Championship for more than 12 months, before being defeated by Bret Hart at *Survivor Series* in November.

Michaels takes the mic

January 2: This episode of *RAW* saw a change from the usual commentary team, as "The Heartbreak Kid" Shawn Michaels joined legendary commentator Gorilla Monsoon behind the microphone. Taking a break from his in-ring work, Michaels provided entertaining commentary for a few weeks of *RAW*. Michaels was not the first and would not be the last guest announcer on *RAW*. Monday nights had featured a host of announcers, including Bobby Heenan, Jim Cornette, and Kevin Kelly. But it was the iconic duo of Jim Ross and Jerry "The King" Lawler who would provide the soundtrack to the Attitude Era.

Captain Kirk vs. The King

January 9: Fans were thrilled when *Star Trek* star William Shatner—whose new show, *Tech Wars*, immediately followed *RAW*—appeared on Jerry Lawler's *King's Court*. Lawler declared that appearing on *King's Court* had to be a high point in Shatner's life; Shatner replied that "chewing gum" was more memorable. Their verbal sparring soon spilled into physical confrontation, ending when Shatner monkey-flipped "The King" to cheers from the crowd. Bret "Hit Man" Hart then added insult to injury by leaping into the ring and raising Shatner's hand in a victory celebration.

January 9: William Shatner, *Star Trek*'s Captain Kirk, claims that "chewing gum" is more memorable than appearing on *King's Court*.

The return of Sycho Sid

February 20: Following his victory in the 1995 *Royal Rumble*, Shawn Michaels described himself as a marked man in the run-up to *WrestleMania XI*. Speaking to Jerry Lawler on his *King's Court* talk show, Michaels claimed he needed protection, and his bodyguard would be none other than Sycho Sid. The crowd gawped as the monster, standing 6ft 9in (2.06m) and weighing 317lbs (144kg), made his way to the ring for the first time in WWE since 1992.

RAW's 100th episode

February 27: The emphasis was on action rather than celebration for *RAW*'s 100th episode. The highlight of a thrilling evening was a war of words between "The Beast from the East" Bam Bam Bigelow and former New York Giants linebacker Lawrence Taylor, whose animosity dated back to a shoving match at the *Royal Rumble* in January. Their verbal confrontation would lead to their legendary main event at *WrestleMania XI* at the Hartford Civic Center.

RAW's 100th episode saw a host of quality matches with Owen Hart (top) making short work of Larry Santo and Doink (bottom right). Lex Luger (bottom left) had a tougher match with Tatanka, whom he defeated via countout. The show culminated in a video segment in which "The Beast from the East" Bigelow clashed with football legend Lawrence Taylor (far left).

Battling brothers

March 27: Just six days ahead of *WrestleMania XI,* the Hart brothers, Bret and Owen, took part in a classic match in *RAW*'s main event. Almost exactly a year after their encounter at *WrestleMania X,* the pair picked up where they left off in a frenetic No Holds Barred Match. Announcers Jim Ross and Gorilla Monsoon questioned whether either competitor would have much left in the tank for *WrestleMania,* before the match was ended by Bret clamping the Sharpshooter on his brother, forcing him into submission.

Bodyguard bother

April 3: The *RAW* immediately following *WrestleMania* is traditionally one of the year's most exciting shows and this one proved no exception. Following his match with Shawn Michaels for the WWE Championship the previous evening, Diesel was magnanimous in victory. Diesel said that on another night it might well have been him asking for a rematch and acknowledged his great friend's performance, agreeing to the match. He did issue one piece of advice for Michaels: to leave his bodyguard Sid at home.

Michaels and Sid would have a confrontation later that evening, with Michaels admonishing Sid for his role in his defeat at *WrestleMania XI.* The big man from Arkansas did not take this well. He clotheslined Michaels from behind and powerbombed his former charge in front of a stunned crowd. Sid later revealed that he had secretly joined the Million Dollar Corporation—part of a dastardly plot engineered by manager Ted DiBiase.

March 27: Bret Hart applies his trademark Sharpshooter to defeat his brother, Owen.

1995

INTRODUCING...

Triple H

April 24: When Greenwich snob Hunter Hearst Helmsley entered the ring to fight John Crystal on April 24, few would have predicted that, as Triple H, he would go on to become a 14-time World Heavyweight Champion and one of the greatest Superstars of all time. The future Triple H made short work of his opponent, pinning him after a devastating neck-breaker. The "King of Kings" would subsequently go on to create many memorable *RAW* moments over the next 23 years, from co-founding D-Generation X to being Chief Operating Officer.

The snooty Hunter Hearst Helmsley wouldn't fully evolve into the Triple H we know today until he joined up with Shawn Michaels to form D-Generation X in 1997.

INTRODUCING...

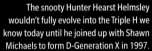

Sunny

May 8: This edition featured a vignette showing WWE Hall of Famer Sunny alongside her partner Chris Candido, alias Skip, on WWE screens for the first time. As part of fitness fanatic villains Bodydonnas, Sunny mocked fans and Superstars alike for their lack of physical perfection. The original WWE Diva would go on to lead Skip and partner Zip to the WWE Tag Team Championships the following year. She later managed a series of championship-winning teams, including The Godwinns and The Smoking Gunns and was inducted into the WWE Hall of Fame in 2011.

Sunny hosted several WWE shows, providing entertaining guest commentary and ring announcing.

Michaels' winning return

May 22: Following a seven-week absence after Sid's powerbomb attack, Shawn Michaels made his return to *RAW*. He was up against another member of the Million Dollar Corporation, the gargantuan King Kong Bundy—a hugely dangerous match, given Michaels' recent return from injury. In a hard-fought encounter, he defeated Bundy with Sweet Chin Music as his friends Diesel and Bam Bam Bigelow celebrated backstage. The pair then joined him in the ring, and Michaels and Diesel shared a trademark high-five.

May 22: Shawn Michaels executes a flying crossbody to King Kong Bundy.

June 12: Lex Luger narrowly avoids a leg drop from the gigantic Yokozuna.

Yokozuna's advance

June 12: Having battled extensively throughout previous years, by a twist of fate Lex Luger was pitted against Yokozuna in a qualifying match for the *King of the Ring* tournament. Yokozuna won following interference from his ringside aides, Mr. Fuji and Jim Cornette. Luger was lured outside the ring when Mr. Fuji stole the American flag from Luger's flag bearer. Yokozuna attacked Luger from behind and used a leg drop on him, leaving him prone in the ringside area as he beat the ten count and advanced to the *King of the Ring* tournament.

Trash talking

July 10: In a battle of the giants, the WWE Champion Diesel was gearing up to face his challenger, Sycho Sid, at *In Your House 2* on July 23. Adding extra unpredictability to the proceedings, a Lumberjack Stipulation Match was announced, with both men choosing 14 lumberjacks each to stand ringside. This episode saw Sid, along with the Million Dollar Man, reveal his henchmen—a diverse range of Superstars including IRS, Tatanka, Henry Godwinn, the Blu brothers, and Mantaur.

Goldust debuts

July 24: This episode was the first chance for the WWE Universe to meet the bizarre Goldust, and the character immediately courted controversy. With his androgynous look and frequent quoting of films, both fans and WWE Superstars were perplexed by the newcomer, who successfully pinned Marty Jannetty in his first match. Goldust—the son of "The American Dream" Dusty Rhodes—would go on to have a legendary WWE career, winning an array of championships over the decades.

July 24: Addressing the WWE Universe in a pre-match vignette, the flamboyant Goldust makes a huge impact on his debut.

Following his run as the "Franchise" of ECW, Shane Douglas showed up on WWE *RAW*. Going by the moniker Dean Douglas, he addressed the WWE Universe in front of a chalkboard, which he raked with his nails to gain attention. He then proceeded to lecture fans and WWE Superstars alike, proclaiming his arrival. Douglas would have a short-lived WWE career and, despite winning the Intercontinental Title, was unable to match his ECW success.

Hall of Famers square off

August 14: In a cross-generational match-up, featuring two of the greatest Superstars of all time, Shawn Michaels faced off against the legendary Jerry "The King" Lawler in this main event. A former multiple heavyweight champion across several wrestling promotions prior to his arrival in WWE, Lawler had the experience advantage, forcing Michaels to rely on his repertoire of high-flying maneuvers. The match ended in a disqualification when Sid interfered, attacking Michaels, only for Michaels to be saved by his upcoming *SummerSlam* opponent, Razor Ramon.

> "You see, I was born a star, it was a gift from that great one in the sky; no editing, just pure talent!"
>
> **Goldust (August 14, 1995)**

1995

The Bulldog turns nasty

August 21: "The British Bulldog" Davey Boy Smith was a fan-favorite for most of his legendary career. On this occasion, however, he drew boos from the fans when he attacked his partner Diesel during an impromptu match with "Men on a Mission" Mabel and Mo. Diesel was then brutalized by the gigantic Mabel who had designs on the WWE Championship.

First shots in the Monday Night Wars

September 4: This was without doubt one of the most important dates in sports entertainment. It was the first time "The Big Two" promotions of WWE and WCW had televised shows head to head on opposing channels. Several years of ratings wars would ensue before, in 2001, WWE claimed victory. However, WCW fired the first shot with the surprise appearance of Lex Luger—whom fans still believed to be a WWE Superstar—who stunned the crowd when he showed up at the Mall of America on WCW's live *Nitro*.

Undertaker action

September 25: The newly intensified rivalry with WCW had a galvanising effect on *RAW*, with a series of marquee matches being added to the schedules. One such match featured "The Phenom of WWE," Undertaker, taking on the newly villainous British Bulldog. Undertaker eventually triumphed in a competitive encounter following the interference of Mabel. After a sustained attack, Undertaker was saved by Shawn Michaels, The Smoking Gunns, and Diesel to close the show.

September 25: The British Bulldog locks a half Boston Crab on the prone Undertaker.

Six-man show-stealers

October 9: This episode of *RAW* featured one of the strongest opening matches ever, with a six-man tag featuring legendary names: Diesel, Shawn Michaels, and Undertaker against The British Bulldog, Yokozuna, and Owen Hart. As expected, the match was hugely competitive, with non-stop action and several high-impact moves. It was won when The British Bulldog pinned Diesel, following a Yokozuna leg drop behind the official's back.

Steel cage drama

October 16: A rare Steel Cage Match main event on *RAW* saw Bret Hart defeat Jerry "The King" Lawler's dastardly dentist Isaac Yankem in a hard-fought match. Typically, Lawler tried to interfere in the match by blocking the escape of Bret Hart; however, he was then bundled by WWE officials into a cage of his own, which was raised above the ring to prevent any further obstructions. Despite Lawler throwing Yankem the key to the main cage, Hart still managed to triumph by escaping as Yankem looked on.

October 16: Bret "Hit Man" Hart attempts to escape the cage against Isaac Yankem.

October 23: Alundra Blayze tussles with the mighty Bertha Faye.

Blayze of glory

October 23: After losing the Women's Championship to the mighty Bertha Faye at *SummerSlam,* revenge was very much on the menu when Alundra Blayze faced her foe on *RAW*. Toward the end of the closely fought match, Faye's boyfriend, Harvey Wippleman, tried to lend a hand by capturing Blayze, but Blayze freed herself from his grasp. Blayze then regained the Championship by pinning the surprised Faye, ending her reign at just 57 days. Faye took out her rage on Wippleman, chasing him all the way to the backstage area.

Elsewhere in WWE

November 19: *Survivor Series* featured an epic match, between Bret "Hit Man" Hart and Diesel, in which Hart won his third WWE Championship. Elsewhere, the team of Shawn Michaels, Ahmed Johnson, The British Bulldog, and Sid defeated Yokozuna, Owen Hart, Razor Ramon, and Dean Douglas in a traditional *Survivor Series* Elimination Match.

Shawn Michaels collapses

November 20: In one of the more distressing moments in *RAW* history, the regular broadcasting of the show was disrupted when Shawn Michaels passed out immediately following his match with Owen Hart. Michaels had only just made his return to the ring following an altercation outside the ring, and his dramatic collapse led to speculation that his head injuries hadn't, and potentially wouldn't, heal. Visibly shocked, Mr. McMahon abandoned the announcing booth to care for Michaels, who was surrounded by Emergency Medical Technicians and WWE officials, before being stretchered from the ring.

It's psychological war!

December 18: The "bizarre and androgynous" Goldust was in heavy pursuit of Razor Ramon and, more importantly, his Intercontinental Championship. Using every trick in the book Goldust delivered a "love letter" to his rival, which left "The Bad Guy" Ramon visibly upset. Goldust would continue to confound Ramon, leading up to their match at the 1996 *Royal Rumble*. The plan clearly worked; Goldust triumphed, gaining the first of his three Intercontinental Championship titles.

1996

1996 WAS A MEMORABLE YEAR not just on *RAW* but for WWE in general. It saw the culmination of Shawn Michaels' boyhood dream at *WrestleMania XII*. The year was also highlighted by Michaels' subsequent WWE Championship defences against the likes of Diesel, Vader, and The British Bulldog. Michaels lasted most of the year as Champion before being defeated by Sid at *Survivor Series*. The year was also bookended by the debuts of Stone Cold Steve Austin and The Rock respectively, two figures who went on to spearhead the more adult-focused "Attitude Era" and become arguably the biggest WWE Superstars. In this year, legends such as "Rowdy" Roddy Piper and the Ultimate Warrior also made their presence felt alongside Superstars such as Bret "Hit Man" Hart and Undertaker. As the year progressed, more edgy characters and storylines heralded the emergence of the Attitude Era.

Steve Austin debuts as The Ringmaster
January 8: There is no doubt that Stone Cold Steve Austin is one of the greatest Superstars in the history of WWE. When he made his debut on *RAW,* however, he first appeared under a very different persona: The Ringmaster. He was introduced by "The Million Dollar Man" Ted DiBiase on the *Brother Love Show*, who announced him as the new Million Dollar Champion. DiBiase proclaimed that he had spent the past year scouring the globe to find the perfect person for the job before finding The Ringmaster.

Vader attacks WWE President Gorilla Monsoon
January 22: In a truly shocking moment on his *RAW* debut, Vader launched a devastating attack on the legendary WWE President, Gorilla Monsoon. Vader had attacked an official following his victory over Savio Vega. This heinous act prompted Gorilla Monsoon to come down to the ring and suspend Vader from WWE indefinitely. As Monsoon checked on the injured official, he was then slammed against the turnbuckle by Vader and hit with a devastating Vader Bomb move. The attack would have continued were it not for Shawn Michaels and Razor Ramon running to the ring to save Monsoon.

January 29: The unpredictable "Rowdy" Roddy Piper returns to *RAW* as Acting WWE President.

Rowdy Roddy for WWE President
January 29: The return of "Rowdy" Roddy Piper as Acting WWE President was met by rapturous applause from the crowd as Piper made his first live WWE appearance since *WrestleMania XI* in 1995. The legendary and unpredictable Superstar praised the current batch of Superstars calling them some of the toughest, greatest athletes he had ever seen. Then, in true Piper fashion, he ended the segment by hoisting a bewildered-looking Mr. McMahon up onto his shoulders and spinning him around, to the delight of the WWE Universe.

Piper announces a 60-minute Iron Man Match

February 26: After winning the *1996 Royal Rumble* it was apparent that "The Heartbreak Kid" Shawn Michaels and Bret "Hit Man" Hart would face off at *WrestleMania XII*. However, when acting WWE President Roddy Piper announced on *RAW* that the match would have an Iron Man stipulation, the seed for a truly classic encounter was sown.

Elsewhere in WWE

March 31: *WrestleMania XII* will go down in history as the event where Shawn Michaels achieved his boyhood dream by winning his first WWE Championship. The legendary 60-minute Iron Man Match with the defending Champion, Bret "Hit Man" Hart, finished in overtime drama, and is remembered as one of the greatest *WrestleMania* matches. The gruelling battle ended when Michaels hit Hart with two Sweet Chin Music kicks before Michaels made the pin for the three count. Elsewhere, "Rowdy" Roddy Piper defeated Goldust in an entertaining Street Fight.

INTRODUCING...

Mankind

April 1: Mick Foley, as Mankind, made an instant impact upon his WWE debut on the post-*WrestleMania XII* edition of *RAW* when he picked a fight with Undertaker. The two began a legendary rivalry which spawned multiple matches such as the first-ever Boiler Room Brawl and the legendary Hell in a Cell Match at the *King of the Ring 1998*. Foley is also one of the few Superstars in WWE history to take on several personas. In addition to Mankind, Foley performs as the equally popular Cactus Jack and Dude Love. Famed for his hardcore matches and brutal style, Mankind evolved again into a more loveable and comedic character with a trusty sidekick and tube sock, Mr. Socko. Foley went on to win the WWE Championship three times before being inducted into WWE Hall of Fame in 2013.

Mankind frequently finished off opponents with his debilitating submission hold, the Mandible Claw.

> "Hold on Vin Man. I'm the champ and I haven't finished talking. I've been waiting eleven years for this, so you can stand there and let me finish."

Shawn Michaels (April 1, 1996)

A new WWE Champion

April 1: Shawn Michaels returned to *RAW* a hero following his epic victory at *WrestleMania XII* the previous night. Michaels was interviewed on *RAW* by Mr. McMahon and took the opportunity to thank the WWE Universe and heap praise on his *WrestleMania XII* opponent Bret "Hit Man" Hart. Michaels spent the majority of the year as Champion defending his Title in incredibly entertaining matches that fully showcased him as one of the greatest in-ring performers of all time.

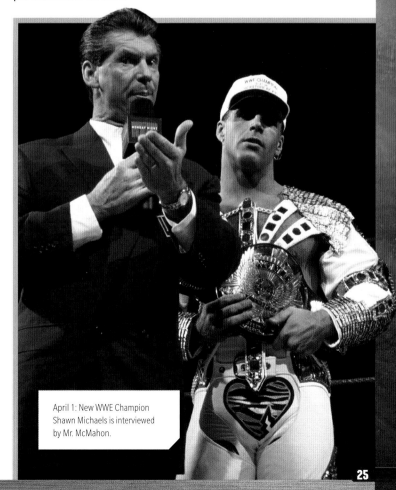

April 1: New WWE Champion Shawn Michaels is interviewed by Mr. McMahon.

1996

Ultimate Warrior attacks Goldust

April 8: The Ultimate Warrior made his return to *RAW* on April 8 in the wake of his quick victory over Triple H at *WrestleMania XII*. The Warrior was in the midst of addressing the WWE Universe when the bizarre Superstar, Goldust, interrupted him in mid flow. The Ultimate Warrior didn't take kindly to this interference and proceeded to verbally tear into Goldust before clotheslining him and forcing him to flee the ring.

Hart to heart

April 15: In a segment taped in Bonn, Germany, Bret Hart reflected on his loss to Shawn Michaels publicly, for the first time. The Hit Man was still visibly upset by the defeat, claiming that, given he had beaten Michaels at the 60-minute mark, the subsequent restart and Michaels' victory should not have happened. Hart also refuted rumors that he may join WCW when he proclaimed that he wasn't greedy for money, but greedy for respect.

Goldust wins the WWE Intercontinental Title

April 22: On the previous episode of *RAW*, Savio Vega thought he had won Goldust's Intercontinental Championship. He had gained the Title controversially when two officials disagreed on the victor of the match after Vega hit Goldust with the Championship Title and subsequently pinned him. While he celebrated, WWE President Gorilla Monsoon entered the ring and announced that the Intercontinental Championship would be vacant and a rematch would occur. On April 22, Goldust had his chance to triumph over Vega, when his manager Marlena caused a distraction while Stone Cold Steve Austin attacked Vega behind the official's back.

April 8: Ultimate Warrior launches at Goldust after the Superstar rudely interrupted him.

Shawn Michaels clears his name

May 20: As part of the rivalry for Shawn Michaels' WWE Championship, The British Bulldog and his manager, Jim Cornette, were pulling out all the stops to gain an advantage over the Champion. Michaels was accused of acting inappropriately towards the wife of The British Bulldog, Diana Hart-Smith, so Michaels used an interview with Jerry "The King'" Lawler on *RAW* to help clear his name. Michaels acknowledged that he had an eye for the ladies, but for him, married women were strictly off limits.

May 20: The wife of the British Bulldog, Diana Hart-Smith, douses Shawn Michaels in water.

Brian Pillman signs with WWE

June 17: In an era where Superstars would jump from WCW to WWE—and vice versa—with regularity, the announcement that "The Loose Cannon" Brian Pillman had signed with WWE was still a surprise to many. Pillman had only recently suffered a serious car accident, which he was lucky to escape with his life. In the press conference to announce his signing, a clearly emotional Pillman fought back tears as he described his gratitude for both surviving the accident and signing with WWE. His sedate mood did not last long; Pillman went on to be one of the more unpredictable and rebellious Superstars in *RAW* history.

Sid is announced as the third man

July 8: Shawn Michaels and Ahmed Johnson revealed the Superstar who would aid them in their match against the dastardly Camp Cornette team at *In Your House: International Incident*. In parallel to the shocking event when Hulk Hogan was announced as the third man to fight for the nWo faction at WCW's *Bash at the Beach* pay-per-view, Camp Cornette's manager, Jim Cornette, went from being incredibly confident that Michaels and Johnson wouldn't be able to find a partner, to shaking in fear when Michaels and Johnson revealed their third man: the maniacal Superstar Sid.

Ahmed Johnson finally loses his undefeated streak

May 27: Going in to the *King of the Ring* tournament the undefeated Superstar Ahmed Johnson was a strong favorite, despite having to face off against the mighty Vader in a qualifying match. Johnson appeared to have Vader under control following a Spinebuster move, but Vader's fellow Camp Cornette member, Owen Hart, leapt from the top rope to deliver a blow from his cast-covered arm which knocked out Johnson. Vader scored an easy pinfall which ended the undefeated streak that Johnson had held since his debut in 1995.

Ultimate Warrior receives an unwelcome gift

June 10: By way of an apology for costing The Warrior an earlier *King of the Ring* qualifying match against Goldust, Jerry Lawler presented his rival with a hand-drawn portrait. When it became apparent that The Ultimate Warrior wouldn't be accepting the gift, Lawler changed tack and smashed the painting over Warrior's head while his back was turned. Warrior brushed off the attack and ran backstage in an attempt to catch Lawler.

June 10: Jerry Lawler smashes a hand-drawn portrait of The Ultimate Warrior across the back of Warrior's head.

July 8: Sid makes his unexpected return to *RAW* to partner with Ahmed Johnson and Shawn Michaels.

1996

A stone-cold rivalry

July 29: Few superstars were as inextricably linked during the Attitude Era as huge rivals Undertaker and Stone Cold Steve Austin. The July 29 main event could be considered as a precursor to the tension between them. On this occasion, Austin emerged victorious after Mankind caused a distraction that caused Undertaker to be counted out of the ring. It wasn't an entirely sweet victory for Austin, however. Undertaker returned to the ring to deliver a Tombstone Piledriver on him.

Crush makes a winning return

August 12: "The Big Hawaiian" Crush looked a far cry from his former colorful self with a meaner, more aggressive look when he defeated Savio Vega upon his return to *RAW*. In his first WWE appearance since 1995, Crush was accompanied by his lawyer, Clarence Mason, who represented him after a recent arrest. The new, meaner Crush defeated Vega and went on to be part of both the Nation of Domination and the biker faction, Disciples of Apocalypse.

Shawn Michaels overcomes gigantic odds

August 19: "The Heartbreak Kid" Shawn Michaels faced a daunting task when he faced the 650lbs (295kg) Yokozuna in an action-packed main event. Despite having his crafty manager Jim Cornette and his stablemates, The British Bulldog and Vader in attendance, Yokozuna still couldn't beat Michaels. Yokozuna succumbed to a stunning Sweet Chin Music maneuver by Michaels and the show ended with Michaels holding the Championship aloft as fireworks burst from the rafters.

Elsewhere in WWE

September 22: The *In Your House 10: Mind Games* pay-per-view event from Philadelphia featured one of the most underrated main event matches of all time. The match, between defending champion Shawn Michaels and Mankind, was fast-paced, brutal, and full of tension. This event also saw the team of Owen Hart and The British Bulldog capture the WWE World Tag Team Championships against The Smoking Gunns.

August 12: A returning and more villainous looking Crush uses his power against Savio Vega.

September 23: Marc Mero executes "The Wild Thing" move on Farooq to claim the Intercontinental Championship.

Marc Mero wins the Intercontinental Championship

September 23: The finals of the Intercontinental Championship tournament saw Mark Mero defeat Farooq in a hotly contested match. In an intriguing subplot, both men were accompanied by two of the most glamorous Divas in WWE history: Sunny (managing Farooq) and Sable (alongside her then husband Mero). The match finished when Mero hit Farooq with his spectacular "Wild Thing" move from the top rope to claim his first and only Intercontinental Championship.

September 30: Two imposters purporting to be Diesel and Razor Ramon cause confusion on *RAW*.

"Diesel" and "Razor Ramon" return to *RAW*

September 30: In one of the more bizarre episodes in *RAW* history, commentator Jim Ross promised to reintroduce Razor Ramon and Diesel the previous week on *RAW*, only for it to transpire that the Superstars were not the original Superstars, Scott Hall and Kevin Nash. In "Ramon's" first match back against Savio Vega on the September 30 episode of *RAW*, Gorilla Monsoon and the other members of the announcing team openly questioned the authenticity of the Superstar to a disgruntled Ross.

Triple H Intercontinental Champion

October 21: In the first of many Championship wins in WWE, Triple H defeated Marc Mero, with the help of Mr. Perfect. Going into the match, there was no indication that Perfect was in cahoots with Triple H, so when the referee was inadvertently knocked out and Mr. Perfect jumped into the ring clutching a steel chair, the WWE Universe expected Triple H to be the one under attack. Instead, Mr. Perfect turned and levelled Mero with the chair, allowing Triple H to score the pinfall as Mero's horrified wife, Sable, looked on.

Brian Pillman gets an unwanted visitor

November 4: In one of the most controversial moments in not just *RAW* but WWE history, Brian Pillman pulled a gun on Stone Cold Steve Austin when he attempted to invade his home. Being interviewed via satellite link by Kevin Kelly, Pillman was visibly on edge, with Austin circling the property. Once Austin broke in via the back door, the cameras showed Pillman standing up and taking aim at Austin only for the satellite feed to disconnect leaving viewers in suspense. Fortunately, no one was hurt, but the graphic nature of the segments shocked and intrigued in equal measure.

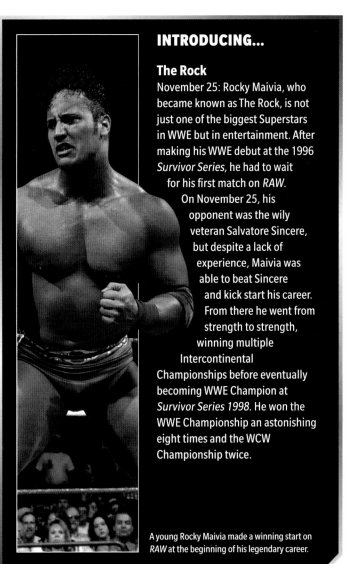

INTRODUCING...

The Rock

November 25: Rocky Maivia, who became known as The Rock, is not just one of the biggest Superstars in WWE but in entertainment. After making his WWE debut at the 1996 *Survivor Series*, he had to wait for his first match on *RAW*. On November 25, his opponent was the wily veteran Salvatore Sincere, but despite a lack of experience, Maivia was able to beat Sincere and kick start his career. From there he went from strength to strength, winning multiple Intercontinental Championships before eventually becoming WWE Champion at *Survivor Series 1998*. He won the WWE Championship an astonishing eight times and the WCW Championship twice.

A young Rocky Maivia made a winning start on *RAW* at the beginning of his legendary career.

1997

POSSIBLY THE MOST CONTROVERSIAL year in WWE history, the defining moment of 1997 was undoubtedly the Montreal Screwjob in November. But this infamous incident simply underlined the new direction WWE and *RAW* had been taking all year, with edgier, more reality-based programming leading the way. Classic elements of WWE remained though: several WWE Superstars reigned as Champion, including Shawn Michaels and Bret "Hit Man" Hart; younger Superstars like The Rock and Stone Cold Steve Austin continued to grow in prominence; and the emergence of factions—such as D-Generation X—made for compelling viewing. Seeds were also sown for clashes that would become cornerstones of the following year's programming, such as the gradual introduction of Undertaker's brother Kane and increased tensions between Austin and Mr. McMahon.

Sid makes it personal

January 6: In the lead-up to their confrontation at the 1997 *Royal Rumble*, the WWE Champion Sid was doing everything in his considerable power to rile his upcoming opponent "The Heartbreak Kid" Shawn Michaels. Sid went as far as attacking the son of Michaels' mentor and manager, Jose Lothario. Sid powerbombed Pete Lothario onto a wooden table toward the end of the night's show. This was the final straw for Michaels. The furious Heartbreak Kid ran to tend to Pete, all the while shouting threats to Sid into the camera. The show ended with a replay of the attack, raising the stakes for the pair's big match.

Repeat of the Rumble

January 20: Stone Cold Steve Austin had won a controversial victory at Sunday's *Royal Rumble* match and the impact was still sorely felt the following day. The night's main event was due to be Stone Cold Steve Austin vs. Undertaker, but before it could begin, a slighted Bret "Hit Man" Hart attacked Austin. Undertaker then entered the ring to take out his own anger on Austin, while Hart and Vader had to be held apart in the locker room. Tensions exploded as Hart and Vader rushed into the ring and referees struggled to retain control of the quarrelling quartet. The four competitors would eventually settle their differences at *In Your House: Final Four* in order to decide who would face the WWE Champion at *WrestleMania*.

History and heartbreak

February 13: A special Thursday edition of *RAW* opened with a surprising win as a young Rocky Maivia pinned the defending Intercontinental Champion Triple H to win the Title. It would be the first of many Championships for The Rock in WWE and one of the earliest battles against his great rival, Triple H.

As one career was taking off, another was seemingly coming to an end. In one of the most famous moments in *RAW* history, the WWE Champion Shawn Michaels was forced to vacate his beloved Title live on air. An MRI scan had revealed that he had suffered accumulated damage to his knee and, on medical advice, would have to retire. The Heartbreak Kid was visibly heartbroken as he explained that, alongside the injury, the pressure of the Championship and his hectic schedule had also caused him to lose his smile.

February 13: A tearful Shawn Michaels is forced to give up his WWE Championship.

February 24: ECW makes a surprise invasion on *RAW*.

Big city invasion

February 24: *RAW* was visiting Manhattan, New York, and Jerry Lawler had issued an open challenge to their Philadelphia-based rivals ECW to join them. No one expected the overwhelming response that followed. As the opening match finished, ECW's The Eliminators—consisting of John Kronus and Perry Saturn—invaded the ring and performed their devastating Total Elimination move on a defenseless match official. The owner of ECW, Paul Heyman, then jumped into the ring to proclaim that Lawler's challenge had been accepted. There was rapturous applause from a crowd that included many local ECW fans.

The British Bulldog triumphs

March 3: In a *RAW* held in Berlin, Germany, The British Bulldog took on his brother-in-law and tag team partner, Owen Hart, to become the first ever WWE European Champion. The match was the culmination of a tournament which saw eight WWE Superstars battle across eight nights in eight German cities. In a technically excellent match between the reigning WWE Tag Team Champions, it was The Bulldog who would emerge victorious when he countered a Victory Roll to make WWE history.

Bret "Hit Man" Hart turns his back on fans

March 24: On this edition, Bret "Hit Man" Hart called out his fans, or some of them at least, for a lack of support and respect. Hart apologized to his fans in Europe, Asia, and the rest of the world, before launching into a bitter tirade against his fans in the USA. He criticized the fans' vocal support for Superstars such as Stone Cold Steve Austin and Shawn Michaels, comparing it to their unfavourable reactions to his results. Hart continued his rant against America, its fans, and WWE management before he was interrupted by an injured Shawn Michaels. Michaels came in to defend the fans, but received a vicious attack from Hart for his troubles. Hart would later reform the Hart Foundation as an anti-American faction.

The war of words continues

April 7: Continuing one of the most intense rivalries in WWE history, Shawn Michaels used this episode of *RAW* to respond to the brutal attack Bret "Hit Man" Hart had made on him two weeks earlier. Michaels was incredibly candid, stating that he and the Hit Man truly loathed each other, both in front of the cameras and behind the scenes. Michaels continued his criticism, as Hart Foundation Members The British Bulldog and Owen Hart watched on backstage. The pair eventually marched down to the ring to attack Michaels, but he was able to fend them off with a steel chair.

Shamrock steps in

April 28: While on tour, Vader had attacked a Kuwaiti television reporter. Now Vader was back in the United States, it was left to Jim Ross to take him to task over his actions during an in-ring interview. Vader, predictably, did not take kindly to the line of questioning and proceeded to threaten Good Ol' JR. For a while it looked like JR was in severe trouble, until Ken Shamrock hit the ring and executed a Belly-to-Belly Suplex on Vader to save the day.

April 28: Ken Shamrock hits Vader with a powerful kick.

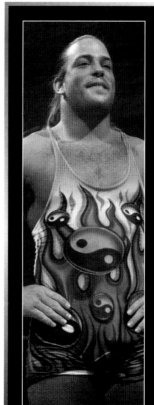

INTRODUCING...

Rob Van Dam

May 12: Rob Van Dam made his WWE debut as part of the 1997 ECW invasion, and was nicknamed "Mr. Monday Night" by Jerry Lawler. However, he wouldn't become a full-time member of the WWE roster until July 9 2001. From then, Van Dam forged an enviable career with acclaimed in-ring work and innovative attacking maneuvers. He won multiple championships along the way, but perhaps his finest night was the ECW *One Night Stand* pay-per-view in 2006, where he defeated John Cena for the WWE Championship in front of the frenzied ECW fan base in the Hammerstein Ballroom, New York.

RVD's first match on *RAW* was against a young Jeff Hardy, before the latter found fame as one half of the Hardy Boyz.

Bad reaction

May 19: Neither party had taken the news well when Stone Cold Steve Austin and Shawn Michaels were told they would be tag team partners at the upcoming WWE Tag Team Championship Match. With each proclaiming the other couldn't be trusted, it wasn't long before a brawl broke out between the unlikely partners. Despite their incredible individual talents, few believed these two rivals would be able to function as a team against their well-drilled opponents, the Hart Foundation.

An unlikely victory

May 26: Once the bell rang for the WWE Tag Team Championship Match, the unhappy team of Stone Cold Steve Austin and Shawn Michaels combined surprisingly well against the duo of Owen Hart and The British Bulldog. In a hard-fought encounter, both teams had moments of offence and near falls; however the match ended when Michaels hit The Bulldog with Sweet Chin Music, allowing Austin to make the cover. The remainder of the Hart Foundation angrily invaded the ring in retaliation, resulting in a mass brawl.

WrestleMania rematch

June 2: Sid had barely been seen since losing the WWE Championship to Undertaker back at *WrestleMania* in March. Now he was back, explaining that, although he had previously left the result unchallenged due to the honor with which Undertaker had defended the Title, that respect had been destroyed when Undertaker had failed to stand up to his scheming manager, Paul Bearer. Sid now called for a rematch. The hard-hitting clash between the two finished with Sid receiving a Tombstone Piledriver and Undertaker securing the victory.

New factions forming

June 23: *RAW* opened with a new-look Nation of Domination, which now included a previous fan-favorite, Ahmed Johnson. Johnson claimed he had made this move to gain more championship shots and be a bigger player in WWE after being held down by the powers that be. But Johnson and the rest of The Nation would be interrupted by a former member, Crush. Crush announced the formation of his own faction, The Disciples of Apocalypse, with the intimidating brothers Skull and 8-Ball as his fellow members.

Paul Bearer's shocking revelation

June 30: For weeks Paul Bearer had been teasing a surprise announcement, a dark secret that he planned to reveal to Undertaker. Finally, Bearer revealed that Undertaker's brother Kane, who had been presumed dead, had in fact survived the house fire that had killed Undertaker's parents. Bearer implied that it was Undertaker himself who had started the blaze and was therefore responsible for the deaths of his parents and the emotional and physical scars of his brother. Now rumor had it that this mysterious relative was out to seek his revenge. The WWE Universe waited with bated breath to see what would unfold.

Elsewhere in WWE

July 6: The *In Your House: Canadian Stampede* pay-per-view live from Calgary, Alberta, Canada, featured one of the finest matches of the year when the Hart Foundation took on the team of Stone Cold Steve Austin, Goldust, Ken Shamrock and the Legion of Doom in front of a raucous crowd. Undertaker also defended his WWE Championship against Vader.

June 2: Undertaker pins Sid in a *WrestleMania* rematch.

Alternative alter ego

July 14: Due to Shawn Michaels' injury, Stone Cold Steve Austin was in need of a new partner for his WWE Tag Team Championship Match against The British Bulldog and Owen Hart. Austin had previously refused an offer of help from Mankind, labeling him a "freak" and instead went to the ring alone. However, the man behind Mankind was really Mick Foley, who refused to take no for an answer. Now wearing tie-dye and calling himself Dude Love, Foley declared he would save the day as the numerical disadvantage began to take its toll on Austin. Despite Austin's reservations, "The Dude" was an effective partner and they retained the Championships.

July 21: Bret Hart and Mr. McMahon grabbed one another at ringside during a match between The Patriot and Triple H.

Bad blood

July 21: 1997 would go on to be defined by the infamous Montreal Screwjob, but an earlier confrontation was a sign of things to come. This edition of *RAW* was held in Halifax, Nova Scotia, and the Canadian crowd erupted in support of their countryman Bret "Hit Man" Hart, when he confronted Mr. McMahon. While Hart and Mr. McMahon would go on to have more significant physical confrontations down the road, this was the first time the two had put hands on each other and underlined the serious bad blood between them.

The Patriot scores a surprise victory

July 28: After months of outspoken rants against the United States, Bret "Hit Man" Hart was on shaky ground with fans when *RAW* returned to US soil for this week's edition. It would have been impossible to find him a more symbolic next opponent than The Patriot. Despite an impressive start to his WWE career, The Patriot was still a massive underdog going into the match. Experienced Hart appeared to have the match under control until the official was rendered unconscious. As Hart attempted to revive him, guest commentator Shawn Michaels decided to make his presence felt. Michaels jumped out of the announcing booth, distracting Hart and allowing The Patriot to score a Rollup Pinfall from behind. The now-conscious official made the three count, giving The Patriot a surprise victory over Hart.

Commissioner Sgt. Slaughter makes an example

August 4: When WWE Hall of Famer Sgt. Slaughter was appointed WWE Commissioner he wasted little time in whipping the troublemaking Hart Foundation into line. A prime example was enforcing Brian Pillman's promise of wearing a dress, following his loss to Goldust at the previous evening's *SummerSlam*. Reluctant Pillman was forced to wear a dress in his *RAW* match against Bob Holly, with Slaughter pushing him through the curtain and down to the rampway.

Stone Cold rage

September 8: Following his devastating neck injury at *SummerSlam*, Stone Cold Steve Austin was unable to defend his Intercontinental Championship. On this edition of *RAW*, Commissioner Slaughter announced that Austin would be stripped of the Title and a tournament would be set up to crown a new Champion. Predictably, Austin did not take the news well. He first hit Slaughter with a Stone Cold Stunner, but also later took out his anger on the Hart Foundation and Mr. McMahon.

A man of many faces

September 21: Before his WWE career began, Mick Foley had wrestled as Cactus Jack all over the world. Since joining the company he had competed as Mankind and Dude Love, however, the third side of his personality had never been seen on WWE. He chose a fitting opportunity to unleash it: a Street Fight with Triple H at the iconic Madison Square Garden. The New York crowd who were familiar with Cactus Jack from his time in ECW responded with loud cheers at the sight of the popular character.

September 21: Mick Foley celebrates with the fans as he debuts his anarchic and violent Cactus Jack character.

1997

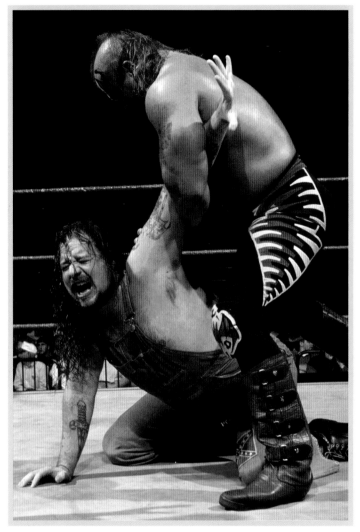

October 13: Animal dominates Phineas Godwinn in a Career vs. Championship Match.

Teams dominate the day

October 13: The stakes couldn't have been higher for the legendary Legion of Doom on this episode of *RAW*: win the WWE World Tag Team Championships against The Godwinns, or retire. Fortunately for the WWE Universe, Legion of Doom partners Hawk and Animal prevailed. They won the Championships and remained in active competition. The Championship win was the first for the pair since the summer of 1991.

Another team was also forming out of the ring and it would go on to have a seismic impact on WWE. A new group comprising Shawn Michaels, Triple H, Chyna, and Ravishing Rick Rude appeared on the Titantron to mock the in-ring Hart Foundation. When their name was announced by Michaels as D-Generation X, the faction became official. D-Generation X would go on to become a significant force on *RAW* over the years, with two of the founders, Michaels and Triple H, still enjoying occasional reunions some 20 years later.

Jarrett speaks out

October 20: Jeff Jarrett made a surprise return to *RAW* with a controversial interview. Jarrett openly acknowledged his previous position at WCW and called out his former boss, Eric Bischoff, by name. At a time where backstage happenings were kept off camera, this interview truly pushed the envelope. Jarrett spoke candidly about his former employers, contract situation, and his reasons for previously leaving WWE. He would go on to forge a successful WWE career before returning to WCW in 1999.

Elsewhere in WWE

November 9: *Survivor Series* in Montreal will go down in history as the most controversial pay-per-view of all time. The main event, in front of a partisan Canadian crowd, saw Shawn Michaels defeat Canadian Bret Hart for the WWE Championship. With Bret Hart locked in his own finisher, The Sharpshooter, Mr. McMahon told the timekeeper to ring the bell and awarded the Championship to Michaels even though Hart hadn't actually submitted. It would go on to be infamously known as the Montreal Screwjob.

The Montreal fallout

November 10: Following the mindblowing events of the night before at *Survivor Series*, Shawn Michaels further riled an angry Canadian audience by proclaiming that WWE wasn't big enough for both him and his rival Bret "Hit Man" Hart. He bragged that he had run Hart down south to WCW with the other "dinosaurs."

November 10: A confident Shawn Michaels showcases both his WWE European and Heavyweight Championships.

"I have no sympathy for Bret whatsoever, none."

Mr. McMahon (November 17, 1997)

Infamous interview

November 17: In one of the most searing interviews in WWE history, Mr. McMahon sat down with Jim Ross to give his thoughts on the controversial *Survivor Series* events. In a groundbreaking segment Mr. McMahon openly acknowledged the issues behind the scenes between himself and Bret "Hit Man" Hart and candidly spoke about the incident. McMahon admonished Hart for not handling his wish to depart the company in the right way. He exclaimed to fans that, as the owner of WWE, he had been forced into a corner. The interview concluded with the immortal line "Bret screwed Bret." The interview helped shape the villainous Mr. McMahon character and usher in a new era of reality-TV drama in WWE programming.

Michaels rubs salt in the wounds

November 24: With the aftermath of *Survivor Series* continuing to unfold, events on *RAW* were becoming increasingly unpredictable. Following the announcement from Shawn Michaels that he wanted to settle the controversy once and for all, some fans were expecting Bret "Hit Man" Hart to accept the challenge. The WWE Universe was left disappointed when the Hit Man's entrance music played, but the man who emerged from the curtain was a far shorter imposter, wearing an ill-fitting mask.

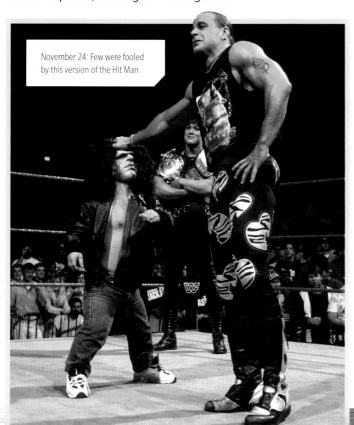

November 24: Few were fooled by this version of the Hit Man.

Traffic violation

December 1: In their heated rivalry for the Intercontinental Championship, Stone Cold Steve Austin would stop at nothing to gain an advantage against The Rock. On this occasion, Austin drove his pick-up into the arena as The Rock took on Vader. Austin watched the match from the driver's seat, radio blaring and drinking beer. The Rock would win via countout, despite the distraction, but the taunting message had certainly been received.

December 1: Stone Cold Steve Austin salutes the WWE Universe from the roof of his pick-up truck.

A growing rivalry

December 8: While Stone Cold Steve Austin and Mr. McMahon had taken part in a few run-ins before this point, this was the first time Mr. McMahon declared himself plainly as Austin's boss. In his typical style, Stone Cold was not impressed and proceeded to verbally chew out the Chairman of WWE. This would set the tone for one of the most spectacular rivalries in WWE history.

Speaking from the Hart

December 15: Owen Hart used this episode of *RAW* to speak to the WWE Universe for the first time since the *Survivor Series* and the departure of his brother Bret. He used the opportunity to announce that, unlike his fellow Hart Foundation members, he would be staying with WWE. With a new, more aggressive persona Owen made it clear that he wanted to be seen as his own man, fight for his role on the WWE roster, and ultimately the WWE Championship.

RAW defeats *Nitro* in the ratings war

December 22: WCW *Nitro* infamously defeated *RAW* in the TV ratings for 83 straight weeks. Although it would take some time for *RAW* to wrestle the mantle back fully, this episode saw *RAW* defeat *Nitro* in the second hour of head-to-head programming. This may have been a small victory at the time, but it was a significant sign of things to come and a vindication that the new creative route WWE was embarking on would ultimately reap dividends.

1998

1998 WILL GO DOWN IN HISTORY as the tipping point in the Monday Night War, where WWE finally overtook the ratings of their rival WCW. Stone Cold Steve Austin emerged as the figurehead of the upcoming Attitude Era, while Superstars such as Undertaker, Kane, Mick Foley, and the emerging D-Generation X also helped contribute to unmissable TV, week in, week out. As the year progressed, The Rock started his journey to becoming one of the greatest Superstars of all time. After starting the year as a hated member of the Nation of Domination, The Rock evolved into a fan-favorite, and then shockingly turned on the WWE Universe to join the Corporation—all within a 12-month period. The year, however, would largely belong to Austin and his ongoing rivalry with Mr. McMahon. This massive clash created some of the most iconic *RAW* moments of the year.

Undertaker shocks Shawn Michaels

January 5: In the lead-up to their Casket Match for the WWE Championship at the *1998 Royal Rumble*, Shawn Michaels had been constantly one-upping Undertaker. On this occasion the tables were turned, when Michaels saw a casket marked with D-Generation X graffiti wheeled down to the ring to replicate Undertaker's entrance. Michaels was clearly expecting a fellow D-Generation X member to emerge; however, a look of panic took over him when his allies Triple H and Chyna emerged from the backstage area shouting warnings. It was Undertaker who instead erupted from the casket. Undertaker dragged Michaels inside and closed the lid behind them in order to exact his displeasure.

Austin and Tyson face off

January 19: Sparks were sure to fly when the "Baddest Man on the Planet," Mike Tyson, entered the same arena as "The Texas Rattlesnake," Stone Cold Steve Austin. After Tyson was introduced to the WWE Universe by Mr. McMahon, it didn't take long for the rattlesnake to strike. Stone Cold marched to the ring and proceeded to talk trash at Tyson. When Austin's taunts became too much for the boxer he shoved Austin. The two men had to be separated by WWE officials, but Tyson had certainly made his presence felt.

Dangerous dumpster

February 2: In one of the more breathtaking moments in *RAW* history, it appeared as if the New Age Outlaws had put not just the careers of Cactus Jack and Chainsaw Charlie at risk, but their lives. The finishing move of the pair's match saw Cactus Jack dropping an elbow from the base of the Titantron onto Chainsaw Charlie, who was at the bottom of a dumpster. The New Age Outlaws emerged as both men were recovering inside the dumpster, and pushed it from the ten-foot-high entrance ramp to the ground. WWE officials and Emergency Medical Technicians rushed over to revive the stricken pair as the shaken crowd looked on.

The legendary Legion of Doom implode

February 23: In a shocking scene that no one in the WWE Universe thought possible, the fabled Legion of Doom turned on each other and came to blows. Frustrated at their lack of success against the New Age Outlaws, the team of Hawk and Animal took their anger out on each other following their defeat, and proceeded to brawl in the middle of the ring. Fans were noticeably shocked as the beloved team were pulled apart by WWE officials.

January 5: Undertaker stands tall after outsmarting his rival, Shawn Michaels.

March 2: Shawn Michaels didn't take long to endear himself to "the Baddest Man on the Planet."

Raising the stakes

March 2: In this edition of *RAW*, Mike Tyson was revealed as the newest member of D-Generation X. The news was unveiled as Shawn Michaels and Tyson were nose to nose in the center of the ring, teasing a fight. Suddenly, Michaels reached out and ripped off Tyson's t-shirt, revealing a D-Generation X shirt underneath. Michaels, Triple H, and Tyson embraced and celebrated. The team's new addition would further stack the deck against Michaels' nemesis, Stone Cold Steve Austin.

Since Kane's terrifying introduction to WWE, his brother Undertaker had been clear that he would never fight his own flesh and blood. On this episode of *RAW*, months of provocation finally came to a head when Undertaker returned in the most dramatic way possible, via a bolt of lightning to a coffin. Undertaker sat upright and faced his brother. He told Kane that he couldn't be destroyed and that Kane would rest in peace at *WrestleMania XIV*.

Triple H becomes European Champion

March 17: Owen Hart allowed Triple H to provoke him into putting his European Championship on the line in an impromptu match, despite Hart being injured. Even with the obvious disadvantage of a cast on his ankle, Hart competed well and the contest was looking evenly matched. That was until Chyna interfered on behalf of Triple H. Chyna marched to the ring while the official was distracted and hit Hart's injured ankle with a baseball bat. She rolled Hart back into the ring, leaving him as easy prey for Triple H who applied an ankle lock and forced the match to be stopped in his favor.

An action-packed post-*WrestleMania* show

March 30: The *RAW* following *WrestleMania* is traditionally one of the more incident-filled episodes of the year. This show was no exception. Firstly, it featured the shocking return of X-Pac, who had defected from WCW to help form the rebooted D-Generation X. Later in the same episode, Triple H, Chyna, and X Pac would be joined by the New Age Outlaws to make the faction stronger than ever. The final major incident was Stone Cold Steve Austin hitting Mr. McMahon with the Stone Cold Stunner. Austin was given a simple choice by McMahon: to follow him obediently or flout his authority and face the full power of WWE management. The crowd cheered as Austin made it clear he would stand up to McMahon, whatever the consequences.

Appealing to the audience

April 13: This episode finally saw WWE overtake their southern rivals WCW, after the latter had enjoyed an 83-week winning streak in the ratings. The momentum following *WrestleMania* was riding high for *RAW* thanks to the Austin vs. Mr. McMahon rivalry and a host of fresh and edgy characters capturing the public imagination. Finally, *RAW* scored a 4.6 Nielsen rating ahead of WCW *Nitro's* 4.3. The two shows would trade victories until the fall, when *RAW* began to totally dominate.

The scheduled main event that night was McMahon against Stone Cold Steve Austin, but with an added stipulation: Austin would compete with one hand tied behind his back. In a series of entertaining vignettes throughout the night, McMahon had been shown training with his stooges, Pat Patterson and Gerald Brisco. The match was ultimately cancelled though, following an interruption by Dude Love. Love would go on to attack Austin and apply the devastating Mandible Claw to floor the Champion.

1998

April 27: D-Generation X take the ratings war with WCW literally, as they invade an episode of *Nitro* in an armored car.

D-Generation X invade *Nitro*

April 27: On this Monday night *RAW* was being held in Hampton, Virginia, while its rival programme *Nitro* was being hosted across the bridge in Norfolk. The rebellious WWE team D-Generation X took full advantage of *Nitro* being in such close proximity. The faction rode toward the rival show in an armored car and declared war on WCW. Although DX were eventually denied entry to the building, the series of vignettes was hugely entertaining. This was perhaps the most direct shot fired in the Monday Night Wars.

Val Venis makes his in-ring debut

May 4: Val Venis was the perfect example of the sort of edgy Superstar that helped catapult *RAW* into domination during the period. The former adult movie star came down to the ring wearing a towel which he would then provocatively remove after uttering his catchphrase "Hello ladies." On this episode of *RAW* he defeated Too Cold Scorpio and would go on to forge a successful and gold-laden career for over a decade in WWE.

May 4: Edgier characters such as Val Venis are a far cry from the Superstars who had debuted in the early 1990s.

Austin has Mr. McMahon arrested

May 25: In the continuing rivalry between Steve Austin and Mr. McMahon the stakes seemed to rise week by week. On this occasion, Austin got his boss arrested. McMahon had been bragging about assaulting Austin in front of the live crowd, which Austin claimed was a confession of crime. The police agreed, cuffing the fuming McMahon and leading him away from the ring kicking and screaming. To add insult to injury, Austin continued to taunt McMahon as the boss's stooges Brisco and Patterson were also cuffed for good measure.

Kane pins Undertaker to earn a Championship shot

June 1: While Undertaker had been victorious against his brother Kane in their high-profile match at *WrestleMania XIV,* Kane was able to gain some semblance of revenge on this edition of *RAW.* He even became number-one contender for the WWE Championship to boot. In a typically hard-fought affair, the brothers traded moves that would have finished lesser men. Eventually, following a distraction from Mankind, Kane was able to hit Undertaker with a Tombstone Piledriver to earn the right to face reigning Champion Stone Cold Steve Austin at the upcoming *King of the Ring.*

July 13: The formidable duo of Mankind and Kane would go on to capture the WWE World Tag Team Championship on two occasions.

INTRODUCING...

Edge

June 22: Edge's *RAW* debut was unspectacular—he made short work of his opponent, Jose Estrada, earning a countout victory. However, Edge would go on to become one of the most decorated WWE Superstars in history, winning the WWE Championship four times and the World Heavyweight Championship seven times. Together with Christian, Edge was also part of one of the greatest WWE tag teams of all time. The popular duo won the WWE Tag Team Championships on seven occasions. Edge was inducted into the WWE Hall of Fame in 2012.

Edge began his career as a mysterious competitor, before evolving into one of WWE's most beloved Superstars.

Austin regains the Championship

June 29: Following a controversial and unexpected loss to Kane at the previous night's *King of the Ring*, Austin was in the mood for revenge. He didn't have to wait long, as Kane accepted the challenge from Austin for a rematch later that night. Kane was made to pay for his actions and eventually succumbed to the Stone Cold Stunner as Austin settled the score to rapturous cheers. This would be Austin's second WWE Championship and he would retain the gold until September.

The *Brawl for All* begins

July 6: In a new concept for *RAW*, the *Brawl for All* saw Superstars taken out of their comfort zone and away from professional sports entertainment to compete for the cash prize of $25,000. The unusual tournament involved an element of boxing and led to some surprising losses for big names. The tournament was won by Bart Gunn, although he would not be so successful when he faced professional boxer Butterbean at *WrestleMania XV*. Gunn was knocked out in just 35 seconds!

Kane and Mankind capture Tag Team Gold

July 13: The team of Kane and Mankind were crowned WWE World Tag Team Champions in a victory against The New Age Outlaws, with a little outside help. Following a Frog Splash from the Nation of Domination's D'Lo Brown, the Outlaws' Road Dogg was an easy target for Kane, who picked up the victory. The winning duo didn't have time to rest on their laurels, though, as they were called back into action later that very same evening against the same opponents. This time they had the added stipulation of Undertaker and Stone Cold as guest referees following some negotiations from D-Generation X leader, Triple H. The match ended in a no contest when a mass brawl broke out at the end of the show.

Undertaker chokeslams Mr. McMahon

July 20: The tension between Undertaker and Mr. McMahon had been simmering over several weeks. On the previous Monday night, Undertaker had told Mr. McMahon he could go to hell. Clearly stung by the insult, McMahon looked for retaliation in this episode of *RAW,* when he wished the same sentiments against Undertaker. The "Deadman" was furious and immediately hit Mr McMahon with a devastating chokeslam. Undertaker's rage was not satisfied however, as he then chokeslammed Gerald Brisco and Sgt. Slaughter, who had run to the aid of their boss.

1998

Star-studded Tag Team Match

August 10: Arguably the most talent-filled match in *RAW* history saw Stone Cold Steve Austin and Undertaker defend their WWE World Tag Team Championships in a Four Corners match. Their opponents read like a Who's Who of top WWE Superstars: The Rock and Owen Hart, The New Age Outlaws, and Kane and Mankind were all duos competing for the gold. The match finished with Kane pinning his brother Undertaker, securing victory for himself and partner Mankind.

Jacqueline captures the Women's Championship

September 21: The Women's Championship had been vacant for many years, until Hall of Famer Jacqueline defeated Sable to become the first active Champion since 1995. Jacqueline had the experience advantage over her opponent; however it required an interference from her partner Marc Mero to secure the victory. As Mero was also Sable's estranged husband, it was a double injustice for her. Sable was left screaming with anger, as Mero and Jacqueline celebrated in the backstage area.

September 21: Jacqueline became the first Superstar since Alundra Blayze to hold the Women's Championship.

Mr. Socko makes his WWE debut

October 5: Despite being known as a "Hardcore Icon" and "King of the Death Match" Mick Foley will also be remembered as the man who gave life to Mr. Socko. A simple tube sock with a crudely drawn face, Mr. Socko was originally used to try and cheer up Mr. McMahon during his stay in hospital but went on to become a cult character to the WWE Universe. Things went from bad to worse for McMahon after Mr. Socko's visit—he was brutally attacked in his hospital room by Stone Cold Steve Austin, who had disguised himself as a doctor.

October 12: The Big Bossman makes his return to WWE to ensure order for Mr. McMahon.

The Big Bossman returns to WWE

October 12: After a five-year absence, the Big Bossman made a dramatic return to WWE. He first appeared as an intimidating presence shrouded in a balaclava but was soon unveiled as Mr. McMahon's bodyguard, wearing a simple uniform and carrying his trusty Nightstick. He used the tool to impose punishment on Stone Cold Steve Austin during the main event. The newly villainous Bossman would see great success in WWE until he left the organisation again in 2003.

The Rock takes on his former teammates

October 19: The demise of the Nation of Domination had coincided with The Rock's meteoric rise as a solo star, and their growing divisions were cemented in this episode of *RAW*. The Rock had taken over from Farooq as leader of the Nation some time ago; however disquiet was now growing among his fellow members. The Rock was out to show who was boss, after being attacked and suffering a big splash from Mark Henry outside of the ring the previous week. At first, The Rock was able to defeat D'Lo Brown with a Rock Bottom, despite the ominous presence of Mark Henry waiting outside the ring. After the bell, Brown and Henry launched another attack on The Rock as the WWE Universe tried to cheer on their hero.

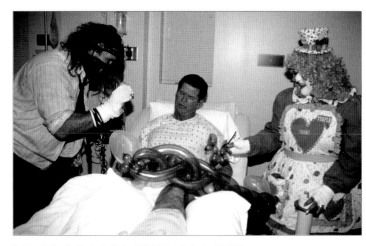

October 5: Despite the best efforts of Mick Foley, Mr. Socko didn't lift the spirits of Mr. McMahon during his hospital visit.

Fighting against the system

November 9: The Rock was all set up to face his former partner, Mark Henry, in the night's main event, but if he lost he would have to leave WWE forever. It appeared to the WWE Universe that Mr. McMahon had done everything possible to stack the deck against The Rock. Earlier in the show The Rock had been attacked, presumably at McMahon's behest, and it seemed doubtful he would even be able to compete. Indeed, as the match drew near, McMahon proclaimed that The Rock wouldn't show up. The Rock not only showed up but defeated Mark Henry and saved his WWE career. To McMahon's anger, it was his own son Shane who made the three-count, following a family argument earlier in the show.

Fighting for the system

November 16: Following the shocking conclusion of the 1998 *Survivor Series,* where it emerged that The Rock and Mr. McMahon had been aligned all along, the WWE Universe were looking for answers. The Rock was happy to provide them and provoked jeers from the crowd as he embraced Mr. McMahon in the centre of the ring. He went on to claim he wasn't a sell-out and was just doing what he had to do to get to the top of the world and become Champion. The Rock's alignment with Mr. McMahon and the Corporation would put him on a direct collision course with Stone Cold Steve Austin—the two would eventually face off at *WrestleMania XV* the following year.

Michaels is the new WWE Commissioner

November 23: Shawn Michaels started the year as the WWE Champion and he finished it as WWE Commissioner. Michaels, who had only appeared sporadically since *WrestleMania* was greeted by rapturous applause from the WWE Universe as his appointment was announced. This joy would prove short-lived, however, as later in the show Michaels would turn on his friend X-Pac and cost him the WWE Championship. The crowd were stunned as Michaels grabbed a steel chair from X-Pac's opponent, The Rock. Instead of defending his friend, Michaels turned the chair on X-Pac and joined the Corporation.

The Corporation don't see the funny side

December 14: D-Generation X are almost as well known for their parodies as they are for their in-ring success and controversial antics. On this occasion their victims were the Corporation, showing that with DX, imitation isn't the sincerest form of flattery. With Triple H going under the name of "The Crock," D-Generation X had the WWE Universe rolling in the aisles, but the members of the Corporation fuming with rage.

November 16: The newly crowned "Corporate Champion," The Rock, makes his entrance on *RAW.*

"The Rock did what The Rock had to do, to get to the top of the world."

The Rock (November 16, 1998)

November 23: Shawn Michaels became WWE Commissioner while he was out of action with a devastating back injury, holding the role until 2000.

September 28, 1998: The Brothers of
Destruction, Kane and Undertaker, face off.

1999

1999 WAS, WITHOUT A DOUBT, one of the defining years in WWE history. This year saw the company solidify their lead in the infamous Monday Night Wars, with *RAW* as their flagship show. From ratings wins, and defections from the competition, to new Champions and the debuts of several Superstars who have attained legendary status with the company, it truly had everything. While the creative content of the show continued to push the envelope, 1999 can also be defined by great ring work, and exciting young stars such as Chris Jericho and Big Show rubbing shoulders with mainstays of the Attitude Era such as The Rock and Steve Austin.

Foley in shock win

January 4: In a surprise twist, Mick Foley as "Mankind" won his first WWE Championship against The Rock. WCW announcers mocked Foley's attempt on air, but the joke was soon on them as viewers switched over to *RAW*. Defecting fans were rewarded by seeing the ultimate underdog, Mick Foley, win his first WWE Championship in a result that had Mr McMahon incandescent with rage.

Chyna makes history

January 11: Chyna became the first women to qualify and later compete in the *Royal Rumble*. The episode hinged around a DX vs. Corporation mini-rumble where the winner would win the coveted number 30 spot. It first appeared as if Vince McMahon had won it, but then Chyna came out to eliminate him and make history.

Mr. McMahon forfeits title shot

January 25: Having won the *Royal Rumble* on January 24, Mr. McMahon made a few announcements the next night on *RAW*. He awarded The Rock the $100,000 bounty for helping him eliminate Austin in the match. He then announced that he was forfeiting his title shot at *WrestleMania*, the first time a winner had done so.

WWE *RAW* Saturday Night electrifies Canada

February 13: This was the first time the show was ever shown on a Saturday. It drew a crowd of 41,432 fans to the Toronto Skydome, making it the best-attended *RAW* event to date.

Elsewhere in WWE

February 14: Big Show made his WWE debut at *St Valentine's Day Massacre*. He made his *RAW* debut the following night as part of Mr. McMahon's Corporation. Eighteen years later, the Big Show is still a fixture of *RAW* and continues to confound and amaze with his vast size and powerful array of moves.

The poster for the *Massacre* shows Mr. McMahon holding a bunch of roses.

The Rock defeats Mankind

February 15: This episode of *RAW* saw one of the key moments of the legendary rivalry between The Rock and Mankind play out in Birmingham, Alabama. The pair had been battling over the WWE Championship for several weeks, with the Title swapping back and forth between them in a series of brutal encounters. On this occasion The Rock got the best of Mankind in an epic Ladder Match, capturing the WWE Championship for the third time with the help of his then fellow Corporation member, Paul Wight—a man who would soon be known to all as the Big Show.

February 15: The Rock uses a ladder to his advantage on his way to winning the WWE Championship from his long-time foe, Mankind.

Undertaker wages psychological warfare

February 22: As part of the ongoing rivalry between Undertaker's Ministry and Vince McMahon's Corporation, Undertaker had taken to playing mind games. In this episode, he burned Mr. McMahon's childhood teddy bear on the show. Later he would again reduce McMahon to tears when he invaded McMahon's Connecticut home and left the Ministry's symbol burning on the front lawn.

February 22:Mr. McMahon can only look on as Undertaker torches his childhood teddy bear. Mr. McMahon would crawl on his knees to the bear when Undertaker tossed it aside.

Soaked in beer

March 22: Stone Cold Steve Austin had had enough of the Corporation. As Mr. McMahon, Shane, and The Rock stood around berating Stone Cold, he decided it was time for a little payback. Austin drove a beer truck into the arena, and proceeded to hose down the members of the Corporation as the crowd cheered. Austin couldn't resist aiming the hose at his own mouth, too.

Ken Shamrock rescues Stephanie McMahon

March 29: Ken Shamrock went above and beyond the call of duty in this episode of *RAW*. As a member of the Corporation, he took it upon himself to attack several members of the Ministry of Darkness in order to help find the kidnapped Stephanie McMahon. Shamrock, also known as the World's Most Dangerous Man, even incurred a symbolic Bloodbath during his quest.

The Rock throws Stone Cold Steve Austin off a bridge

April 12: Around a year previously, Stone Cold Steve Austin threw Intercontinental Champion The Rock's Championship Title into a river in one of the highlights of their rivalry. On this edition of *RAW* it would be The Rock who would have the upper hand. The Rock goaded Austin into meeting him on a bridge over the Detroit River where a brawl started between the two. In a parallel of the events of the previous year, the show ended when The Rock threw Stone Cold from the bridge into the river, tossing in his WWE Championship after him for good measure.

Stone Cold Steve Austin destroys The Rock's car

April 19: A week after he was thrown into the river by The Rock, Stone Cold got his revenge. No stranger to commandeering different types of vehicle, Stone Cold excelled himself when he ran over The Rock's new car in his Austin 3:16 Monster Truck.

April 19: Stone Cold Steve Austin flattens The Rock's Lincoln Continental with his customized Austin 3:16 Monster Truck.

March 22: A soaked Mr. McMahon runs for cover as Stone Cold Steve Austin aims a stream of beer at him.

1999

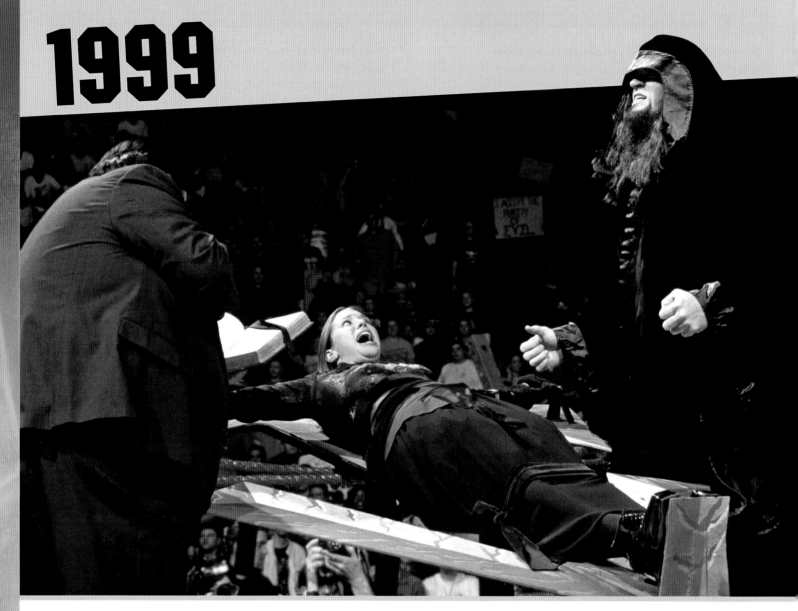

Undertaker tries to marry Stephanie McMahon

April 26: In one of the more disturbing moments in *RAW* history, Undertaker attempted to marry Stephanie McMahon in a Black Wedding Ceremony. Using Stephanie as an unwilling pawn in his battle with Vince McMahon, it looked as if no one would be able to stand in the way of "The Deadman." However, Stephanie was freed by an unlikely savior: Stone Cold Steve Austin brawled his way through the ranks of the Ministry of Darkness and stopped the ceremony, despite his long-standing rivalry with Mr. McMahon.

An unlikely Union is formed

May 3: The Union may not go down in history as a faction to rival the nWo or D-Generation X but the group, founded on this episode of *RAW*, was a force to be reckoned with. Made up of disgruntled former Corporation employees, the short-lived group consisted of Mankind, Big Show, Test, and Ken Shamrock, all of whom had tasted championship gold during their time in WWE.

Undertaker defeats The Rock

May 17: Undertaker is rightly regarded as the king of the Casket Match, having defeated an impressive list of WWE Superstars. A rarity of a match for *RAW*, he faced off against The Rock, eventually locking him in a casket with help from Triple H.

April 26: Undertaker ties Stephanie McMahon to his symbol in an attempt to marry her and gain a psychological advantage in his long-running rivalry with Mr. McMahon.

May 3: Members of The Union—the "Hardcore Icon" Mick Foley, the gargantuan Big Show, the formidable Test, and the "World's Most Dangerous Man" Ken Shamrock—gather to face down the Corporation.

RAW is Owen

May 24: Following the tragic death of Owen Hart, the entirety of this episode of *RAW* was dedicated to him. WWE Superstars wore black armbands in his honor and shared their memories of Owen in front of and behind the camera. The affection shown for Owen that night was touching and reflected not just his popularity with fellow Superstars but his amazing in-ring career.

Mr. McMahon is revealed as the Greater Power

June 7: Few moments in WWE history are as well remembered as Vince McMahon revealing himself to be the mysterious Greater Power. After weeks of speculation as to who was secretly controlling Undertaker and his Ministry of Darkness, it was finally revealed to be the boss himself. As he pulled away his hood, he uttered the now-iconic phrase with a diabolic grin: "It was me, Austin, it was me all along."

June 28: Stone Cold Steve Austin raises his arms in victory after a hard-fought bout against his nemesis, Undertaker.

Stone Cold captures the WWE Title

June 28: Stone Cold Steve Austin captured the WWE Championship for the fourth time in this action-packed edition of *RAW*. Facing Undertaker in the main event, Austin defeated his long-standing foe with his trademark Stone Cold Stunner in front of a frenzied crowd in Charlotte, North Carolina. Austin would hold the Title for 55 days before losing it to Mankind at *SummerSlam*.

The Hardy Boyz capture their first WWE gold

July 5: In beating The Acolytes (later to be known as the APA, consisting of Ron Simmons and John Bradshaw Layfield) the Hardy Boyz took one of the first major steps in their monumental careers. In front of a vocal crowd in their home state of North Carolina, the Hardy Boyz won the first of multiple Tag Team Titles when Matt pinned Layfield following the use of their manager Michael Hayes' cane to secure the win.

June 7: After weeks of speculation Mr McMahon is revealed to be the Greater Power in control of Undertaker and his vile Ministry of Darkness.

1999

Ben Stiller drops in on *RAW*

July 26: Whilst celebrity guest hosts wouldn't become a fixture of *RAW* until years later, the show has always attracted interest from stars in other walks of life. On July 26, popular comedian Ben Stiller appeared on Jeff Jarrett's segment on *RAW* to talk about his newest film. When he became a bit too attentive to Jarrett's valet, Debra Marshall, he was attacked by Double J. It took D'Lo Brown to intervene and save Stiller, carrying him off to the locker room.

D'Lo Brown makes Eurocontinental history

August 2: D'Lo Brown became the first ever "Eurocontinental Champion" when he defeated Jeff Jarrett for the Intercontinental Title on *RAW*. As he already held the European Championship, which he had won from Mideon at *Fully Loaded*, his victory gave him a special place in the record books for holding the two titles at the same time. His status would be short-lived, however—he lost both titles to Jarrett a month later at *SummerSlam*.

August 23: Triple H holds up the WWE Championship alongside Shane McMahon, who made the three-count after knocking out the designated match official.

INTRODUCING...

Chris Jericho

August 9: Chris "Y2J" Jericho had one of the most memorable debuts in WWE history. After weeks of the Millennium Countdown clock ticking down, Y2J emerged on *RAW* with a barrage of fireworks and fan hysteria. His immediate verbal sparring session with The Rock would become the stuff of legend. Jericho's career became equally legendary, with the Canadian going on to win every major championship possible in WWE. Over the years he would introduce the WWE Universe to new moves and personas—and his infamous "List of Jericho."

Chris Jericho has shown himself to be equally gifted on the microphone and in the ring throughout his glorious WWE career.

"Welcome to... *RAW* is Jericho!"

Chris Jericho (August 9, 1999)

Triple H wins the WWE Championship for the first time

August 23: There are few Superstars in history with a record of success that is comparable to that of Triple H, or "The Game." On this edition of *RAW* he won the WWE Championship for the first time when he defeated Mankind, who had only won the Title the previous evening at *SummerSlam*. This was the first of nine WWE title reigns for the "Cerebral Assassin," Triple H.

The Rock 'n' Sock Connection capture their first WWE Tag Team Championships

August 30: As far as unlikely duos go, the "Rock 'n' Sock Connection" have to be up there. The team consisting of The Rock and Mankind was clearly an odd couple, the former being the charismatic "People's Champion" and the latter being the hardcore legend, yet frequently hilarious, owner of a tube-sock-turned-mascot—Mr. Socko. The pair would go on to win the World Tag Team Championships three times, but this was their first on *RAW*, when they defeated the formidable alliance of Undertaker and Big Show.

The British Bulldog makes surprise return to *RAW*

September 13: Few will forget the iconic moment when The British Bulldog Davey Boy Smith won the Intercontinental Title at *SummerSlam 1992* in front of a capacity crowd at Wembley Stadium in London, England. His return to WWE caught many by surprise seven years later, when he appeared on *RAW* and announced his intention to win the WWE Championship before he retired.

September 13: The British Bulldog returned to WWE with a new look and a new attitude in 1999.

Mr. McMahon relinquishes the Title

September 20: Mr. McMahon relinquished the WWE Title after just four days in order to set up a Six-Pack Challenge Match at *Unforgiven*. Mr. McMahon had won the Title by defeating Triple H on *SmackDown* with the help on an unlikely ally, Stone Cold Steve Austin.

This Is Your Life, Rock

September 27: Together with his tube-sock hand puppet, Mr. Socko, Mankind hosted a hilarious segment parodying the 1950s TV show *This Is Your Life* to honor his tag team partner, The Rock. It was Mankind's way of making up to The Rock after several clashes over the year. Following the format of the TV show, Mankind invited people from The Rock's past to come on. One by one they were revealed—a home-economics teacher, a high-school football coach, and a former high-school sweetheart. As things soon started unraveling on the trip down Memory Lane, Mankind asked Yurple the Clown to lead the singing of *Happy Birthday* to The Rock.

RAW invades WCW territory

October 11: *RAW* was held at the Georgia Dome. Just a few months earlier, the thought of *Monday Night RAW* coming to the heartland of WCW for a live show would have been unimaginable. A huge feather in the cap for WWE at the time, running a show in front of a jam-packed crowd during the Monday Night Wars emphasized their superiority over the competition. It proved to be another defining moment in the battle against Ted Turner's company.

Ivory captures the Women's Championship

October 25: On this episode of *RAW*, Ivory defeated the Fabulous Moolah for the Women's Championship. This match was especially notable as the Fabulous Moolah, accompanied by her great friend Mae Young, was 76 years old at the time.

September 27: Balloons rain down on The Rock as part of Mankind's birthday tribute to his tag team partner.

1999

Kurt Angle embarks on a legendary career

November 15: Kurt Angle is undoubtedly one of the greatest performers ever to set foot in the ring. He made his in-ring *RAW* debut in November 1999, when he defeated fellow WWE Hall of Famer The Godfather in a short match with a trademark suplex.

In the same episode of *RAW,* The Rock suffered a rare defeat in a Number One Contendership Match with the Big Bossman. Far removed from his early days in the WWE as a fan-favorite, the Big Bossman was aggressively pursuing the WWE Champion, Big Show. This victory allowed him the chance to challenge Show for his title, an attempt which ultimately proved unsuccessful.

November 15: Following his Olympic Gold Medal triumph in 1996, it didn't take Angle long to introduce the WWE Universe to his "Three I's": intensity, integrity and intelligence.

Wedding crasher

November 29: Stephanie McMahon was due to marry Test in a ceremony on *RAW*. As the couple were about to take their vows, Triple H interrupted the ceremony. He objected that Stephanie couldn't marry Test because she was already married—to him. The wedding party could only look on as Triple H showed them a video of his wedding to Stephanie at a drive-through chapel. This act took Triple H's psychological warfare on Mr. McMahon to a new level.

"Santa Claus" attacks Mankind

December 20: Few WWE Superstars are as transfixed by Christmas as Mick Foley, which made it a cruel twist of fate that he was attacked by several versions of "Santa Claus" during a Boiler Room Brawl. The Santas were later revealed as Triple H's allies—the New Age Outlaws. Triple H, also disguised as Santa, would go on to win the match, leaving a stricken Mankind on the boiler room floor.

November 29: Mr. McMahon, Stephanie, and Test, along with the wedding party, look on in shock as Triple H plays the video.

Mankind is fired from WWE

December 27: The Rock defeated Mankind in a Pink Slip on a Pole Match, meaning Mankind was "fired" from WWE. Of course, Mick Foley would have many more iconic moments in WWE to come—however, on this episode of *RAW* it really did appear that his career would be over following the loss. As he made his way out of the arena, fans saluted one of the true heroes of the Attitude Era.

December 20: Showing that not everyone was feeling the Christmas spirit, Mankind is attacked by the New Age Outlaws in a Boiler Room Brawl.

December 27: The Rock beats Mankind in getting to the pink slip.

2000

THIS YEAR WWE DOMINATED its rival WCW in terms of ratings, and the McMahon–Helmsley alliance dominated programming. Aside from the continued excellence of Triple H, 2000 saw several new stars emerge, most notably Kurt Angle, who won the WWE Championship in October. Angle was also involved in a memorable love triangle with Triple H over the affections of Stephanie McMahon. Stone Cold Steve Austin made a welcome return to the ring, having recovered after being hit by a car at *Survivor Series 1999*. The entire McMahon family was also heavily involved in WWE programming, with the battle for full ownership of the company providing many entertaining moments. With Superstars such as The Rock, Triple H, Undertaker, Kurt Angle, and the returning Austin at the height of their powers, the year 2000 is remembered as one of the greatest and most successful in WWE history.

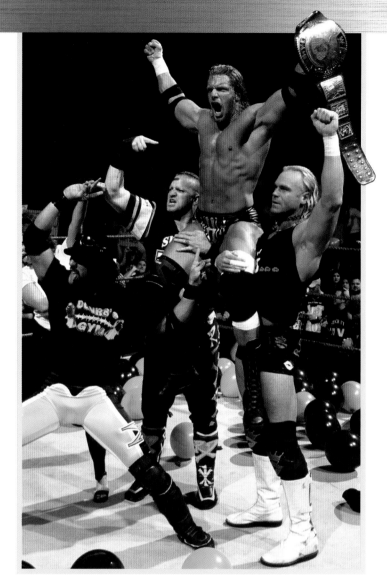

January 3: Triple H celebrates winning his third WWE Championship with fellow D-Generation X members.

The Rock leads a mass protest

January 10: Uniting 50 WWE Superstars around a single goal may seem like an impossible task, but The Rock managed to achieve this feat as a protest against the McMahon-Helmsley era. Specifically, the WWE locker room was united over the treatment of Mick Foley. The Rock threatened a mass walkout, unless the recently fired Foley was reinstated to WWE. Triple H eventually bowed to the pressure and reinstated the hardcore icon. Foley would later challenge Triple H to a match at the upcoming *Royal Rumble,* which would go down as one of the most entertaining and brutal of the year.

Triple H claims the WWE Championship

January 3: The first *RAW* of the new millennium set the tone for the year when a thrilling show was capped by Triple H claiming his third WWE Championship. Facing off against the defending Champion, Big Show, it proved a hard-fought encounter, with Triple H using his attritional abilities to counteract Big Show's sheer size and power. Triple H secured the win after his DX cohorts distracted the official, allowing Triple H to hit Big Show with a low blow, followed by his signature Pedigree.

"Triple H and Stephanie, bring your candy asses out here and face The Rock!"

The Rock (January 10, 2000)

The Radicalz make their first WWE appearance

January 31: The introduction of The Radicalz to WWE television was without question one of the standout moments of the Attitude Era. The group, consisting of Perry Saturn, Eddie Guerrero, Chris Benoit, and Dean Malenko, had all been fixtures at WCW, and such a mass jumping of talent was truly unprecedented. This group initially appeared as members of the crowd; however, it did not take long for them to make an impact. They attacked Road Dogg and performed their signature moves on him and Mr. Ass Billy Gunn, to the delight of the live crowd.

The Radicalz' shocking alignment

February 7: It was revealed that Mick Foley had played a huge part in persuading new fan-favorites The Radicalz to jump ship to WWE. *RAW* opened with The Radicalz acknowledging Foley's role and inviting him to join them in the ring. Triple H then came out to address Foley and make their upcoming match at *No Way Out* a Career vs. Title match. The shocking twist came when Triple H walked confidently into the ring surrounded by The Radicalz and Foley and announced that the group should prove their loyalty to the man (Triple H) who gave them their WWE contracts. The group proceeded to attack Foley as the stunned crowd looked on.

March 13: The Rock lays the smackdown on Big Show.

The Rock earns a title shot

March 13: With The Rock facing off against the gigantic Big Show, and with the surprise addition of The Rock's foe, Shane McMahon, as a match official, the odds didn't look good for "The Great One." In fact, it looked like it would take a miracle for The Rock to earn a WWE Championship shot at *WrestleMania 2000*! However, a miracle arrived, in the form of Mr. McMahon. As the match seemed to be coming to its inevitable conclusion, a limousine containing Mr. McMahon arrived. Mr. McMahon knocked Triple H out with a right hand, then marched down to the ring and did the same to his son, Shane. He then donned Shane's striped shirt and made the three-count as The Rock pinned Big Show!

A winning combination

March 27: In one of the most star-studded main events in *RAW* history, the team of The Rock and Mr. McMahon defeated Shane McMahon and Big Show with Triple H and Mick Foley as match officials. The match eventually broke down when Triple H dropped an elbow on his fellow official, Foley, preventing him from making a three-count. This prompted an irate Mr. McMahon to strike Triple H and knock him out of the ring. In the ensuing melee, Mick Foley applied his Mandible Claw to Big Show, allowing The Rock to hit Shane with his Rock Bottom maneuver and secure the win.

> ### Elsewhere in WWE
>
> **April 2:** *WrestleMania 2000* took place at the Arrowhead Pond in Anaheim, California. The showcase event of the year was main-evented by a Fatal 4-Way between Triple H, The Rock, Mick Foley, and Big Show, who each had a different member of the McMahon family in their corner.

Eddie Guerrero is European Champion

April 3: As well as capturing his first European Championship, Eddie Guerrero won the heart of Chyna. She had previously avoided the advances of "Latino Heat" Guerrero, and accompanied her ally, Chris Jericho, to the ring. With the official dazed, Chyna slid into the ring and counted an unofficial three-count for Jericho; as she raised his hands in victory she hit him with a low blow and pulled Guerrero on top of Jericho. Chyna then revived the official who counted the fall as Guerrero secured the Championship. He then embraced Chyna in front of a pained and crestfallen Jericho.

A Championship win overturned

April 17: While Triple H was distracted after shoving over WWE official Earl Hebner, Chris "Y2J" Jericho pounced, hitting "The Game" with a spinning heel kick and then a moonsault off the ropes to secure the pin. The crowd went wild as Y2J grabbed an unexpected win against the seemingly indomitable Game. Jericho's reign would last only a matter of minutes as Triple H, along with Stephanie and Shane McMahon, physically intimidated referee Hebner to make him reverse his decision.

April 17: After seemingly losing his Championship to Chris Jericho, Triple H resorts to physical intimidation, alongside his brother-in-law, Shane McMahon.

2000

Inside a steel cage

May 1: The Rock once again beat the odds to retain his WWE Championship against Shane McMahon in this Steel Cage main event. With Mr. McMahon and Triple H lurking outside the ring and stooge Pat Patterson as the match official, The Rock had his work cut out to emerge from the cage with his precious Championship intact. It looked as if the numbers at ringside had finally taken their toll on The Rock, until an unlikely savior arrived in the form of referee Earl Hebner, who came down to the ring and slammed the cage door on Triple H, allowing The Rock to escape.

May 1: The Rock hits guest official Pat Patterson with the Rock Bottom.

Shawn Michaels' surprise return

May 15: Before a raucous Cleveland crowd, Shawn Michaels made a surprise return appearance in this episode. The fans were stunned, however, when Michaels then resigned as WWE Commissioner after admitting that he hadn't been sufficiently available to do his job and curb the McMahon-Helmsley Era. The WWE Universe were clearly disappointed at Michaels' resignation, but they soon found reason to cheer when Michaels announced himself as the special guest referee for the upcoming Iron Man Match for the WWE Championship between The Rock and Triple H at *Judgment Day*.

Kane unites with Undertaker and The Rock

May 29: Undertaker and The Rock were forced to face each other in the main event. The match was made even more volatile when Mr. McMahon announced that it would be a Lumberjack Match. The Lumberjacks consisted of Triple H and his allies, meaning that the two in-ring opponents were surrounded by hostility. As expected, the match eventually broke down, with the Lumberjacks attacking the two men until the intervention of the "Big Red Machine," Kane. The returning Kane cleared the ring and the show closed with him standing over a prone Triple H and holding his WWE Championship aloft.

May 29: The returning Kane signals his intention to fight for the WWE Championship.

Crash Holly and the Hardcore Championship

June 12: Few Superstars are more synonymous with the WWE Hardcore Championship than Crash Holly, who won the Title an astonishing 22 times—second only to Raven, who had 27 reigns. The 24/7 rule was the predominant reason for such a high turnover of Champions. According to this wacky rule, the Title was constantly on the line day or night, as long as a WWE official was present. One beneficiary was Mr. McMahon's comedic stooge Gerald Brisco. However, in this *RAW* episode, Brisco was defeated for the Hardcore Title by Holly, following an accidental shot from a trash can by Brisco's ally, Pat Patterson.

June 26: "I get to make the matches! I get to make the decisions!" Mick Foley enjoys the reaction from the crowd as he makes his WWE return as Commissioner.

Mick Foley becomes WWE Commissioner

June 26: Once Mick Foley was announced as the new WWE Commissioner by the previous incumbent, Shawn Michaels, he wasted little time making his mark. Foley mocked Triple H, who had arrived in the ring to confront Michaels, accusing Triple H of "whining" about not being the number-one contender for the WWE Championship. He also impersonated Triple H, claiming that no one would ever have to listen to "a boring, 20-minute, Triple H promo again!" Foley then turned his attention to the newly crowned King of the Ring, Kurt Angle, laughing out loud at his crown, scepter, and robes.

Triple H receives a Stinkface

July 3: Following his match with Rikishi, Triple H was the recipient of one of the most feared moves in sports entertainment, Rikishi's humiliating signature move, the Stinkface. After Triple H was counted out, Chris Jericho rolled Triple H back into the ring—whereupon the 425lbs (205kg) Rikishi rubbed his rear end all over Triple H's face as his wife, Stephanie McMahon, looked on, horrified.

July 10: "I want you to accept my gift and ride what a real American rides!" Kurt Angle's provocative gift of a scooter is guaranteed to enrage Undertaker.

Kurt Angle's peace offering

July 10: "American Hero" Kurt Angle had been getting under Undertaker's skin over recent weeks, so it was no surprise that "The Deadman" called Angle to the ring, to settle things once and for all. Undertaker was particularly incensed that Angle had poured milk on his brand-new Titan motorcycle. Angle ducked out of an impromptu match, but brought "The American Badass" an insulting "peace offering"—a tiny scooter. Undertaker chased Angle to the backstage area, speeding after him on his Titan hog.

Marriage problems?

July 31: With *RAW* appearing at Georgia Dome—the heart of WCW territory—the WWE Universe expected an epic show, and they weren't disappointed. In recent weeks, Triple H and Stephanie McMahon-Helmsley had been having marital problems. Stephanie had caught Triple H in a compromising position with Trish Stratus, under the guise of wrestling training. This episode's main event was meant to be Triple H and his wife against The Rock and Lita; however, when Triple H accidentally called Stephanie "Trish" in training, she walked out of the building. Triple H tried to postpone the match but Commissioner Foley arranged for Trish to partner "The Game." The match ended with Lita pinning Trish, following her trademark Moonsault. The Rock then hit Triple H with a chair and he passed out on Trish in a *very* compromising position!

Tazz and Lawler come to blows

August 7: Tazz had taken exception to comments Jim Ross had previously made about him on commentary, and to say he overreacted would be an understatement. As Tazz approached "Good Old" JR, he called him a "redneck scumbag," and proceeded to knock the cowboy hat from his head, earning a slap from JR. Tazz continued to provoke the announcer, until JR's partner, Jerry "The King" Lawler, intervened and hit Tazz. The two combatants were then separated by the officials.

2000

Lita wins the Championship

August 21: Hall of Famer Lita will go down as one of the all-time great Women's Champions. This episode of *RAW* saw her lift the Championship for the first time against Stephanie McMahon-Helmsley in a main event that featured The Rock as special guest referee. Stephanie was not alone—she had both Kurt Angle and her husband, Triple H, in her corner; however, when Kurt Angle accidentally incapacitated Triple H when aiming for The Rock, she had nowhere to go. Lita hit Stephanie with her trademark spectacular Moonsault finishing move for the pin.

August 21: WWE Hall of Famer Lita proudly holds her first Women's Championship aloft.

September 4: In a great display of teamwork, Edge and Christian target Undertaker and keep him from tagging his partner The Rock—shortly before the match descends into chaos!

The underdogs have the edge

September 4: Despite being one of the greatest teams in WWE history, Edge and Christian were still underdogs in their Championship defence against The Rock and Undertaker. In a pulsating main event, both teams had chances to win and several near falls. It was an interference from Kane, who had been on guest commentary, that enabled the Champions to hit The Rock with a devastating Con-Chair-To and secure the victory.

Elsewhere in WWE

September 21: In *SmackDown*, Kurt Angle added further intrigue to his relationship with Stephanie McMahon. Leading up to his match at the *Unforgiven* pay-per-view event with her husband, Triple H, Angle attacked "The Game" with a sledgehammer. As Triple H writhed in pain, Angle proceeded to kiss Stephanie!

Stone Cold looks for answers

September 25: Following his return to WWE at *Unforgiven* the previous evening, Stone Cold Steve Austin kicked off *RAW* with a typically powerful address to the WWE Universe. Austin proclaimed that he was going to continue to drink beer, raise his middle finger and do what he wanted, when he wanted! He also announced that he was on a mission to discover who had run him over and put him out of action for nine months.

Kurt Angle celebrates his first Championship win

October 23: Kurt Angle had much to celebrate on this episode of *RAW*, not least the feat of becoming WWE Champion within his first year of active competition. He was announced, to jeers, by his business partner, Stephanie McMahon, as fireworks erupted and streamers and balloons fell from the ceiling. His over-the-top celebrations were soon interrupted by Commissioner Foley who awarded The Rock a rematch that night in a Triple Threat Match also containing Triple H. Angle would retain his Championship via disqualification following an interference from Rikishi.

October 23: Kurt Angle celebrates his first WWE Championship win along with Stephanie McMahon in a less than understated style.

Rikishi admits to running over Stone Cold

October 9: In a shocking twist to Mick Foley's investigation into Stone Cold Steve Austin's mystery assailant, Rikishi confessed he was the culprit. Mick Foley had found evidence to prove it was Rikishi, he just didn't know why. The response from Rikishi was astonishing—he had done it for his cousin, The Rock; and not just for his cousin, but for the people of Samoa. The Rock, who was not involved in the incident, looked disgusted as his cousin repeated that he was the one who did it, and that he'd do it again.

Triple H reveals he was behind attack on Austin

November 6: Triple H revealed himself to be the man behind Rikishi's attack on Stone Cold Steve Austin in dramatic fashion. After interfering in the Triple Threat main event between Austin, Rikishi, and Kurt Angle, Triple H attacked Austin with his trademark sledgehammer. He then put on a black glove and proceeded to attack Austin alongside Rikishi before telling him the search was over and he was responsible for nearly ending his career.

Mick Foley fired as WWE Commissioner

December 18: Stephanie McMahon, who had previously been at odds with her father, reaffirmed her allegiance by gleefully announcing that Mr. McMahon had full control of the company again. Mr. McMahon used his newly regained power immediately by uttering the infamous line, "You're fired" to WWE Commissioner Mick Foley, making sure he would once again finish the year badly. Injury was then added to insult when Kurt Angle levelled Foley with a steel chair, leaving him helpless in the ring as Mr. McMahon wished him a Merry Christmas.

October 9: WWE Commissioner Mick Foley discovers it was Rikishi who had run over Steve Austin.

2001

2001 WAS ONE OF THE MOST incident- packed in the history of sports entertainment. It saw the end of the Monday Night Wars through the purchase of WCW by WWE, which, alongside the fall of ECW, effectively ended all outside competition. Naturally, the year was dominated by the invasion of WWE by WCW and ECW Superstars, leading to many twists and unforgettable moments. Many new Superstars emerged this year, such as Booker T and Rob Van Dam. Kurt Angle continued to thrill fans with his in-ring skill and charisma, and the McMahon family drama continued to entertain all. The year would eventually belong to Chris Jericho, who would finish 2001 as the first ever Undisputed WWE Champion.

Triple H returns
January 8: Triple H made an impactful return to *RAW* when he cost Stone Cold Steve Austin a chance of winning the WWE Championship by interfering in his match with Kurt Angle. Austin had all but won the match, but as the WWE official was making the count The Game pulled him out of the ring and knocked him out as Austin looked on, stunned. "The Texas Rattlesnake" then invited Triple H into the ring and the two had a brutal brawl which ended when The Game knocked Austin out with a metal pipe.

Test wins the European Championship
January 22: Despite standing at 6ft 6in (1.98m) in height and weighing in at 285lbs (129kg), the formidable Test was still the underdog going into his match against the vastly experienced European Champion, William Regal. The WWE Universe looked on in shock as Test dominated the match and disposed of Regal in a matter of minutes to claim the Championship. He would go on to hold the Championship for an impressive 69 days before losing to Eddie Guerrero at *WrestleMania X-Seven*.

Former ECW Champion Justin Credible debuts on *RAW*
February 12: In an unexpected defection from ECW, Justin Credible came to the aid of X-Pac against the reigning Intercontinental Champion, Chris Jericho. X-Pac, who had himself returned to *RAW* when he attacked Jericho earlier that night, was suffering retribution at the hands of Jericho following a match with Brian Christopher. As Jericho stood over the prone X-Pac, Credible ran to the ring and levelled the Canadian with a steel chair in front of a stunned crowd.

February 12: Former ECW Champion Justin Credible makes a surprise appearance on *RAW*.

January 8: The returning Triple H interrupts a potential three-count.

The Rock and Austin face off

February 26: In the lead-up to their legendary match at *WrestleMania X-Seven*, The Rock and Stone Cold Steve Austin opened *RAW* by facing off in the ring. The two legends had very clear messages for each other. Austin told The Rock to stay healthy until the match, while The Rock told Steve Austin that all he had to do was get ready. Austin helped preserve The Rock's health later that night when he saved The Great One following a vicious attack from Kurt Angle, Albert, and Perry Saturn.

February 26: The Rock and Stone Cold Steve Austin face off prior to their *WrestleMania* encounter.

March 5: ECW owner Paul Heyman proves to be a thorn in JR's side on commentary.

Paul Heyman joins and The Hardy Boyz triumph

March 5: Following Jerry Lawler's departure, he was replaced on commentary by none other than Paul Heyman. At this point Heyman was known purely as the owner of ECW ,and no one was expecting him to show up on *RAW*. Heyman clearly had friction with fellow commentator "Good Old" JR right from the get-go, and the clashing styles of the two announcers provided some hugely entertaining moments.

In the same edition, The Hardy Boyz captured the WWE Tag Team Championship for the fourth time against their great rivals, The Dudleys. The Hardys had Christian to thank for the win—he hit D-Von Dudley with a steel chair, allowing Matt Hardy to use the Twist of Fate for the win. This would be far from the end of issues between the two teams.

Shane shamed and Titles change hands twice

March 19: In an honorable act, Shane McMahon called out his own father and offered to fight him at *WrestleMania* in defence of his mother, Linda, who had been suffering terrible treatment from her husband. Vince McMahon not only signed the contract for the match but set up an attack from his son-in-law, Triple H. "The Game" leveled Shane with a Pedigree as Mr. McMahon and Stephanie looked on in delight. Mr. McMahon then told Shane that he would never forgive his wife Linda for giving birth to him.

In an unprecedented series of events on *RAW*, the WWE Universe witnessed not one, but two, Title changes on the same night. The first change occurred after the debuting former ECW superstar, Rhyno, gored Jeff Hardy, allowing Edge to make the pin and capture the Championships for the sixth time. This wouldn't last long, however, as The Dudleys would capture the Championships against Edge and Christian following an interference from another unexpected debutant, their little brother Spike Dudley.

2001

March 26: In a historic moment, Shane McMahon reveals he has beaten his father to buy WCW.

Mr. McMahon ends the Monday Night Wars

March 26: *RAW* opened with a shot of Mr. McMahon watching both *RAW* and *Nitro* simultaneously on two televisions. He went on to explain how he had bought his competition and would address WWE and WCW fans and Superstars alike in a historic simulcast. As the simulcast began Mr. McMahon described how WCW was dead and buried and that the deal would be signed at *WrestleMania*. At the same time, at *Nitro* in Panama City, Florida, Shane McMahon emerged to huge cheers. The sight of Shane McMahon in a WCW ring was surreal enough, but when Shane announced he had beaten his father to the deal and was the new owner of WCW, it cemented its place as one of the most shocking twists in the history of sports entertainment.

Elsewhere in WWE

April 1: At *WrestleMania X-Seven*, 67,925 fans packed the Reliant Astrodome in Houston, Texas. The event, full of excellent matches, finished with an epic main event between The Rock and Stone Cold Steve Austin. Austin would triumph to win his fifth WWE Title and shockingly align with his old enemy, Mr. McMahon.

Things go from bad to worse for The Rock

April 2: This episode of *RAW* saw the deck stacked even more firmly against "The People's Champion," The Rock. After Stone Cold Steve Austin had done the unthinkable and aligned with Mr. McMahon at *WrestleMania* in order to win the WWE Championship, The Rock found himself up against two powerful enemies. Two would soon become three when, after The Rock was locked in a steel cage and beaten down by Austin and McMahon, Triple H ran to the ring, seemingly to his aid, as the crowd cheered. As Triple H and Austin stared each other down they suddenly both turned on The Rock, with Triple H knocking him down with a sledgehammer.

Triple H regains the Intercontinental Championship

April 16: Following his dramatic and surprising loss to Jeff Hardy on *SmackDown*, "The Game" was determined to win back the Intercontinental Championship. Triple H succeeded, but only after the interference of his new ally, Stone Cold Steve Austin, who first attacked Matt Hardy and then stalked towards Lita at ringside. This distraction allowed Triple H to level Jeff Hardy with the Pedigree and claim the Intercontinental Championship for the fourth time.

Stephanie McMahon falls victim to the Stink Face

May 7: When Rikishi defied the orders of Stephanie McMahon and WWE Commissioner William Regal to apply the Stink Face to Mick Foley, retribution was never going to be far away. On this night, however, there would be retribution for none other than Stephanie herself. Following the main event of Stone Cold Steve Austin vs. Rikishi, Stephanie fell victim to the Stink Face herself as a delighted Foley looked on. The show closed with Stephanie looking horrified as laughter filled the arena.

Angle hits Shane with the Angle Slam

May 21: In typical fashion, Kurt Angle decided to celebrate winning back his medals with a ceremony live on *RAW*. With tickertape falling from the ceiling, Angle was clearly overjoyed and determined to share this with the WWE Universe. His celebrations were short-lived when the WCW owner, Shane McMahon, came down to the ring to rain on Angle's parade. Angle took exception to this and hit Shane with an Angle slam from atop a medal stand, and then proceeded to hook the devastating ankle lock on the screaming Shane.

May 21: Kurt Angle looks on in anger as Shane McMahon interrupts his medal ceremony.

June 18: Diamond Dallas Page rides to the ring before he reveals himself to the WWE Universe.

DDP revealed to be the stalker of Undertaker's wife

June 18: After weeks of speculation as to who was stalking Undertaker's wife, Sara, it was revealed to be none other than former WCW World Champion Diamond Dallas Page. Page revealed himself in dramatic fashion as he rode masked to the ring on a motorcycle in a similar fashion to Undertaker. As he stood in the center of the ring and suddenly pulled off his mask he was greeted by gasps from the astonished WWE Universe.

The WCW invasion begins at Madison Square Garden

June 25: After attacking Stone Cold Steve Austin at the *King of the Ring* the previous evening, both Austin and Mr. McMahon were out for revenge against the WCW contingent of Booker T and Shane McMahon. Things wouldn't go their way, however, as the crafty Shane McMahon lured both Austin and Kurt Angle to the nearby WWE New York restaurant in their quest for revenge. With Austin and Angle out of the picture, Mr. McMahon was left alone. He was soon attacked from behind in the center of the ring by Booker T, with Shane McMahon looking on. The show closed with the WWE locker room chasing Booker T out of their symbolic home in Madison Square Garden.

July 2: Booker T levels Buff Bagwell in a lacklustre WCW main event on *RAW*.

WCW main event Monday Night *RAW*

July 2: In an event that no one thought they would ever see, two WCW Superstars faced off in the main event of *RAW*. With WCW Diva Stacy Keibler as the ring announcer and Arn Anderson alongside Scott Hudson on commentary, the match between Booker T and Buff Bagwell for the WCW Championship certainly had a unique feel. The match itself wasn't an all-time classic, and the fans erupted as Stone Cold Steve Austin and Kurt Angle hit the ring to attack Booker T and interrupt the action.

2001

ECW and WCW join forces against WWE

July 9: This action-packed episode of *RAW* saw not just one, but two shocking twists. Firstly, following a match between Chris Jericho and Kane against WCW's Lance Storm and Mike Awesome, ECW superstars Rob Van Dam and Tommy Dreamer invaded the ring to attack the WWE Superstars. As they proceeded to beat them down, several more WWE Superstars such as Raven, Tazz, and the Dudley Boyz ran down to help their colleagues. However, in a shocking twist, they turned against the WWE, united by their former boss Paul Heyman. The intrigue wouldn't end there, as the main event of *RAW* saw WCW and WWE united to take on the ECW invasion. However, the two rival promotions would soon unite against WWE as Shane McMahon revealed the new owner of ECW was none other than his sister, Stephanie, merging the two companies in their war with WWE.

July 23: Kurt Angle clotheslines D-Von before a narrow defeat at the hands of the Alliance.

Heroic Kurt Angle battles three WCW opponents

July 23: In a Tag Team Table Elimination Match, Kurt Angle was left on his own after the unfortunate elimination of his partners Christian and Edge at the hands of the Dudley Boyz and Booker T. Despite the numerical disadvantage, Angle fought bravely, eliminating both D-Von Dudley and Booker T, leaving just himself and Bubba Ray standing as the match drew to a close. As Angle appeared to be in control, Stone Cold Steve Austin jumped the Olympic gold medallist from behind, allowing Bubba Ray to powerbomb him through a table.

July 9: Shane reveals his sister, Stephanie, as the new owner of ECW.

Stone Cold Steve Austin clears house

July 16: In one of the more iconic moments of the era, Stone Cold Steve Austin marched to the ring and viciously attacked multiple WCW and ECW Superstars in order to leave the WWE standing tall prior to the *Invasion* pay-per-view. Austin hit multiple Stone Cold Stunners as Kane and Undertaker chokeslammed the remaining invaders, leaving themselves alongside Chris Jericho and Kurt Angle as sole survivors amongst the carnage. Austin would go on to shockingly turn on the WWE and join the Alliance at the *Invasion*.

"Finally The Rock has come back to the WWE."

The Rock (July 30, 2001)

The returning Rock commits to WWE

July 30: Speculation had been mounting as to whether the returning Rock would commit to WWE or join the Alliance on this episode of *RAW*. As the show drew to a close, The Rock arrived in a limousine. A host of photographers surrounded the car as he marched into the arena with purpose. As The Rock arrived in the ring, Shane, Stephanie, and Mr. McMahon all pitched for his services as the Great One stared impassively. The crowd were aghast when he suddenly hit Mr. McMahon with the Rock Bottom and appeared to join the Alliance. However, they erupted as he then hit Shane with the same move and announced he was WWE through and through.

Kurt Angle crashes Stone Cold appreciation night
August 20: In a truly iconic moment, Kurt Angle drove a milk truck to the ring and proceeded to douse the Alliance, as the WWE Universe went wild. In a moment which echoed Steve Austin's famous beer truck *RAW* invasion several years previously, it would be Austin who would fall victim to Angle on this occasion. The crowd erupted as Angle chugged two cartons of milk on the hood of the truck as the soaked Alliance slipped around the ring.

Christian turns on Edge
September 3: This unexpected *RAW* moment saw one of the greatest teams in WWE history split up in violent fashion. Following his defence of the Intercontinental Championship against Lance Storm, Edge was attacked by his disgruntled opponent after the bell. His brother and partner Christian ran down to make the save and the two embraced in the ring to cheers from the crowd. Suddenly Christian turned and hit Edge hard with a steel chair, leaving him knocked out on the mat. The jealous Christian then attacked Edge with his own *King of the Ring* trophy in a vicious attack before WWE officials intervened.

Tajiri defeats Chris Kanyon
September 10: The Invasion made it possible for WCW Championships to be defended on WWE programming, which made for a wide array of matches and incidents. One such example was Tajiri defeating Chris Kanyon for the WCW United States Championship on *RAW*, several weeks after Kanyon had been awarded the title on *Smackdown*. Tajiri, accompanied by the beautiful Torrie Wilson, defeated Kanyon with a spinning kick after temporarily blinding him with green mist in a popular victory.

August 20: Kurt Angle chugs back milk after his attack on the Alliance.

September 10: Tajiri uses green mist to defeat Chris Kanyon for the WCW United States Championship.

The Rock defeats Rob Van Dam

September 24: The Rock retained the WCW Championship against Rob Van Dam thanks to the accidental help of Stephanie McMahon. In the middle of the main event, Stephanie got into an altercation with the WCW official Charles Robinson and pushed him against the ropes. Little did she know that RVD was up there, getting ready for a Five Star Frog Splash. When Robinson hit the ropes, RVD lost his balance, which allowed The Rock to hit him with a Rock Bottom to retain the Championship.

September 24: RVD clotheslines The Rock before his defeat at the hands of the "People's Champion."

Stone Cold captures the WWE Championship

October 8: In an epic main event on *RAW*, Kurt Angle put his WWE Championship on the line against the returning Stone Cold Steve Austin. Perhaps unsurprisingly in a match between two of the all-time greats, the match was a classic and had fans in the arena and at home at the edge of their seats. The match ended when William Regal, the WWE Commissioner, turned on Angle and hit the Olympian with the Championship Title. This wasn't enough to finish Angle, however; it still required Austin to pull him up and execute another Stunner to seal the win and the Championship.

The Rock and Chris Jericho capture the Tag Team Titles

October 22: In the lead-up to *Survivor Series*, the rivalry between WWE and the Alliance was at fever pitch. This episode of *RAW* saw WWE claim four Championships on the same night with the highlight being the main event between Chris Jericho and The Rock and the Dudley Boyz. Despite the individual talent of the WWE pairing, the Dudley Boyz were a formidable unit, with Stacy Keibler on the outside lending an air of unpredictability. The match finished with the "People's Champion" hitting the Rock Bottom for the win. He presented his teammate Jericho with his newly won Tag Team Championship as well as his WCW Championship.

October 8: The returning Stone Cold Steve Austin is able to overcome Kurt Angle.

Ric Flair returns to *RAW*

November 19: Following the *Survivor Series* that ended the Alliance, this was a historic episode of *RAW*. It opened with Mr. McMahon firing Paul Heyman and replacing him with the returning Jerry "The King" Lawler, but the excitement didn't end there. In the final segment of the show, Mr. McMahon and WWE hero Kurt Angle were interrupted by the legendary Ric Flair who received a gigantic ovation as he strutted to the ring. Flair then revealed he had purchased the WWE stock Shane and Stephanie had sold, making him and Mr. McMahon partners in business and co-WWE owners.

Undertaker turns on Jim Ross

November 26: In an unexpected moment, Undertaker turned on Jim Ross and forced him to join Vince McMahon's "Kiss My Ass Club." Undertaker explained that he had been kissing Mr. McMahon's ass for eleven years and that unless Jim Ross thought he was better than him he'd have to do the same thing. To add insult to injury, Undertaker put Jim Ross's trademark hat on Mr McMahon's head before forcing him to do the deed.

Chris Jericho retains his Undisputed Championship

December 24: Chris Jericho himself is known to mention it occasionally, but on December 9 at *Vengeance*, he defeated The Rock and Stone Cold Steve Austin on the same night to become the Undisputed WWE Champion. Jericho was forced to defend his Championship the night before Christmas in a Triple Threat Match against both Kurt Angle and The Rock. Despite having two impressive opponents, Jericho was able to prevail and finish the year on top.

Kurt Angle shockingly joins the Alliance

October 29: Throughout the Invasion, only a few Superstars stood up for WWE. One was Kurt Angle, who had been the hero in multiple encounters throughout the year. His loyalty to WWE is what made his subsequent betrayal all the more hurtful. Following a Street Fight between Vince and Shane McMahon, an open brawl ensued between members of the Alliance and the WWE. When Stone Cold Steve Austin hit the Stunner on The Rock, Angle ran to the ring with a steel chair. Fans naturally thought he was there to save The Rock, and were stunned as he levelled Jericho, and then The Rock, Undertaker, and Kane for good measure.

The Rock captures the WCW Championship

November 5: In an event which played right into the hands of the Alliance, Chris Jericho reacted badly to losing the WCW Championship to The Rock. When The Rock finally got the pin with a surprise roll-up at the end of a hard-fought match, Jericho did not take the loss lying down. He attacked The Rock first with the Championship itself and then a steel chair, as the crowd looked on. With cracks beginning to appear between two of the top WWE Superstars, it appeared that momentum was now turning towards the Alliance.

December 24: Chris Jericho proudly displays both the WCW and WWE Championships as Undisputed Champion.

2002

THE PAST AND THE FUTURE of WWE collided in 2002. Legends returned to the ring and Superstars who would become the biggest names of the new millennium debuted. As the company changed its name to simply WWE, change was widespread. The WWE locker room was divided between *RAW* and *SmackDown* as part of the first-ever WWE Superstar Draft. The world was also shocked by changes in the boardroom when Mr. McMahon hired his most despised rival as the General Manager of *RAW*.

Games Superstars play

January 7: Mr. McMahon despised the other co-owner of WWE, Ric Flair. The two executives were set to square off at the *Royal Rumble* event later in the month. To get under Flair's skin ahead of this, McMahon dressed up as Flair and mocked his trademark strut and "Wooooo" catchphrase. Flair tried putting an end to the impersonation, but McMahon fought back, driving Flair into the ringside steps and leaving his rival in a heap.

Meanwhile, the new year meant a new start for Triple H, who had injured his quadriceps muscles eight months earlier. The future of his in-ring career had been in doubt during an extensive surgery and rehab process. Fortunately, Triple H returned to WWE and *Monday Night RAW*, receiving one of the loudest ovations in WWE history. He declared that "The Game" was back and would enter the Royal Rumble Match.

Before death do we part

February 11: Two years after their wedding and just in time for Valentine's Day, Stephanie McMahon and Triple H were set to renew their marriage vows. Stephanie had recently told Triple H that she was expecting their first child. But it was all a lie. Stephanie wasn't pregnant, she just wanted to ensure that she would be able to continue to profit from Triple H's successes. When Triple H learned of her deception, he dumped Stephanie—right in the middle of their vow renewal ceremony.

January 7: Mr. McMahon mocks Ric Flair by imitating his peroxide-blonde hair and his flashy fashion sense.

February 11: Stephanie McMahon roars at her soon-to-be-ex-husband after he ruins their wedding vow renewal.

Elsewhere in WWE...

February 17: Mr. McMahon felt that WWE co-owner Ric Flair was a "cancer" in WWE that had ruined the company. In order to save his creation, McMahon felt he needed to inject WWE with "poison" to eliminate the cancer. To do so, he brought in the New World Order (nWo) faction—"Hollywood" Hulk Hogan, Kevin Nash, and Scott Hall—who many believed had destroyed WWE's rival WCW. The nWo debuted at the *No Way Out* pay-per-view, promising to wreak similar havoc on WWE and its Superstars.

Clash of generations

February 18: This episode brought a face-off of the two biggest sports entertainment icons of their generations. On one side was Hulk Hogan, who ruled WWE in the 1980s before defecting to rival company WCW and forming the New World Order faction. On the other was The Rock, the third generation Superstar who had become a household name. Upon Hogan's return to WWE, The Rock challenged Hogan to an Icon vs. Icon Match at *WrestleMania X8*.

February 18: The Rock lays down a challenge to "Hollywood" Hulk Hogan for an Icon vs. Icon Match at *WrestleMania X8*.

Undertaker destroys Flair's friends and family

February 25: Undertaker was ready for a fight at *WrestleMania X8*, and wanted his opponent to be the 16-time World Champion and co-owner of WWE, Ric Flair. But Flair refused the challenge. Undertaker was undeterred, and started attacking Flair's friends and family. Targets included Flair's son, David, and best friend, retired Superstar Arn Anderson. Flair finally accepted the challenge, putting an end to the attacks.

Unexpected relationships

March 11: WWE Superstar Diamond Dallas Page was all about having a good attitude and optimistic outlook on life. Page was mentoring his friend Christian in the power of positivity, helping him get back to his winning ways after a losing streak. Once Christian started winning matches, however, he felt he no longer needed DDP. Christian attacked his former friend, leading to a match between the two at *WrestleMania X8*.

While friends became rivals, enemies were also becoming allies. Perhaps no two WWE Superstars had traded more heated or insulting words than Stephanie McMahon and Chris Jericho. However, when Jericho learned he would be defending the WWE Undisputed Championship against Stephanie's ex-husband Triple H at *WrestleMania X8*, he turned to Stephanie hoping to form an alliance. Stephanie, wanting to get revenge on Triple H for leaving her, agreed to help Jericho, despite their former differences.

March 11: Stephanie McMahon presents her new charge, the Undisputed WWE Champion, Chris Jericho.

INTRODUCING...

Brock Lesnar

March 18: The night after *WrestleMania X8*, the WWE Universe was introduced to "The Next Big Thing" Brock Lesnar during *Monday Night RAW*. The rookie, who would go on to be one of the most dominant Superstars in WWE history, made his presence known by destroying Al Snow and Maven mid-match. Lesnar's agent and advocate Paul Heyman cheered on at ringside, while all of WWE realized a devastating force had arrived.

Brock Lesnar makes his impactful mark on WWE, debuting the night after *WrestleMania*.

Biggest Names Ever for the Biggest Prize

May 13: Throughout the 1980s and 1990s, two of the biggest names in sports entertainment were Hulk Hogan and Ric Flair. These two legends also faced each other for the Undisputed WWE Championship in a match that saw interference from X-Pac, Big Show, and Stone Cold Steve Austin, leading to a Hogan victory, retaining his Title as Champion for a while longer.

Frog Splash specialists

May 27: Eddie Guerrero and Rob Van Dam both used the same finishing move, the high-flying Frog Splash. They shared a rivalry over who performed the move better, with both Superstars believing themselves superior. This led to a Ladder Match on *RAW* for Guerrero's Intercontinental Championship, which Van Dam won. Ironically, neither Superstar was able to use the Frog Splash move during the match and settle the long-standing debate.

March 25: The co-owners of WWE, Mr. McMahon and Ric Flair, kick off the first ever WWE Brand Extension Draft.

First draft

March 25: Following the purchase of rival sports entertainment companies WCW and ECW, WWE had an overabundance of Superstars. To give as many Superstars as possible a chance for success, the WWE Board of Directors created a "Brand Extension" where half the roster would appear on *RAW*, run by WWE co-owner Ric Flair, and the other half on *SmackDown*, run by Mr. McMahon. Flair and McMahon selected their Superstars as part of the first ever WWE Superstar Draft. Flair's first pick was Undertaker while McMahon selected The Rock.

Stone Cold signing

April 1: Following the draft, one Superstar, Stone Cold Steve Austin, remained a free agent. Both Ric Flair and Mr. McMahon were determined to convince Austin to sign with their respective brand. Austin made his decision, and joined *RAW*, but not before giving both McMahon and Flair a Stunner for their troubles.

The Immortal One and the Dead Man

April 29: "Dead Man" Undertaker was the number-one contender to "The Immortal One" Hulk Hogan's Undisputed WWE Championship. Hogan was due to defend against Undertaker at the *Judgment Day* pay-per-view in May, but *RAW* nights in the preceding weeks also saw tensions rise between the pair. In this edition, Undertaker verbally insulted Hogan during an in-ring interview, which Hogan responded to with a physical attack. Later in the evening, Undertaker retaliated by interrupting Hogan's match against William Regal.

May 27: Rob Van Dam knocks Eddie Guerrero off the ladder in their match for the Intercontinental Championship.

June 3: Founding member of the New World Order Kevin Nash introduces a surprisingly limber Shawn Michaels to the nWo.

Michaels is nWo

June 3: When Shawn Michaels—a founding member of D-Generation X—joined his close friend Kevin Nash in the nWo, Michaels became the third Superstar in history to be a part of both factions, following X-Pac and "Ravishing" Rick Rude. Despite still being unable to compete in the ring because of an injured back, Michaels promised the WWE Universe that the nWo would return to its past dominance now that he was a member.

Winner gets all

June 10: Ever since Ric Flair returned to WWE in 2001 and announced that he had purchased half the company, he and Mr. McMahon had had countless battles over the future of WWE. But none was more serious than this night's: a No Holds Barred Match for 100% ownership of the company. With some help from Brock Lesnar, Mr. McMahon claimed a victory and once again became the sole owner of WWE.

Stone Cold goes home

June 17: Despite signing with *RAW* only two months earlier, Stone Cold Steve Austin disagreed with the direction of WWE and quit. Rumors were flying that "he" was coming back to *RAW*. Mr. McMahon assumed that the returning "he" was Austin, hoping to rejoin the company. McMahon went to the ring and called Austin out so he could confront him about quitting. McMahon and the WWE Universe were shocked when the rumored "he" was actually The Rock. The Rock insulted McMahon and then promised the WWE Universe that while Austin might have quit, he would be with WWE forever.

June 17: Mr. McMahon, who was expecting a returning Steve Austin, is shocked by the return of The Rock instead.

2002

McMahon calls for "Ruthless Aggression"

June 24: Two weeks after becoming the sole owner of WWE, Mr. McMahon called a meeting of the *RAW* Superstars. He told them he was disappointed in them, because none of them were determined enough to achieve great success. McMahon called on the all the WWE Superstars to prove to him they wanted to be successful by showing him "Ruthless Aggression."

June 24: With the entire *RAW* roster surrounding him, Mr. McMahon issues a challenge for more "Ruthless Aggression" in the ring.

Elsewhere in WWE...

June 27: A young fresh-faced rookie named John Cena was watching RAW at home and heard Mr. McMahon's call for "Ruthless Aggression." Cena decided to show McMahon that one day he would be the biggest Superstar in WWE. Cena debuted four nights later on *SmackDown*, accepting an open challenge from Kurt Angle and kick-starting a long and legendary career.

Rookie John Cena debuts, facing off against Kurt Angle.

Dust Vader

July 1: In earlier weeks, Goldust had taken to imitating famous characters from TV and movies, but none was more entertaining than when he impersonated *Star Wars* villain Darth Vader. Clad in a mask and cape like the movie character and even carrying a lightsaber, Goldust quoted Vader's lines to other Superstars, at one point claiming to be Big Show's father!

INTRODUCING...

Eric Bischoff

July 15: Throughout the 1990s, WWE and rival sports entertainment company WCW were engaged in a fierce ratings battle over their respective Monday night TV shows. WWE was led, of course, by Mr. McMahon while WCW's leader was a controversial young executive named Eric Bischoff. Bischoff led WCW's *Nitro* show to ratings wins for nearly two years. There was no one McMahon despised more than Bischoff. So, it shocked the world when Mr. McMahon hired Bischoff as the new General Manager of *Monday Night RAW.*

The world is shocked as the former president of WCW, Eric Bischoff, is introduced as the new *RAW* General Manager by Mr. McMahon.

> "*Nitro* beat *RAW* 84 weeks in a row... If there's one person who can take this struggling franchise and turn it into a national media powerhouse, well, it would be me."

Eric Bischoff (July 15, 2002)

July 22: Rob Van Dam flies toward Jeff Hardy in their Intercontinental and European Title Unification Match.

Unification and breakups

July 22: Jeff Hardy and Rob Van Dam were both known for their high-flying in-ring style. Their Ladder Match unifying the WWE Intercontinental and European Championships was about as high flying as it could be. In the end, it was RVD who came out the victor, adding (and retiring) the European Title to his Intercontinental Championship.

Five years earlier, Shawn Michaels and Triple H had formed D-Generation X, but very soon afterwards, Michaels had to retire from in-ring competition because of an injured back. The time had come for Michaels to begin his return to the ring. His best friend Triple H had a plan, and the two original members of DX reformed the faction. The reunion was short-lived, however, as Triple H attacked Michaels minutes later, turning from friend to foe.

Ever since his impactful debut four months earlier, Brock Lesnar had been dominant on *RAW*. However, *SmackDown* General Manager Stephanie McMahon saw an opportunity to build her brand. Stephanie snuck backstage during this edition of *RAW* and signed Lesnar to a *SmackDown* exclusive contract. A furious *RAW* General Manager Eric Bischoff watched as Stephanie and Lesnar left in the same limousine.

Three Minute Warning

July 29: Eric Bischoff hired cousins Rosey and Jamal to act as his "muscle," enforcing his will on *RAW*. He called them "Three Minute Warning," because he would give the Superstars who'd earned his wrath three minutes to comply before being attacked by the giant enforcers. The pair's first attack was on elderly, retired Superstars Fabulous Moolah and Mae Young.

Formal unification

August 26: Only a month after his European Title win, Intercontinental Champion Rob Van Dam had the opportunity to unify his Title with another WWE Championship. This time it was the WWE Hardcore Championship held by his good friend and fellow ECW alum Tommy Dreamer. The back-and-forth contest ended when RVD pinned his opponent, winning the match and retiring yet another Championship.

Rivalry had also spread outside the ring to announcers Lillian Garcia and Howard Finkel. Each believed they were the true voice of WWE matches. Finkel further antagonized Garcia with his sexually inappropriate comments. This led to a Tuxedo vs. Evening Gown Match between the two. Garcia won by stripping Finkel down to his underwear, helped by several other female WWE Superstars who had been offended by his comments.

August 26: Rob Van Dam lands his vicious "rolling thunder" move on top of a ladder that's already on top of Tommy Dreamer.

2002

A new World Champion

September 2: Brock Lesnar had recently won the Undisputed WWE Championship. Since he was now a *SmackDown*-exclusive Superstar, Lesnar refused to defend the Title on *RAW*. To compensate, General Manager Eric Bischoff decided to create a *RAW*-exclusive championship, the World Heavyweight Championship, and presented the Title to Triple H.

September 2: Triple H celebrates his new World Heavyweight Championship, gifted to him by Eric Bischoff.

INTRODUCING...

Randy Orton

September 23: Following in the footsteps of his grandfather and father, rookie Randy Orton debuted in the ring. Introduced to *RAW* by legendary commentator Jim Ross, Orton defeated Steven Richards in his first match. The young Superstar would go on to become one of the most significant Superstars to ever compete in WWE, winning countless championships and gaining legions of fans.

Randy Orton joins RAW as a third generation Superstar.

Spin the wheel, make the deal

October 7: When *Monday Night RAW* arrived in Las Vegas, Eric Bischoff wanted to liven things up for the WWE Superstars. Inspired by the games of chance that surrounded them, he created *RAW Roulette*—a giant wheel featuring lots of different match types. Superstars would spin the wheel to learn what kind of match they'd be competing in. That included the chaotic main event: an eight Superstar, four-team Tables, Ladders, and Chairs Match for the Tag Team Championship. Champions The Hurricane and Kane faced Bubba Ray and Spike Dudley, Christian and Chris Jericho, and Rob Van Dam and Jeff Hardy. Kane, forced to fight alone because The Hurricane had been attacked backstage, retained the Titles single-handedly.

Elimination addition

November 11: Heading into the annual *Survivor Series* pay-per-view, Eric Bischoff announced an innovative new match concept: The Elimination Chamber. A mix of several older match types, the Chamber would feature six WWE Superstars competing in a massive steel structure. On this edition of *RAW*, Bischoff revealed the blueprints for the Chamber.

Elsewhere in WWE...

November 17: Shawn Michaels reached the apex of his five-year journey back from injury to WWE competition by winning the World Heavyweight Championship at *Survivor Series*. He visited *RAW* the next night to celebrate this victory in the ring, before being told by Eric Bischoff that he would defend the Title the very next week.

Jim Ross competes in the ring

December 23: Despite the festive season, Eric Bischoff was in a bad mood, and took it out on *RAW* commentators Jim "JR" Ross and Jerry "The King" Lawler. Bischoff forced JR and Lawler to compete in a Tag Team Match against William Regal and Lance Storm that night, or be fired. JR was terrified, as he had never competed in the ring. Lawler worked hard to protect his friend and commentary partner, fighting off William Regal. Thanks to some additional interference from the Dudley Boyz, JR pinned Regal to get the victory in his very first match.

The *Survivor Series'* survivor

November 18: Scott Steiner had been a big part of WWE's competition, WCW. Calling himself "The Big Bad Booty Daddy," Steiner had decided not to join WWE when the company purchased WCW. But after a year and a half watching *RAW* from home, Steiner decided to enter WWE and prove that he was the best Superstar in the world. Debuting the night before at *Survivor Series*, Steiner came to *RAW* and declared war on the WWE Superstars.

Michaels' first match on *RAW* in five years

November 25: For the first time in five years, Shawn Michaels competed in the ring on *RAW*, defending his newly claimed World Heavyweight Championship against Rob Van Dam. Michaels' *RAW* return match would end prematurely, however, as Triple H interrupted the match by attacking both Superstars.

November 25: Rob Van Dam challenges Shawn Michaels to a match for the World Heavyweight Championship.

December 23: The Dudley Boyz celebrate Jim Ross' unexpected debut and even more shocking victory.

2003

THE START OF THE YEAR brought a milestone for *RAW*—its tenth anniversary. It also turned out to be a year of evolution, both for *RAW* and WWE. Anti-authority rebel Stone Cold Steve Austin returned for his final match, and then became part of the management he'd fought against throughout his career. The Rock faced another icon from WCW; Ric Flair and Triple H recruited a pair of young Superstars to form Evolution; and The Legion of Doom— arguably the greatest tag team in sports entertainment history—returned for a final shot at the Tag Team Championships. As the company looked to the future, *RAW* was where that future was defined.

Pose Down
January 6: Triple H and Scott Steiner were both proud of their physiques. As the two chiseled Superstars prepared for their match at the *Royal Rumble* pay-per-view, they faced off in a bodybuilding "pose down" in the ring. Triple H got the better of his opponent as he'd selected the six "judges," who attacked Steiner.

January 6: Triple H and Scott Steiner go eyeball to eyeball as they perform press-ups during their bodybuilding pose challenge.

The Next Evolution
January 20: Ric Flair and Triple H believed they were the greatest of the past and present in sports entertainment, and they wanted to craft the future of WWE in their image. To do so, they recruited a pair of young, up-and-coming Superstars, Randy Orton and Batista. The foursome, who would call themselves "Evolution" in the weeks to come, made a statement attacking Triple H's rival Scott Steiner during a match.

Electrocution!
February 3: Orton and Batista, doing Triple H's bidding, searched backstage for Scott Steiner, but instead found Goldust. The Evolution duo taunted Goldust, until a fight between the three broke out. Orton and Batista fought Goldust throughout the backstage area, finally throwing him into a wall of electrical panels. Goldust was electrocuted, apparently suffering nerve damage that caused him to twitch and stutter.

WrestleMania rivalries
March 3: Booker T won the World Heavyweight Championship five times in WCW, and wanted a chance to win it for the sixth time at *WrestleMania XIX*. In this episode of *RAW*, the current Title holder, Triple H, dismissed Booker T's challenge, claiming that Booker's five Championship reigns weren't all that impressive as WCW was a joke. After weeks of challenges and attacks Booker finally earned his Championship Match at *WrestleMania*. Their epic encounter concluded with Triple H winning with his Pedigree finisher.

It had been nearly a year since Stone Cold Steve Austin had left WWE. When Austin quit, The Rock returned and spoke out against Austin's decision. Now Austin was back, ready to dominate WWE once again. And The Rock had a challenge for Austin: a match at *WrestleMania XIX*.

January 20: Randy Orton, Ric Flair, Triple H, and Batista unite to form Evolution.

The Rock Concert

March 24: The Rock had found success in Hollywood, and was back in WWE to face Stone Cold Steve Austin at *WrestleMania*. The Rock wanted to show the WWE Universe he could do anything in the world of entertainment. So, he brought his trusty six-string guitar to the ring and sang songs insulting the fans, Austin, and even Sacramento, the city where *RAW* was taking place. His "Rock Concert," as he called it, ended prematurely when Austin charged the ring and destroyed the guitar.

> "What you see in this ring before you is the greatest example of Evolution you will ever see."
>
> **Triple H (February 3, 2003)**

March 24: The Rock shows off his singing talent in his very first "Rock Concert."

March 3: Steve Austin stares down The Rock, as the greatest rivalry in *RAW* history kicks off one last time.

Elsewhere in WWE...

March 30: The Rock and Steve Austin had faced each other in the main event at three *WrestleMania* events. Austin won the first two encounters, while The Rock pulled out a victory in this year's *WrestleMania XIX*. As a result of nagging injuries, this was the last time Stone Cold Steve Austin would compete in the ring.

INTRODUCING...

Goldberg
March 31: Bill Goldberg was one of the biggest names in WCW. His 173-match winning streak was unparalleled. He debuted on *RAW* the night after *WrestleMania XIX*, warning The Rock that he was "next" and hitting him with a mighty spear shoulder block. Goldberg would go on to win the World Heavyweight Championship before defeating Brock Lesnar at *WrestleMania XX* a year later. Goldberg returned to WWE 12 years later, winning the Universal Championship.

Six years after debuting in WCW, Goldberg makes The Rock his number-one WWE target.

With friends like these...
April 7: Triple H and Kevin Nash had been friends for many years, so no one was more shocked than Triple H when Nash returned after many months away from *RAW* and attacked "The Game." Nash wanted Triple H's World Heavyweight Championship and wasn't going to let a little thing like friendship stand in the way. Triple H and Nash would face each other in several pay-per-view matches, culminating in a *Hell in the Cell* match in June. Triple H and Evolution attacked Nash weekly on *RAW* leading up to each match.

Highlight Reel debuts
April 28: Chris Jericho hosted his new *Highlight Reel*, which would eventually become one of the most famous talk-show segments in *RAW* history. "In honor of the occasion," Jericho's first guest was Goldberg, with whom Jericho had shared an intense rivalry years earlier in WCW. A newcomer to WWE, Goldberg had caused quite a commotion in the WWE Universe by spearing The Rock the day before. Jericho's first question was, "Who in the hell do you think you are, Goldberg?"

Meanwhile, the WWE Board of Directors had grown concerned about *RAW* General Manager Eric Bischoff's repeated abuses of power. To help reign Bischoff in, the Board had hired a surprising new co-General Manager, Stone Cold Steve Austin. Austin's first act as Co-GM was to give Bischoff a Stone Cold Stunner. It was a new era for the management of *RAW*.

April 28: Newly hired Stone Cold Steve Austin gives his Co-GM Bischoff a Stunner as a hiring bonus.

The Legion of Doom try for one more title

May 12: The Legion of Doom—Road Warrior Hawk and Road Warrior Animal—were considered by many to be the greatest tag team of all time. The L.O.D. returned to *RAW* after a four-year absence to compete for the WWE World Tag Team Championships, held by Rob Van Dam and Kane. Although RVD and Kane retained the Titles, the L.O.D. received an incredible ovation from the WWE Universe in what would be the team's final WWE match.

For the 17th time

May 19: Triple H was forced to defend the World Heavyweight Championship against his idol and Evolution teammate, Ric Flair. Triple H had assumed Flair would just let him win to keep the Title, but Flair, a 16-time World Champion himself, put everything he could into the match, hoping to win a 17th title. Ultimately, Triple H conquered his mentor and kept the Championship.

May 19: Triple H extends a respectful hand to his mentor Ric Flair, prior to their World Championship Match.

The people's *Peep Show*

June 2: On the heels of Chris Jericho's *Highlight Reel* talk show, his friend Christian also wanted to create a talk segment on *RAW*. Thus was born *The Peep Show*, named for Christian's "peeps"— his name for his fans. The Rock, who hadn't been seen in WWE for two months, was Christian's first guest. Determined to conduct the show himself, The Rock seized the mike and mingled with the crowd, while taunting the hapless Christian.

May 12: Road Warrior Animal sets Rob Van Dam up for the Legion of Doom's devastating Doomsday Device finishing move.

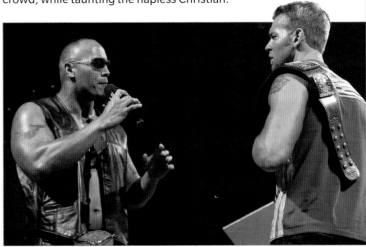

June 2: The Rock gives Christian an earful on the debut of Christian's talk segment, *The Peep Show*.

2003

June 23: The monster known as Kane removes the mask he'd worn since his debut, revealing a horrifying visage.

June 30: Gail Kim debuts and wins the Women's Championship.

The men behind the masks

June 23: Mick Foley was known around the world as "The Hardcore Legend" because of his violent, high-risk in-ring style. Also known as the wild Cactus Jack, the fun-loving Dude Love, and the masked mauler Mankind, Foley had retired from WWE and become a bestselling author. He appeared on *RAW* to promote his latest book when co-General Manager Steve Austin invited him to the ring. Austin celebrated Foley's career and presented him with a framed WWE Hardcore Championship Title.

This episode also featured a momentous revelation: Since surviving a devastating fire that had killed members of his family, Kane had worn a mask to hide facial scars. After losing a match against Triple H (thanks to interference from Evolution), Kane was forced to remove his mask. As he did so, Kane revealed that his scars were as much mental as physical. Removing his mask brought the emotions Kane had tried to repress to the surface and he took out his anger on his tag team partner, Rob Van Dam.

Seven-woman Battle Royal

June 30: Seven of WWE's top female Superstars competed in the ring in a Battle Royal to crown the new WWE Women's Champion. One of these women was Gail Kim, who, on her first night on *RAW*, threw Victoria out of the ring to win the Title.

Reflections on Montreal

July 7: Nearly six years after the infamous "Montreal Screwjob" between Shawn Michaels, Mr. McMahon, and Bret "Hit Man" Hart, Michaels returned to Montreal. The WWE Universe in Montreal were not happy to see Michaels, and booed him loudly, still angry about Michaels' role in their countryman Hart being robbed of the WWE Championship.

Kane is fired up

July 14: Following his unmasking a month earlier, Kane, still clearly troubled that he had become a figure of fun for his scarred appearance, sat down with commentator Jim Ross for a special interview. Part way through, however, Kane snapped. Screaming "You need to feel my pain!," Kane attacked JR, doused him with gas, and set him on fire!

Goldberg vs. Evolution

August 11: Ever since arriving in WWE a few months earlier, Goldberg had had one goal in mind: winning the World Heavyweight Championship held by Triple H. Before he could face Triple H, however, Goldberg had to defeat Triple H's Evolution teammate Ric Flair in a match specially refereed by Randy Orton, also a member of Evolution. The match was a setup, as all of Evolution attacked Goldberg, hoping to soften him up for his impending showdown with Triple H.

Hair vs. Hair

August 18: Chris Jericho blamed Kevin Nash for a recent loss and challenged him to the first "Hair vs. Hair" battle on *RAW*, in which the loser would have his head shaved by the winner. Nash accepted, but lost the bout when Jericho cheated by using brass knuckles to knock him out. Following the match, Jericho happily shaved off Nash's long locks.

August 25: Shane McMahon turns the tables on Kane by throwing him into a fire Kane has started. Shane's revenge on Kane for his attacks on Shane's mother, Linda, was seemingly complete.

Hellfire

August 25: Shane McMahon wanted revenge on Kane after the "monster" had attacked Shane's mother, WWE CEO Linda McMahon, for not giving him a Championship Match. When Kane interfered in one of Shane's matches, Shane fought back, pursuing Kane outside the arena. Kane jumped Shane and, while he was stunned, poured gasoline into a nearby garbage dumpster and set it on fire. Kane planned to throw Shane into the burning dumpster, but, at the last moment, Shane kicked Kane, "The Devil's Favorite Demon," into the flames instead.

August 18: Chris Jericho shaves Kevin Nash's hair after winning their "Hair vs. Hair" match.

2003

The Coach vs. The King

September 1: Jonathan Coachman felt disrespected by his announcing colleague Jerry "The King" Lawler and interfered in a match Lawler had a week earlier. Lawler demanded payback, and competed against Coach. Coach wasn't a trained Superstar, but, with help from broadcasting partner Al Snow, got the pin!

The State of *RAW*

September 8: As co-General Manager of *RAW*, Stone Cold Steve Austin had plenty of opinions. He delivered an address he called "The State of *RAW*," in which he made some new matches, announced some new rules, and gave Chris Jericho a Stunner.

A Spear for the boss

September 22: Goldberg was celebrating his World Heavyweight Championship victory from the night before when he was interrupted by *RAW* co-General Manager Eric Bischoff. Bischoff bragged that Goldberg owed him his entire career, since Bischoff had first hired Goldberg in WCW. Feeling disrespected, Goldberg smashed Bischoff with a hard-hitting Spear.

September 1: Jonathan Coachman struggles with Jerry "The King" Lawler.

September 22: Goldberg stands over a fallen Eric Bischoff after giving the *RAW* General Manager a vicious Spear.

Fight for the mic

September 29: For the better part of a decade, Jim Ross had been the voice of *Monday Night RAW*. But Jonathan Coachman wanted to take JR's spot as the lead announcer on *RAW*. Eric Bischoff decided that the two announcers should face each other in a match to decide which one would become the lead announcer. The two announcers attacked each other with leather straps. Eventually, and despite the 20-year age difference, Ross defeated Coachman with a Stone Cold Stunner to keep his job.

September 29: Jonathan Coachman punishes Jim Ross in their match to decide the future voice of *Monday Night RAW,* but JR later claimed victory.

Batista collects the bounty

October 20: Triple H had set a $100,000 bounty on Goldberg. Several Superstars had tried to gain this prize for putting Goldberg out of action. The winner was Batista, who returned after several months away recovering from a biceps injury. Batista attacked Goldberg, delivered a brutal beat-down, and collected the bounty.

RAW roulette

November 24: Eric Bischoff was less than thrilled to be returning to "boring" Salt Lake City for *RAW*. To liven things up, he brought back "*RAW* Roulette," where matches of all types were made simply by spinning a giant roulette wheel.

Outside help

December 1: Eric Bischoff had Stone Cold Steve Austin removed as co-General Manager of *RAW*, assuming he would have all the power on the show, but the WWE Board of Directors had a different idea. The Board hired WWE legend Mick Foley to serve as an "Outside Consultant," and keep Bischoff's abuses of power in check.

Spitting on a legend

December 15: Mick Foley was set to have his first match in four years, against Randy Orton. If Foley won, he would become the sole General Manager of *RAW*. If he lost, Eric Bischoff would fill that role. As Foley walked to the ring, he reconsidered competing and walked away from the match. Orton confronted Foley in the parking lot, calling him a coward. To add to this insult, Orton spat in Foley's face.

October 20: Batista powerbombs Goldberg after returning to claim the $100,000 bounty Triple H had placed on Goldberg's head.

December 15: Mick Foley walks away from facing Randy Orton to a chorus of boos from the crowd.

2004

AFTER YEARS of being the motorcycle-riding "American Badass," Undertaker returned to his creepy "Deadman" ways at the beginning of 2004. This year also saw the introduction of a new Diva, discovered by way of the first ever WWE *Diva Search*. *RAW* also traveled across the pond, and was broadcast from Great Britain for the very first time. The year ended with yet another groundbreaking moment as two WWE Superstars, and future Hall of Famers, shattered WWE's glass ceiling as Trish Stratus and Lita were the first women to compete in the main event on *Monday Night RAW*.

Legend Killer and the King
January 5: Following attacks on iconic WWE Superstars such as Mick Foley, Randy Orton had rechristened himself "The Legend Killer." He reinforced that moniker when he hit retired Superstar Jerry "The King" Lawler with an RKO. Commentator Lawler had entered the ring to confront WWE manager Teddy Long, who had insulted Memphis, Tennessee—that night's *RAW* location and Lawler's hometown—when he was hit with the sneak attack.

Canadian love triangle
January 26: Chris Jericho, Christian, and Trish Stratus all originally hailed from Canada, but that wasn't the only thing that linked the three. They were also involved in a tangled love triangle, with Jericho and Christian both vying for Trish's affections. Christian confronted his rival about it on this edition of *RAW*. The former friends faced off at *WrestleMania XX* two months later. Christian won the match and, more importantly, Trish's heart.

Deadly rivalries
February 2: The previous November, Kane had defeated his brother, Undertaker, in a "Buried Alive" match. Undertaker, who had taken to calling himself the "American Badass," hadn't been seen since. However, Kane started receiving terrifying messages on *RAW* from beyond the grave, promising Undertaker would rise again.

Meanwhile, Goldberg, a *RAW* Superstar, was engaged in a more lively conflict with *SmackDown* Superstar Brock Lesnar. As Goldberg was a *RAW* Superstar, he was banned from showing up or interfering with Lesnar's WWE Championship defense match, scheduled for the next *SmackDown* pay-per-view *No Way Out*. However, on *RAW*, former General Manager and current "*RAW* Sheriff" Stone Cold Steve Austin gave Goldberg a ticket to the event, with the loaded warning, "Don't do anything I wouldn't do." Goldberg attended the event and cost Lesnar the Title, leading to a match between the two at *WrestleMania XX*.

February 2: Kane receives a dire warning from his brother, Undertaker, that appears to be from the great beyond.

February 2: Thanks to Steve Austin's gift of a ticket, Goldberg attends his rival Brock Lesnar's match at the *No Way Out* pay-per-view event.

RVD and Booker T win the Titles

February 16: Since the end of 2003, Randy Orton and his Evolution teammates had made life miserable for Mick Foley, and Foley had had enough. Evolution's Ric Flair and Batista were defending the World Tag Team Championships against Rob Van Dam and Booker T when Orton tried to interfere in the match. Tired of Orton's attitude, Foley raced to the ring, cutting off Orton and attacking Batista. Foley's interference allowed RVD and Booker T to win the Tag Team Championships, although Foley's conflict with Evolution was far from over.

Bischoff vs. McMahon

February 23: Throughout the 1990s, during the "Monday Night Wars" between WWE and rival company WCW, the two organizations were led by Mr. McMahon and Eric Bischoff respectively. Bischoff had challenged McMahon to a bout in that period, but a match had never been held. During this edition of *RAW*, however, the long-awaited match finally happened, with special referee Stone Cold Steve Austin. Just as the match started gaining momentum, with Mr. McMahon gaining the upper hand, Brock Lesnar raced to the ring and attacked Austin, ending the match prematurely.

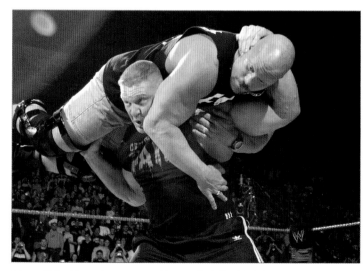

February 23: Brock Lesnar interrupts a match between Bischoff and McMahon to give referee Steve Austin an F-5.

> ## "Your days of beating and beating and beating on Mick Foley, those days are over!"

The Rock (March 1, 2004)

Rock and Sock reunite

March 1: To combat the numbers game in his war with Evolution, Mick Foley turned to his former tag team partner, The Rock. Known as "The Rock and Sock Connection," Foley and The Rock had been one of the most popular tag teams in WWE history. Their reunion on *RAW* led to a match at *WrestleMania XX* against three members of Evolution: Ric Flair, Batista, and Randy Orton.

March 1: The Rock, alongside Mick Foley, warns Evolution that, come *WrestleMania XX*, they will feel the united wrath of the Rock and Sock Connection.

Elsewhere in WWE

March 14: Last seen as the "American Badass," the Undertaker returned to battle Kane at *WrestleMania XX*, returning to his original form as the "Deadman." And he was not alone. His longtime manager and mentor Paul Bearer also returned to WWE.

2004

Playing the Lottery

March 22: The annual WWE Superstar Draft Lottery was held in this edition of *RAW*, and provided some historic moments before ending in a widespread brawl. John Cena appeared on *RAW* for the very first time. Though he wasn't drafted on the show, he did perform a rap before making an unsanctioned pick. The result was that *RAW* stalwart Triple H was traded to *SmackDown*. The shocking move did not stick, though, and he was traded back to *RAW* later in the week, before even making his *SmackDown* debut.

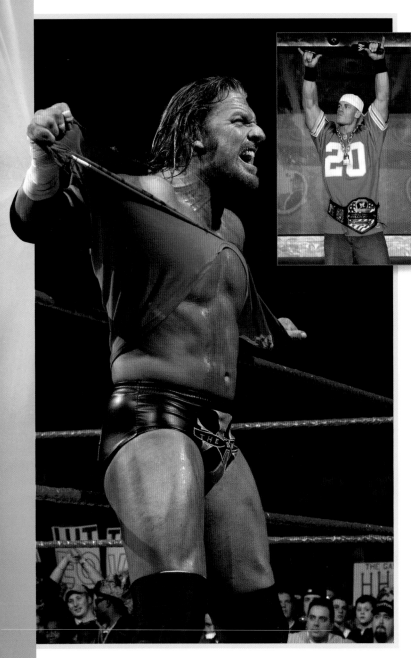

INTRODUCING...

Eugene

April 5: Eric Bischoff's nephew Eugene joined the *RAW* roster, where he was mentored by William Regal. Uncle Eric loathed his nephew, but Eugene was able to rise above this challenge and become an important part of *RAW*. He would go on to win the WWE Tag Team Championships with Regal.

Before making his debut, Eugene had been an avid fan of WWE and had learned a lot from watching the matches on TV.

Monstrous kidnapping

May 3: Whether it was based on real feelings, or was purely an effort to get inside Matt Hardy's head, Kane had started stalking Lita, Hardy's girlfriend. Kane then perpetrated his most nefarious act yet—kidnapping Lita, tying her to a chair, and holding her hostage in a boiler room. Although rescued by Hardy, the kidnapping had a traumatic effect on Lita.

Christian, Trish, and Tomko terrorize Chris Jericho

May 24: Christian and Trish Stratus' rivalry with Chris Jericho got taken to the next level as Christian and Trish utilized their recently hired bodyguard, Tyson Tomko, to conduct a brutal attack on Jericho. Tomko proved himself useful to his new employers, building a sustained working relationship as the pair's enforcer.

May 24: Trish Stratus and Tyson Tomko stand over a fallen Chris Jericho following their brutal attack.

March 22: John Cena (inset) appears for the first time on *Monday Night RAW*, while Triple H shows his anger about being drafted to *SmackDown*.

Rocks and hard places

June 21: After not being seen since his match at *WrestleMania XX*, The Rock returned and confronted one of his *WrestleMania* opponents, Randy Orton, in the ring. While not a scheduled match, The Rock verbally sparred with Orton before attacking him. The Rock would appear just twice more on *RAW* in 2004. After that, he wouldn't be seen live on the show for seven years.

The summer saw heartache continue for Matt Hardy. Lita was the love of his life, and as such Hardy wanted to marry her. Desiring a fairytale outcome, he proposed to her in the middle of the ring, but the romantic moment had a tragic conclusion when Kane interrupted and announced that he, not Hardy, was the father of Lita's unborn child.

June 21: Matt Hardy proposes marriage to his longtime girlfriend Lita, unaware of the devastation he would soon feel.

General Manager Eugene

July 5: With *RAW* General Manager Eric Bischoff taking the night off, the GM duties fell to Bischoff's eager-to-please nephew Eugene. Eugene made matches through unusual but fun means, including awarding a Title Match to the winner of a game of musical chairs. The WWE Universe loved Eugene and his unique way of running *RAW*.

July 5: Newly assigned *RAW* General Manager Eugene shows off his personalized, and inflatable, office space.

Regal attacks Evolution

July 19: Ever since Eugene arrived on *RAW*, William Regal had been assigned to look out for him. Although he hated the assignment at first, Regal had grown fond of Eugene. As such, he was enraged a week earlier when Evolution beat up his friend. This week, Regal proved his affection for Eugene by unloading a vicious attack on Evolution in revenge.

The Viper un-evolves

August 16: After winning the World Heavyweight Championship at *SummerSlam* the night before, Randy Orton boasted about becoming the youngest World Champion in history. He held a celebration of his victory in the ring. His Evolution teammates, Ric Flair, Triple H, and Batista, joined him in the ring for the party. Orton's celebration ended prematurely as Triple H gave him a thumbs-down, attacking the champ and kicking him out of Evolution.

2004

Nice day for a dark wedding

August 23: Kane defeated Matt Hardy at *SummerSlam,* which, according to the stipulations of that match, meant Hardy's girlfriend Lita would marry Kane. Despite Hardy's attempt to prevent the marriage, and the bride's own reluctance, a "Wedding from Hell" was held in the ring. Lita, dressed in a black dress and veil, eventually said "I do" to Kane. Kane menacingly carried Lita away as a devastated Matt Hardy looked on.

Celebrations and infomercials

September 13: Triple H had defeated his former Evolution teammate Randy Orton to once again win the World Heavyweight Championship at the *Unforgiven* pay-per-view one night earlier. On Monday, Evolution held a celebration for the new champ, complete with giant cake. But the party was over when sore loser Randy Orton burst from the cake and attacked Triple H.

Not one to promote cake, debuting WWE Superstar Simon Dean was obsessed with healthy living. He'd even developed his own health plan, complete with supplements and exercise routines. He pitched this health plan, "The Simon System," via a condescending and mean-spirited infomercial that aired during that night's *RAW.*

August 23: Kane kisses his new bride Lita's hand during their frightening wedding ceremony.

INTRODUCING...

Snitsky

September 13: Debuting on *RAW* in a match against Kane, Snitsky would unintentionally cause Lita to miscarry her and Kane's baby. Claiming "It wasn't my fault," about everything, Snitsky would go on to face Kane in several matches before being moved to *SmackDown* and ECW before finishing his WWE career back on *RAW.*

The monster Snitsky shocked the WWE Universe and terrified his fellow Superstars when he joined *Monday Night RAW.*

Elsewhere in WWE

September 20: WWE needed a new Diva to join WWE and conducted a weeks-long reality TV-style competition called *Diva Search.* The wannabe-Divas competed in challenges on *RAW,* and *SmackDown,* with one contestant eliminated each week. On the September 20 edition of *RAW* Christy Hemme was declared the winner of the first-ever WWE *Diva Search.*

Crossing the pond

October 11: For the first time, *RAW* was broadcast from the United Kingdom. With massive Union Jack flags surrounding the *RAW* set, the show was held in Manchester, England, and featured a main event that included Evolution facing Shawn Michaels and Edge.

October 11: Fireworks and pyro in front of massive British flags and an enthusiastic crowd kick off the very first *Monday Night RAW* held in the United Kingdom.

Monstrous Snitsky

November 8: Snitsky had accidentally caused Lita to miscarry her unborn baby two months earlier. Lita was devastated by the accident, but Snitsky didn't feel any remorse. To the disgust of the crowd, he brought a baby doll to the ring and asked Lita what the doll's name was. Adding further insult, Snitsky grew tired of the doll, and kicked it into the audience.

Title deciders

December 6: A World Heavyweight Championship Match a week earlier had ended controversially when the Superstars involved seemed to defeat each other at the same time. Mr. McMahon therefore appeared on the next *RAW* to announce the future of the Title. Defending Champion Triple H assumed he'd have the Title returned to him, but Mr. McMahon disagreed and declared the Title vacant.

Later, and for the first time in *RAW* history, two female Superstars competed in the main event. Trish Stratus and Lita battled for the Women's Championship. Lita used her aerial maneuvers to pin Trish in the center of the ring, and win the Championship. The Title was a victorious end to what had been a traumatic year for Lita.

INTRODUCING...

Daivari

December 13: Manager Daivari debuted on *RAW* with his charge Muhammad Hassan. As a proud Iranian-American and fluent Persian speaker, Daivari was keen to dispel negative stereotypes and media portrayals about the Middle East. While Hassan was only in WWE for a short time, Daivari had a very successful career that included managing other Superstars like The Great Kahli and Kurt Angle, and even pursuing the Cruiserweight Championship himself.

Daivari hoped that his appearance on *RAW* would help to change minds and attitudes about the Middle East.

December 6: Lita flies through the air toward Trish Stratus, tearing the house down in the first women's match to main-event *Monday Night RAW*.

2005

2005 WAS A YEAR of homecomings on *Monday Night RAW*: WWE's flagship program returned to its original network, USA; Shawn Michaels' longtime tag team partner came home to WWE and briefly reformed "The Rockers" with Michaels; John Cena found a new home on *RAW* when he was drafted away from *SmackDown*; and the Superstars of Extreme Championship Wrestling (ECW) returned for *One Night Stand*. *RAW* served as the home of John Cena's rap music video premiere, and Matt Hardy came back to seek revenge against Edge for destroying his relationship with Lita. Finally, the WWE Universe said goodbye to Eddie Guerrero.

Pillow fight!

January 10: A few weeks after Lita and Trish Stratus main-evented *RAW*, a women's match of a very different sort took place on the show as divas Maria Kanellis and Christy Hemme battled each other in a lingerie pillow fight. Hemme got the win after pummeling Maria with her pillow and then pinning her.

Monster mash

January 17: Ever since Snitsky accidentally caused Lita to miscarry her and Kane's baby at the end of 2004, Kane had been on a revenge mission against him. The two monsters battled repeatedly, and in this edition of *RAW*, Kane chokeslammed Snitsky off the entrance stage. Two weeks later, their rivalry would reach its peak as they tore each other apart inside a steel cage.

American hero vs. villain

January 31: Sgt. Slaughter was an American hero. An icon of patriotism, the former Marine drill sergeant stood up against anti-American Superstar Muhammad Hassan. And while Sgt. Slaughter made a noble effort, the younger Hassan came out on top, using his version of a camel clutch submission hold.

January 31: Muhammad Hassan causes Sgt. Slaughter immense pain by trapping him in a camel clutch submission hold.

Viper attacks a Snake and The Rockers reunite

March 14: Randy Orton had built a reputation for being untrustworthy and sneaky. Because of this he'd received a new nickname: "The Viper." Also known as the "Legend Killer," Orton lived up to both nicknames when he hit visiting WWE Legend Jake "The Snake" Roberts with an unexpected RKO maneuver during an interview on Chris Jericho's *Highlight Reel* talk show segment.

Shawn Michaels and Marty Jannetty had begun their sports entertainment careers together as a tag team known as "The Rockers" in 1985. They'd broken up in 1992, but "The Rockers" reunited on *RAW* when Jannetty returned to WWE at Kurt Angle's invitation. Angle wanted to face Jannetty on *SmackDown* as a tune-up match prior to facing Michaels at *WrestleMania*. Michaels insisted on a match as The Rockers before Jannetty faced Angle. The Rockers defeated La Résistance when Jannetty got the pin.

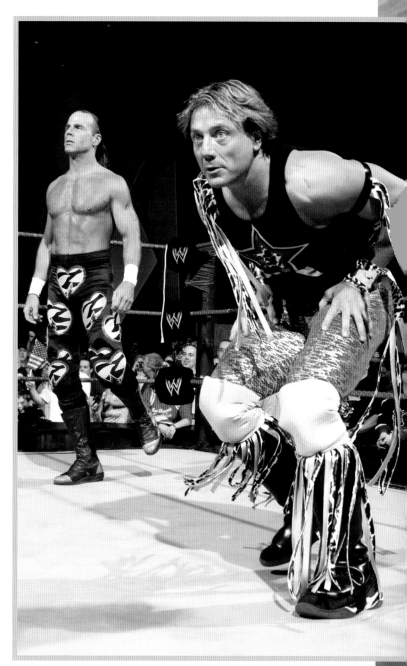

February 21: Batista makes the decision to leave Evolution and face Triple H for the World Heavyweight Championship at *WrestleMania 21*.

Big in Japan

February 7: For the first time, *RAW* was broadcast from Tokyo, Japan. This edition featured Japanese Superstar Taijiri, along with his tag team partner William Regal, winning the WWE Tag Team Championships from La Résistance.

"The Animal" strays

February 21: By virtue of winning the Royal Rumble Match, "The Animal" Batista was granted a championship match at *WrestleMania* against either the *RAW* or *SmackDown* champion. Conventional wisdom said Batista would choose to face JBL and John Cena in a Triple Threat Match for *SmackDown's* WWE Championship rather than square off against his Evolution teammate and *RAW* World Heavyweight Champion Triple H. However, with a thumbs down, Batista chose the match against Triple H, breaking up Evolution for good.

Angle attacks

February 28: Kurt Angle was a *SmackDown* Superstar, and as such wasn't expected to appear on *RAW*. This made his sneak attack on Shawn Michaels all the more surprising. Michaels had previously challenged Angle to a match at *WrestleMania 21* and, through this attack, Angle accepted Michaels' challenge.

March 14: Shawn Michaels is reunited with his longtime tag team partner Marty Jannetty, reforming their legendary team "The Rockers."

2005

Fiery warning

March 28: "The Legend Killer" Randy Orton had set his sights on another legend: Undertaker's undefeated streak on *WrestleMania*. As Orton called out Undertaker in the middle of the ring, the ring posts ignited in fire. It was a warning from Undertaker to the brash young Superstar that this legend wouldn't be killed easily.

Elsewhere in WWE

April 3: Chris Jericho had a brilliant idea for a match: put a WWE Championship Match contract in a briefcase, and hang it 15 feet above the ring. Then, invite six to eight Superstars to compete in a Ladder Match for the briefcase. The winner would be the first Superstar to get the briefcase. He could cash in his Championship Match contract whenever he wanted. Thus the Money in the Bank Match was born, and debuted at *WrestleMania 21*.

Master Lock Challenge

April 18: Superstar "The Masterpiece" Chris Masters was proud of his incredibly chiseled physique and his impressive strength. To demonstrate these attributes, he created the "Master Lock Challenge," in which he claimed no one could escape his Master Lock submission hold. Over the next two years, countless Superstars unsuccessfully tried to win the Master Lock Challenge.

May 23: Paul Heyman, Mr. McMahon, and Eric Bishoff—the leaders of ECW, WWE, and WCW respectively—reflect on their contributions to sports entertainment during the ECW memorial service.

May 9: John Cena leads a group of actors parodying 1980s hit television series *The A-Team* in his music video for the song "Bad, Bad Man."

Music video premiere

May 9: In addition to being the WWE Champion, John Cena, a *SmackDown* Superstar, had recently released his first rap album. The first music video for that album, for the song "Bad, Bad Man," premiered on *RAW*, and featured a number of tributes to 1980s pop culture, including *The A-Team* television series, and a cameo by actor Gary Coleman.

Gold Rush Tournament

May 16: A new number-one contender for the World Heavyweight Championship and a new relationship came out of the finals of the "Gold Rush Tournament." Eight Superstars had competed in the three-week tournament, with Edge and Kane making it to the finals. Edge won the tournament after Lita attacked her husband Kane, ending their relationship and leading to a new one with Edge.

An Extreme memorial

May 23: Eric Bischoff, the former president of WCW (World Championship Wrestling), hated ECW (Extreme Championship Wrestling). When WWE announced they were holding a special ECW reunion pay-per-view event, Bischoff decided to mock ECW with a funeral service for the brand. However, the leader of ECW, Paul Heyman, and the Chairman of WWE, Mr. McMahon, interrupted the funeral, and, in the process, insulted Bischoff and WCW.

> "You know how it is, every member of both rosters, nobody's safe. I got the call, they say John Cena's officially *RAW*. So, I do it how they do it in St. Louis, baby, the Champ is HERE!"
>
> **John Cena (June 6, 2005)**

June 6: WWE Champion John Cena celebrates becoming an official member of the *Monday Night RAW* Superstar roster.

The *RAW* Draft goes Extreme

June 6: In the annual Superstar Draft, *RAW* gained arguably the biggest acquisition in the show's history when WWE Champion John Cena was drafted from *SmackDown* to *RAW*. Monday nights were never the same, once Cena declared "The Champ is here!"

The ECW reunion pay-per-view *One Night Stand* was six days away, and Eric Bischoff had promised to lead a group of both *RAW* and *SmackDown* Superstars to the event to disrupt and ruin it. But the ECW Superstars didn't want to wait until *One Night Stand*. They attacked the WWE Superstars en masse on *RAW*, raising an ECW banner over the ring, marking WWE as their territory, and warning Bischoff's invaders to stay away.

June 6: Invaders from Extreme Championship Wrestling make *Monday Night RAW* their territory.

Elsewhere in WWE

June 12: Despite going out of business in 2001, Extreme Championship Wrestling still had a loyal following of fans and Superstars. In tribute to ECW's lasting legacy, WWE sponsored an ECW reunion event called *One Night Stand*, in which ECW alumni competed in the ring.

2005

Olympic hero gets *RAW*

June 13: In week two of the annual Superstar Draft, Olympic hero Kurt Angle jumped ship from *SmackDown* and landed on *RAW*. Angle's first matter of business was going after Triple H, Batista, and Shawn Michaels, challenging each Superstar to a match.

R-Rated wedding

June 20: After dumping her husband Kane and linking up with Edge, Lita was ready for her second wedding on *RAW* in a year. As Edge and Lita took their vows, Lita joked about breaking former lovers Matt Hardy's and Kane's hearts by finding true love with Edge. Kane, still furious at losing Lita, attacked the couple. He inflicted a tombstone move on the priest, but Edge and Lita escaped.

Welcome to "Carlito's Cabana"

June 27: Carlito loved everything cool, and created a talk show segment that was the epitome of style. Called *Carlito's Cabana*, the set had a Caribbean feel. Carlito's first guest was Rob Van Dam, who had returned to *RAW* from *SmackDown* in week three of the Superstar Draft.

June 20: Kane objects to the wedding of Lita and Edge—much to the bride's surprise!

Hulkamania heartbreak

July 4: It was a dream tag team. Two of the greatest Superstars of all time, "The Heartbreak Kid" Shawn Michaels and Hulk Hogan. The two former WWE Champions united to face Kurt Angle and Carlito. After defeating their opponents, Hogan and Michaels posed in the ring—until Michaels kicked Hogan in the jaw.

July 4: Shawn Michaels stands over his former tag team partner Hulk Hogan after super-kicking the Hulkster and breaking up their team.

July 11: Matt Hardy attacks Edge, seeking revenge for Edge stealing Matt's former girlfriend Lita.

Betrayals and vengeance

July 11: For many years, Lita and Matt Hardy had had an intimate relationship. When the relationship ended, because Lita had fallen in love with Edge, WWE felt it best not to have both Hardy and Edge in WWE, so, in March, Hardy was fired. Watching *RAW* at home on television, Hardy grew angrier and angrier at seeing Edge and Lita together. Hardy finally snapped; he bought a ticket to *RAW*, and proceeded to brutally attack Edge after a match. Security quickly arrested Hardy but, within a matter of weeks, he had been re-hired by WWE.

On this edition of *RAW*, WWE's original talk show segment, *Piper's Pit*, hosted by WWE Hall of Famer "Rowdy" Roddy Piper, made its triumphant return. Piper, who for more than a decade had had a rivalry with Hulk Hogan, wanted answers from Shawn Michaels as to why Michaels had kicked Hogan the week before. Michaels refused to answer Piper's questions, and ended the interview by kicking Piper in the face, as he had Hogan.

Going for gold and a "Battle of the Bands"

July 25: Kurt Angle, an Olympic gold medalist, had held an open challenge in recent weeks where competitors could win his Olympic gold medal if they lasted three minutes with him in the ring. Thus far, Angle had retained his medal. Enter Eugene. Against the odds, he beat the clock, and won the gold medal.

Also on this edition, John Cena and Chris Jericho both performed their musical stylings in a "Battle of the Bands." Cena was a rapper and Jericho was the lead vocalist for a rock band called Fozzy. The winner of the music contest would be selected by the applause of the WWE Universe. Cena's performance of "Bad, Bad Man" ended up the clear winner.

Chavo becomes Kerwin

August 22: Chavo Guerrero had long been proud of his Mexican heritage, but after struggling to find success in recent weeks in WWE, he thought he might have more luck if he competed as an "Anglo-American." Taking on a persona named "Kerwin White," Guerrero played the part of a wealthy suburbanite.

August 22: Kerwin White drives onto *Monday Night RAW* in a golf cart.

Homecoming

September 26: When it premiered in January 1993, *Monday Night RAW* was broadcast live on the USA Network. USA remained the home of *RAW* until the fall of 2000, when it moved to Spike TV. After five years on Spike, *Monday Night RAW* returned to USA Network with a three-hour "Homecoming" special. The Homecoming edition of *RAW* featured countless memorable moments, including Matt Hardy vs. Edge in a "Loser Leaves *RAW*" Ladder Match, Stone Cold Steve Austin giving Stone Cold Stunners to the entire McMahon family, Shawn Michaels facing Kurt Angle in a 30-minute Iron Man Match, Eric Bischoff vs. John Cena for the WWE Championship, Rey Mysterio's *RAW* debut, Triple H attacking his mentor Ric Flair, and much more. *RAW* was back home, and better than ever!

Matt Hardy punishes Edge in a ladder; Rey Mysterio launches into the air; John Cena provides Eric Bischoff with a much needed Attitude Adjustment; and Shawn Michaels drops an elbow on Kurt Angle, all during *RAW*'s "Homecoming" special.

Jim Ross, you're fired!

October 10: One week earlier, Stone Cold Steve Austin had given Stunners to every member of the McMahon family. As punishment, Mr. McMahon declared that someone would be fired, but since Austin wasn't a full-time WWE employee, it would have to be someone else. That someone else was Austin's close friend Jim Ross. Mr. McMahon's wife Linda fired Ross, and added to the humiliation of the moment by kicking him below the belt.

INTRODUCING...

Mickie James

October 10: An avid fan of WWE Superstar Trish Stratus, Mickie James joined WWE so she could be close to her hero. But that closeness quickly turned to stalking. It was all mind games by Mickie James, though. Mind games that led to James defeating Stratus for the Women's Championship at *WrestleMania*. She would go on to become a six-time champion in WWE. James would leave WWE in 2010, but returned in 2016, setting her sights on the new *SmackDown* Women's Championship.

Mickie James carries one of the six Women's Championships she won in her WWE career.

Dr. Heinie

October 24: After he was unceremoniously fired by the McMahon family, Jim Ross underwent colon surgery. Mr. McMahon pretended to be Ross' surgeon, and parodied the medical procedure, pulling a variety of items from a Jim Ross mannequin's rear end, including a fake Jim Ross head.

Raw Styles

November 7: With Jim Ross having been fired, *RAW* was in need of a new lead announcer. The job was given to Joey Styles, who had been the lead announcer in Extreme Championship Wrestling, and had made his WWE announcing debut at the *ECW One Night Stand* pay-per-view in June.

November 7: Legendary voice of ECW Joey Styles joins *RAW* as its lead announcer.

November 14: John Cena set the WWE Championship atop an Eddie Guerrero T-shirt in tribute to Guerrero, who had sadly passed away.

Eddie Guerrero tribute

November 14: Former WWE Champion Eddie Guerrero had passed away unexpectedly just the day before. The entire WWE Superstar roster, backstage personnel, and the McMahon family paid tribute to Guerrero throughout the night. Current WWE Champion John Cena laid the WWE Championship atop an Eddie Guerrero T-shirt, and Eddie's nephew Chavo Guerrero abandoned his Kerwin White persona, promising to proudly carry the Guerrero family name in the future.

Hard lessons from bad attitudes

December 5: Eric Bischoff had been the General Manager of *Monday Night RAW* for three and a half years. Mr. McMahon felt that it was time for Bischoff's performance review, and held that review like a courtroom trial. Dressed as a judge, Mr. McMahon found Bischoff guilty of numerous misdeeds and fired him. As an exclamation point on the decision, Mr. McMahon threw Bischoff into the back of a garbage truck.

Later, Edge kicked off his brand new talk show segment *The Cutting Edge* by mocking Ric Flair. WWE legend Michael "P.S." Hayes charged to the ring to defend Flair's honor. Hayes, a WWE official, had competed in the ring for more than 30 years and felt that current Superstars like Edge didn't show enough respect for people like himself and Flair, who had paved the way for them. Edge ignored Hayes' rebuke and hit him with his metal Money in the Bank briefcase.

December 5: Mr. McMahon, dressed in a judge's black robes, emphatically fires Eric Bischoff by throwing him into the back of a garbage truck.

Tribute to the Troops

December 19: Beginning in 2003, WWE had held an annual event for members of the military serving abroad in places like Iraq and Afghanistan. WWE's *Tribute to the Troops* had been a standalone television special, but this year it was a special episode of *RAW* for the first time. Held in Bagram, Afghanistan, the event featured Superstars JBL and Mick Foley, both dressed as Santa Claus, in a match against each other, with Shawn Michaels vs. Triple H as the main event.

December 19: WWE performs for hundreds of American and Allied soldiers during *Tribute to the Troops* in Bagram, Afghanistan.

2006

2006 BEGAN IN THE MOST SHOCKING of ways as Edge became the first Superstar to cash in the Money in the Bank briefcase, and was crowned Champion. That was only the beginning of a career-defining year for Edge, as he was in *Monday Night RAW's* main event picture for the entire year. But Edge was not alone in the spotlight. John Cena battled everyone from Mr. McMahon to Rob Van Dam, D-Generation X reformed to wreak havoc throughout WWE, and several future champions debuted, including The Miz and Beth Phoenix.

Elsewhere in WWE

January 8: At the *New Year's Revolution* pay-per-view event, Edge cashed in his Money in the Bank briefcase on an already exhausted John Cena, defeating Cena for the WWE Championship. It was the first time the briefcase had been cashed in, and the first time that Edge had won the WWE Championship.

Tough love
January 9: Edge was so happy he'd won the WWE Championship at *New Year's Revolution*, he declared he and his girlfriend Lita would have a "live sex celebration" on *RAW* the following night. But the adult party didn't end well, as Ric Flair interrupted to mock Edge over his seemingly inferior prowess, leading Edge to hit Flair with a chair. John Cena came to Flair's rescue, attacking Edge and putting a premature end to the R-rated celebration.

Not all Superstars had such victorious starts to the year, however. Shelton Benjamin had been on the losing side of several matches, and no one was more disappointed about that than his mother. Mama Benjamin arrived on *RAW* to encourage Benjamin with some tough maternal love. Her strong vocal "encouragement" motivated Benjamin, and in the weeks that followed, he started gaining victories in matches.

TLC with Flair
January 16: In his three decades of in-ring competition, 16-time World Champion Ric Flair had never competed in a Ladder Match. But in seeking his 17th title, Flair competed against Edge in a Tables, Ladders, and Chairs (TLC) Match. Although unsuccessful in capturing the WWE Championship, Flair had at least finally competed in an iconic Ladder Match.

January 16: Edge holds up his WWE Championship in victory after winning the TLC Match against Ric Flair.

Spirit Squad arrives

January 23: Despite their classic uniforms and pom poms, WWE Superstars Spirit Squad were no ordinary cheerleaders. The team were also talented in-ring competitors. They debuted in WWE helping *RAW* announcer Jonathan Coachman win a match against fellow *RAW* announcer Jerry Lawler. One member, Nicky, went on to greater WWE fame as Dolph Ziggler.

The Game dominates

February 20: Triple H was passionate about holding the WWE Championship. He displayed his passion and drive when he defeated Big Show and Rob Van Dam in the finals of the eight-Superstar *Road to WrestleMania* tournament. The tournament had begun two weeks earlier on *RAW* and granted the winner, Triple H, a match against John Cena for the WWE Championship at *WrestleMania 22*.

A hardcore challenge

February 27: Mick Foley himself had long lamented that he'd never had a career-defining *WrestleMania* moment. Therefore when Edge publicly brought up Foley's less-than-stellar *WrestleMania* record, Foley took it very personally. He challenged Edge to a Hardcore Match at *WrestleMania 22* to teach the younger Superstar a lesson in respect. Edge readily accepted the challenge.

The Boss and the Champ

March 27: Mr. McMahon needed to prepare for his impending No Holds Barred Match against Shawn Michaels at *WrestleMania 22*, so he challenged John Cena to a match. In an attempt to prevent interference from Michaels or Cena's own upcoming *WrestleMania* opponent Triple H, both rival Superstars were handcuffed to the ring. McMahon and Cena engaged in a brief match, but it was all a setup. McMahon was disqualified for a low blow. He freed Triple H, who attacked both Cena and Michaels with a sledgehammer.

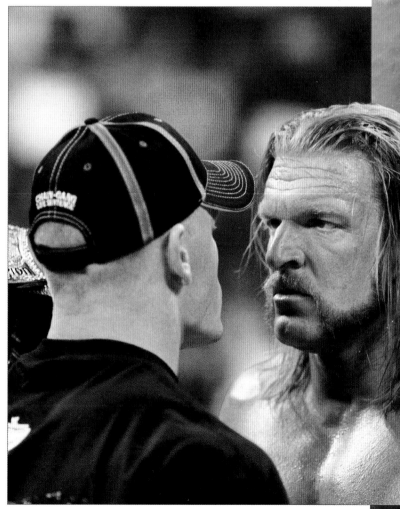

February 20: On the road to their WWE Championship Match at *WrestleMania 22*, John Cena and Triple H stare each other down.

2006

Squad goals

April 3: The *RAW* after *WrestleMania 22* saw victory snatched away as swiftly as it had been secured. After successfully defending the Tag Team Championships at *WrestleMania*, the Champions Kane and Big Show lost the titles to the Spirit Squad. It took all five members of the Squad to defeat the two giants, but at the end of the Monday night match, the cheerleaders were the new champions.

McMahons go to church

April 10: Mr. McMahon had challenged Shawn Michaels to a Tag Team Match at the upcoming *Backlash* pay-per-view event. McMahon would partner with his son Shane, but the father-and-son duo had an unusual condition for their opponent. They suggested Michaels, who was a devout Christian, have God as his tag team partner. On this edition of *RAW*, in order to prepare for this almighty match, the McMahons went to church to try and scout out the opposition. They left disappointed that they hadn't caught a glimpse of their divine opponent.

Seeing double

April 17: For months, Mickie James had stalked Trish Stratus. After defeating Stratus for the Women's Championship at *WrestleMania 22*, James' mind games continued. She impersonated Stratus and even kidnapped Stratus' boyfriend. Stratus didn't give in to James' bizarre assaults, instead turning James' own techniques against her. Stratus attacked James and saved her boyfriend—all while dressed up as James.

Styles gets extremely upset

May 1: Commentator Joey Styles had built his career as the voice of the original ECW wrestling promotion. After becoming the voice of *RAW*, Styles quickly grew disenchanted with the differences between ECW and WWE. These feelings came to a head after an argument between Styles and co-commentator Jerry Lawler grew physical. Styles left commentary, and declared his disdain for WWE, notably Mr. McMahon.

INTRODUCING...

Beth Phoenix

May 8: Known as "The Glamazon," Beth Phoenix raced to the ring to save Trish Stratus from one of Mickie James' attacks on the May 8 edition of *Monday Night RAW*. That began a career that saw Phoenix win four Women's/Divas Championships, a Slammy Award as Diva of the Year, enter the Royal Rumble Match against 29 male Superstars, and be inducted into the WWE Hall of Fame.

The debuting "Glamazon" saves Trish Stratus from another Mickie James attack.

April 17: Trish Stratus (dressed up like Mickie James) slaps Mickie James (dressed up like Trish Stratus) while Stratus' boyfriend looks on.

May 22: Rob Van Dam announces he's going to cash in his Money in the Bank briefcase on John Cena at the *ECW One Night Stand* pay-per-view event.

"I'd like to see this take place somewhere where... the conditions work *extremely* well in my favor."

Rob Van Dam (May 22, 2006)

Going to extremes

May 22: At *WrestleMania 22*, Edge and Mick Foley fought in a brutal Hardcore Match. Nearly two months later, on this edition of *RAW*, and in honor of their vicious match, Foley presented his competitor Edge with the retired WWE Hardcore Championship Title. Declaring that he and Edge would be co-holders of the Championship, Foley proclaimed that he and Edge were the greatest Hardcore Superstars in the history of sports entertainment, angering ECW hardcore legends Tommy Dreamer, Terry Funk, and Paul Heyman, who interrupted their celebration and challenged them to a match at the upcoming *ECW One Night Stand*.

After winning the Money in the Bank Ladder Match at *WrestleMania 22*, Rob Van Dam was entitled to a WWE Championship Match at a time and place of his choosing. Van Dam announced on *RAW* that his match against Cena for the WWE Championship would take place at *ECW One Night Stand*. Van Dam had been a top Superstar in the original ECW company, and knew the ECW fans would give him a home-field advantage over Cena in their match.

Double demons

May 29: Two Kanes? How was this possible? The WWE Universe couldn't believe their eyes when the monster Kane, who had removed his mask three years earlier, was attacked by a mask-wearing double. Masked-Kane attacked Kane in the middle of the ring, giving him a vicious chokeslam. The Masked-Kane haunted Kane for several more weeks until Kane battled back, dragging his imposter away, never to be seen again.

INTRODUCING...

The Miz

June 2 edition of *SmackDown*: The Miz is one of *RAW*'s best-known Superstars, but before joining the show, he began his career as "the host" of *SmackDown*, emceeing segments on the show, including the 2006 *Divas Search*. Soon after, The Miz began his in-ring career, which would lead him to several championships, including the WWE Championship. He would main-event *WrestleMania 27* against John Cena, become a Hollywood movie star, and return to his hosting roots with his *Miz TV* segment on *RAW*.

"The Miz" entertains the WWE Universe as the official emcee of WWE.

2006

The ECW Originals attack

June 5: Extreme Championship Wrestling (ECW) was a sports entertainment organization filled with scrappy and violent underdogs who waged war against WWE. On this edition of *RAW*, when ECW alum Rob Van Dam was signing his contract to face John Cena for the WWE Championship, RVD's fellow ECW Superstars interrupted the contract signing and attacked John Cena, the face of their hated WWE.

June 5: The ECW Originals attack John Cena during his contract signing to face Rob Van Dam.

Elsewhere in WWE

June 13: Following the *ECW One Night Stand* event, WWE launched a new weekly ECW TV series, featuring ECW Originals—veterans of the old ECW brand—and up-and-coming Superstars. One of these newcomers was CM Punk, whose braggadocious style electrified the WWE Universe and irritated his opponents. Punk went on to win eight championships in WWE, including being a five-time WWE Champion.

DX reunited

June 19: In the late 90s, D-Generation X had run amok in WWE, causing chaos wherever they went. After several years apart, DX—Shawn Michaels and Triple H—reformed during this episode of *RAW* and picked up where they'd left off, instituting chaos. Though this time, rather than the entire WWE, DX had their eyes on just one goal: making the McMahon family's lives miserable.

McMahon-eration X

June 26: After reforming a week earlier, D-Generation X continued their efforts to annoy the McMahon family. This week, it was by impersonating Mr. McMahon and his son Shane in the ring. The humorous but unflattering impression wasn't well received by the McMahons or their protectors, the Spirit Squad. Their displeasure obviously didn't bother DX, as they went on to dump buckets of human waste on the McMahons and the Squad, humiliating the WWE boss even further.

Edge recaptures the Title

July 3: Rob Van Dam had won the WWE Championship at *ECW One Night Stand* several weeks earlier, with a helping hand from Edge. Unfortunately for RVD, his happiness didn't last long. Almost immediately Cena demanded a rematch, while Edge also wanted a shot at the Title in return for his earlier help. Cena and Edge both got their wish on this *RAW* edition. The trio competed in a Triple Threat Match that ended with Edge pinning RVD to win the Title.

The Nature Boy's hardcore challenge

July 31: Mick Foley and Ric Flair were both considered sports entertainment legends, but they certainly weren't fans of each other. Flair stood in the center of the ring on *RAW* and challenged Foley to a match at *SummerSlam*, but not just any match: Flair wanted a Hardcore Match, Foley's specialty, to prove he could beat Foley at his own game.

June 26: D-Generation X members Triple H and Shawn Michaels mock the McMahon family by impersonating Mr. McMahon (Triple H) and Shane McMahon (Shawn Michaels).

Disrespecting their elders

August 14: Edge's rivalry with John Cena got taken to a personal level when Edge and his girlfriend, Lita, attacked John Cena's father in his own home. Edge was going to defend the WWE Championship against Cena at *SummerSlam*, and showed the home invasion on *RAW* as a way to get inside Cena's head.

Randy Orton had been calling himself "The Legend Killer" for many months, referencing his attacks on different WWE Hall of Famers and Legends, but he may have bitten off more than he could chew when he threatened to kill the legend of Hulk Hogan at *SummerSlam*. On this edition of *RAW*, Orton brought out an elderly actor impersonating Hogan, enraging the true Hogan. He attacked Orton and vowed to get his revenge by defeating him at *SummerSlam*.

Leaving their mark

August 21: D-Generation X's efforts to emotionally and psychologically break the McMahon family were taken to a whole new level when Triple H and Shawn Michaels found out where the McMahons' personal airplane was kept, and defaced it with DX graffiti. Mr. McMahon was livid but DX was proud of leaving their mark all over the corporate jet.

August 21: D-Generation X's Shawn Michaels and Triple H pose in front of their handiwork after vandalizing the WWE corporate jet.

July 3: Edge celebrates his WWE Championship win after defeating John Cena and Rob Van Dam in a Triple Threat Match.

Elsewhere in WWE

September 17: At the *Unforgiven* pay-per-view event, Trish Stratus won her record-setting seventh Women's Championship by defeating Lita. Stratus had previously announced that the match would be her last before retiring. Stratus kept her word, and bowed out of sports entertainment while still holding the Women's Championship.

2006

Knights of the Booker table

September 25: World Heavyweight Champion and *SmackDown* Superstar Booker T had won the *King of the Ring* tournament. He now demanded that the WWE Superstars bow before him and kiss his feet. However, proud WWE Champion John Cena refused to kneel before the newly crowned king. King Booker called in his loyal servants, Finlay and William Regal, who attacked Cena and forced him to kiss the King's foot.

Cage match

October 2: The rivalry between John Cena and Edge over the WWE Championship reached fever pitch, and there was only one way for the two Superstars to put an end to it: inside a steel cage. John Cena ultimately retained the Championship, although the action wasn't limited to the two rivals. Edge tried to get help from Superstars Lance Cade and Trevor Murdoch. D-Generation X not only put an end to these plans, but also ended up costing Edge the match by hitting him with the cage door.

Notable appearances

October 16: Over the years, DX had mocked and impersonated their rivals, such as the Nation of Domination and the McMahon family. This time, DX got a dose of their own medicine when they were the ones being impersonated. After weeks of frustrating losses in the ring, Edge and Randy Orton teamed up together to form Rated RKO. Their first item of business was to mock DX with some crude impersonations of the other pair.

Also making a mockery was rapper Kevin Federline, who appeared on *RAW* and insulted both the WWE Universe and its hero, John Cena. Cena, who'd had success as a rapper himself, defended the WWE Universe and belittled Federline in return. Federline remained cocky, driving a frustrated Cena to use an Attitude Adjustment to shut him up.

October 16: John Cena delivers an Attitude Adjustment to rapper Kevin Federline.

October 16: Newly-formed tag team Rated RKO (Edge and Randy Orton) impersonate rivals D-Generation X with Edge playing the part of Triple H and Orton as Shawn Michaels.

Elsewhere in WWE

November 5: There were three recognized World Champions in WWE: WWE Champion John Cena on *RAW*, World Heavyweight Champion King Booker on *SmackDown*, and ECW Champion Big Show on ECW. At the *Cyber Sunday* pay-per-view event, all three competed in a "Champion of Champions" Triple Threat Match to determine who the most dominant champion in WWE was. Thanks to interference from rapper Kevin Federline, King Booker won the match.

Bischoff's back

November 6: Former *RAW* General Manager Eric Bischoff returned as General Manager for one night only, and he wasn't in a good mood. Irritated at how he'd been disrespected by certain Superstars, he punished them with difficult matches. The Tag Team Champions Ric Flair and Roddy Piper had to face off against Rated RKO, consisting of Edge and Randy Orton. Meanwhile, announcer Maria was forced into a match against the heavyweight Umaga.

New tag champs

November 13: A week earlier on *RAW,* Rated RKO had competed in a Tag Team Championship match against Champions Ric Flair and Roddy Piper. Because that match had been interrupted by D-Generation X, Rated RKO were given another chance at the Titles in this week's episode. This time Rated RKO defeated Piper and Flair to become Tag Team Champions.

Nicky vs. Dusty

November 20: The Spirit Squad was set to face a team of four legends at *Survivor Series* in a traditional Elimination Match. To warm up for that match, Spirit Squad member Nicky challenged Legends team member Dusty Rhodes for a one-on-one match on *RAW.* Though the Spirit Squad thought it would be an easy match, given Rhodes' age, they were shocked when the veteran and Hall of Famer Rhodes won the match.

Broken Spirit (Squad)

November 27: For most of the year, D-Generation X and the Spirit Squad had battled each other in the ring and out. In their final encounter, DX, with help from Ric Flair, defeated the Spirit Squad once and for all. After the match, Triple H and Shawn Michaels piled the members of the Spirit Squad into a large shipping crate, and mailed the cheerleaders out of WWE.

Biggest Battle Royal

December 18: The night kicked off with the largest Battle Royal in *RAW* history as 30 Superstars competed for a chance to face John Cena for the WWE Championship later in the evening. Edge outlasted the 29 other competitors and went on to try for the title in the night's main event. Despite his dominant victory in the opening Battle Royal, Edge couldn't defeat the mighty Cena.

November 13: Less than one month after forming their team Rated RKO, Edge and Randy Orton celebrate winning the WWE Tag Team Championships.

2007

2007 WAS AN INTENSE YEAR on *Monday Night RAW*. Over the course of this action-packed year, a celebrity billionaire challenged WWE Chairman Mr. McMahon to a match at *WrestleMania*, an iconic Superstar returned after several years to "save" *RAW* from mediocrity, Mr. McMahon uncovered a long-lost son, and the WWE Universe celebrated 15 years of sports entertainment's flagship show.

Contract signing gone awry

January 15: Set to face each other two weeks later at the *Royal Rumble* event for the WWE Championship, John Cena and the mighty Samoan warrior Umaga met in the ring to sign the contract for their match. Umaga's manager Armando Alejandro Estrada insulted Cena, and was given an Attitude Adjustment through the contract-signing table for his troubles.

The Donald makes it rain

January 29: Mr. McMahon had declared this night to be "Fan Appreciation Night." He thanked the WWE Universe for all the money he had made and gave away self-promoting prizes to fans, including a giant copy of a muscle magazine that featured him on the cover. He was interrupted by billionaire reality TV star Donald Trump on the big screen. Trump told McMahon that he was out of touch with fans and that he, Trump, knew what they really wanted. Seconds later, thousands of dollars in cash rained down on the WWE Universe. McMahon protested that the money was just pieces of paper, but the dollar bills looked real enough!

January 29: While thanking the WWE Universe for making him a billionaire, Mr. McMahon is suddenly interrupted by Donald Trump, who has his own ideas about giving fans value for money.

The new contender

February 5: WWE Champion John Cena was looking for an opponent at *WrestleMania 23*. That opponent would be the winner of a Triple Threat Match between Shawn Michaels, Randy Orton, and Edge. Michaels capitalized on the tension between former tag team partners Edge and Orton, pinning Orton for the win.

January 15: John Cena throws Armando Estrada through a table after signing a match contract with Estrada's charge, Umaga.

February 12: Donald Trump challenges Mr. McMahon to a Battle of the Billionaires match at *WrestleMania 23*.

Matchmaking and dealing

February 12: After interrupting Mr. McMahon via the big screen two weeks earlier, Donald Trump appeared live and in person on *RAW*. He had a challenge for Mr. McMahon: a match at *WrestleMania*. Mr. McMahon made a counter-offer—each billionaire would pick a WWE Superstar to represent him in the ring. Trump then dramatically upped the stakes—the losing billionaire would be shaved bald! McMahon accepted, and the Battle of the Billionaires was set for *WrestleMania 23*.

Stone Cold referee

March 5: Nearly a month after taking up Donald Trump's Battle of the Billionaires challenge for *WrestleMania*, Mr. McMahon expressed concern over who would referee the match. The WWE Board of Directors stated that they would choose the referee. After wrongly believing Eric Bischoff, Mick Foley, and Shane McMahon would be the refs, Mr. McMahon was horrified to learn that the Board had chosen McMahon's longtime rival, Stone Cold Steve Austin.

What does "Umaga" mean?

March12: The Rock hadn't appeared in WWE for nearly three years, but the rising Hollywood star felt compelled to make an appearance on *RAW* via the big screen to comment on the upcoming Battle of the Billionaires. The Rock wanted to make a public service announcement, mocking Mr. McMahon's chosen defender, Umaga, telling WWE Universe that "Umaga" was a crude term for a certain part of a monkey's anatomy.

Breaking the Master Lock

March 29: For nearly two years, Chris Master had gone undefeated in his "Master Lock Challenge," in which he invited Superstars to try to get free from his seemingly unbreakable Master Lock hold. Enter Bobby Lashley. The ECW Champion, and Donald Trump's chosen Superstar, was able to escape the hold with ease, becoming the first Superstar to do so.

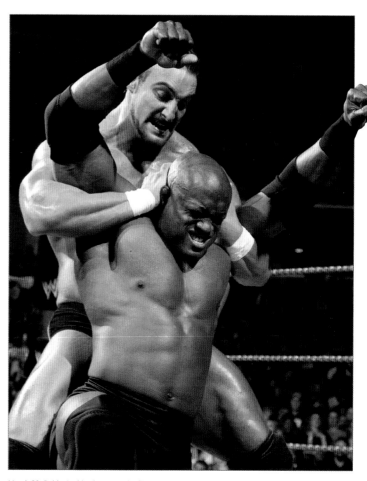

March 29: Bobby Lashley becomes the first Superstar to escape from Chris Masters' powerful Master Lock.

Elsewhere in WWE

April 1: *WrestleMania 23*'s Battle of the Billionaires was the talk of the sports and entertainment worlds: Would Donald Trump lose his famous coiffure? The answer, it turned out, was no, as Trump's champion, Bobby Lashley, defeated McMahon's champion, Umaga. After the match, Trump took great pleasure in helping to shave Mr. McMahon's head.

2007

Team extreme and bald exposure

April 2: It was the night after *WrestleMania 23*, and the WWE Universe was still buzzing from the epic event. At the direction of Mr. McMahon, WWE Tag Team Champions John Cena and Shawn Michaels were ordered to defend their Titles in a ten-team Battle Royal. The Champions were eliminated in the middle of the match, leaving their Titles up for grabs. The Hardy Boyz outlasted the remaining teams, winning the match and the Championships.

Later that night, Mr. McMahon complained about losing his hair following the Battle of the Billionaires. The victor in that match, Bobby Lashley, came to the ring and forcibly removed Mr. McMahon's hat, exposing his newly shaved head.

RAW goes to Italy

April 16: *Monday Night RAW* has been broadcast from locations throughout the world, and on this night made its debut in Italy. The Italian members of the WWE Universe greeted the Superstars with frenzied enthusiasm, and grew even more excited when one of their own, Santino Marella, was invited into the ring for a chance to win the Intercontinental Championship. The world was shocked when Marella pinned Umaga, winning the Title.

April 2: The Hardy Boyz hold their newly captured WWE World Tag Team Championship high after winning a ten-tag-team Battle Royal.

A giant thief

May 7: The Great Khali had won a match against Shawn Michaels to become the number-one contender for John Cena's WWE Championship. But Khali didn't want to wait for his match against Cena to take the Title. He attacked Cena at the end of *RAW* and stole the Title, carrying it with him as he left the arena.

INTRODUCING...

Santino Marella

Apr 16: Santino Marella thought he was just a regular member of the WWE Universe, but when he attended *Monday Night RAW* in his hometown of Milan, Italy, his life was changed forever. Marella was sitting in the front row when the Intercontinental Champion Umaga challenged him to a match. Marella won, and his WWE career took off like a rocket. Marella would go on to win several more championships, and entertain the WWE Universe with his funny antics before retiring from the ring in 2014.

Santino Marella celebrates with his countrymen in Italy after winning the Intercontinental Championship on his debut.

Elsewhere in WWE

April 29: At the *Backlash* pay-per-view, Mr. McMahon defeated Bobby Lashley (with help from Umaga) to win the ECW Championship. McMahon became only the third Superstar to have won both the WWE and ECW Championships in his career.

May 7: After becoming the number-one contender for the WWE Championship, The Great Khali shows the current Champion John Cena what's in store in their upcoming match.

June 18: A federal agent, investigating Mr. McMahon's apparent murder, interviews WWE Champion John Cena.

The first Tri-Brand Draft and no love for Mr. McMahon

June 11: Every year, the WWE Superstars are drafted to different brands. This year's Draft was unique as it featured Superstars being drafted to *RAW* and *SmackDown*, but also ECW.

The draft coincided with Mr. McMahon Appreciation Night. Past and present Superstars appeared on *RAW*, but instead of praising the boss, they lambasted and humiliated him. Disappointed by the response to his Appreciation Night, Mr. McMahon left the arena by the back door, and got into his limousine. Moments later, the limo exploded, seemingly killing Mr. McMahon.

Lashley beats the clock

July 2: Bobby Lashley was already having a record-setting year, having won the ECW Championship and having represented Donald Trump in the Battle of the Billionaires at *WrestleMania 23*. However, he accomplished his greatest feat yet when, on this episode of *RAW*, he won a "Beat the Clock" challenge to become the number-one contender to John Cena's WWE Championship.

June 11: Mr. McMahon Appreciation Night has a shocking end as his fancy stretch limo explodes, apparently with Mr. McMahon inside it.

INTRODUCING...

Cody Rhodes

July 2: Cody Rhodes, the son of WWE Hall of Famer "The American Dream" Dusty Rhodes, joined WWE intent on teaching Randy Orton to respect his legendary father. Cody battled Orton for several months before joining forces with him to form "The Legacy," a stable of second and third-generation Superstars. Cody would go on to forge his own path before teaming up with his older brother Goldust and becoming the mystical Superstar Stardust.

Cody Rhodes stares down Randy Orton as Rhodes' legendary father, "The American Dream" Dusty Rhodes, looks on.

Murder investigation

June 18: One week after the apparent sudden death of Mr. McMahon in the explosion, federal agents launched an investigation. Superstars and WWE personnel were interviewed, without much success. A few months later, Mr. McMahon returned unexpectedly, explaining that he'd faked his death to see who would miss him when he was gone.

Royal conflict

July 30: Booker T won the *King of the Ring* tournament, and started calling himself "King Booker." For three decades, *RAW* commentator Jerry Lawler had called himself "The King." These two sports entertainment monarchs were on a collision course that led to a match on *RAW*, with King Booker losing by disqualification when he wouldn't stop striking Lawler in the corner.

2007

General Manager Regal

August 6: *Monday Night RAW* needed a new leader, so a 20-Superstar Battle Royal was held; the winner would become *RAW's* new General Manager. As the match was coming to its close, Shelton Benjamin, Carlito, and The Sandman battled for victory. The Sandman knocked Benjamin and Carlito to the floor and appeared to have won. Suddenly, William Regal, who had been outside the ring, struck Sandman from behind and eliminated him, winning the contest and becoming General Manager.

King Booker and the King of Kings

August 20: King Booker was on a crusade against all of sports entertainment's other kings. He'd defeated Jerry "The King" Lawler, and now set his sights on Triple H, "The King of Kings." King Booker challenged Triple H to come to the ring and bow before him. But it was a Triple H impersonator who carried out King Booker's orders to pay homage. The real Triple H would get his revenge a week later at *SummerSlam*.

Hornswoggle McMahon

September 10: In August, Mr. McMahon learned that he had an illegitimate son, who was a Superstar on the *RAW* roster. After spending weeks wondering who his offspring was, hoping it was a champion like Randy Orton or John Cena, Mr. McMahon was devastated to learn his son was in fact Hornswoggle!

Father's day

September 17: While Mr. McMahon tried to escape his new son Hornswoggle, Acting General Manager Jonathan Coachman put John Cena's father in a match with Cena's rival Randy Orton. Orton made short work of the elder Cena, giving him a vicious RKO before Cena could intervene and protect his father.

Championship celebration

October 8: Randy Orton had won the WWE Championship the previous night at the *No Mercy* pay-per-view event, and celebrated his win on *RAW*. The celebration was short-lived; Shawn Michaels returned to WWE, after nearly a six-month absence, and attacked Orton.

Santino condemned

November 5: For weeks, Santino Marella had mocked Stone Cold Steve Austin's performance in the action movie *The Condemned*, without repercussions. That would end this week, as "The Texas Rattlesnake" Steve Austin returned to *RAW* and gave Santino a Stone Cold Stunner. Austin celebrated his return with a beer bash in the ring.

Hornswoggle and Khali

November 12: Mr. McMahon wanted his son Hornswoggle to be one of the best competitors in WWE, and set him up in a match with a Superstar three times his size: The Great Khali. Hornswoggle enlisted the help of William Regal for his pre-match training, and Regal ordered Jonathan Coachman to impersonate Khali. Hornswoggle used Coachman-Khali as a "tackling dummy" to practice his moves on. He concluded the training session by leaping from the top rope, connecting with his signature Tadpole Splash, and pinning Coach.

September 10: Hornswoggle hugs an annoyed Mr. McMahon after learning that the Chairman of WWE is his father.

November 19: "The Sexy Beast is back, baby!" Following a lengthy absence, Chris Jericho drinks in the adoration of the WWE Universe.

"This is not a mirage, this is real, this is here, this is now, this is the second coming of Y2J!"

Chris Jericho (November 19, 2007)

Countdown to Jericho

November 19: For many weeks, mysterious messages had been appearing on screen during *RAW*, promising a second coming, alongside a countdown clock. The countdown clock expired, and Chris "Y2J" Jericho returned to WWE after two years away. Jericho proclaimed that *RAW* had become stale with Randy Orton as Champion and that the best way to make WWE exciting again was to take the Championship away from him.

Flair must retire

November 26: Ric Flair was considered by many to be the greatest Superstar of all time. He'd had a 30-year career, was still a strong competitor and, as the crowd cheered, he claimed he was never going to retire. Nonetheless, Mr. McMahon felt it was time for Flair to hang up his boots. The WWE Chairman gave Flair an ultimatum: "The first match you lose, Ric, your career is over."

15th anniversary celebrations

December 10: Marking 15 years as WWE's most important TV show, this episode featured returns of Superstars from throughout the show's first decade and a half, including Hulk Hogan, D-Generation X, Rob Van Dam, and more. The McMahon family, including Hornswoggle, tried to get a family portrait taken, but interference from Triple H ruined the moment. "Million Dollar Man" Ted DiBiase purchased a victory in a Legends Battle Royal from IRS, and Mr. McMahon announced himself as the greatest *RAW* Superstar of all time. That decision was met with anger from the WWE Universe as well as attacks from the truly legendary Superstars in *RAW* history: Mick Foley, Undertaker, and Stone Cold Steve Austin.

"The Million Dollar Man" buys a Battle Royal victory from IRS; Undertaker makes a dramatic entrance; the McMahon family poses for a portrait; Hulk Hogan returns to save Hornswoggle from The Great Khali, all during *RAW's 15th Anniversary Special*.

2008

2008 WAS A YEAR FULL of debuts, returns, and goodbyes. Kofi Kingston, Dolph Ziggler, and the Bella Twins joined WWE, John Cena shocked the WWE Universe with his return at the *Royal Rumble*, and arguably the greatest WWE Superstar of all time, the 16-time World Champion Ric Flair, retired from in-ring competition. Also in this year, the show celebrated its 800th episode and enjoyed a visit from three presidential candidates.

January 14: Mini-Mankind goes after Hornswoggle in the mini-Rumble match.

Champ vs. Champ

January 14: Two weeks before they were set to face each other for the WWE Championship at the *Royal Rumble*, WWE Champion Randy Orton faced Intercontinental Champion Jeff Hardy in the main event, with the Intercontinental Title on the line. The match itself ended quickly in a disqualification. However, Orton and Hardy, still determined to punish each other, continued to battle to the entrance stage. Jeff Hardy climbed the Titan Tron and jumped off in a multi-story Swanton dive, landing on Orton below.

On the same night, to prepare for his Royal Rumble Match debut, Hornswoggle competed in a "mini-Rumble," against little people versions of WWE Superstars such as Batista and Mr. Kennedy. Hornswoggle was on his way to winning the match when things got a bit rough—the full-sized version of The Great Khali entered the Rumble and attacked Hornswoggle. Finlay charged the ring to save Hornswoggle from Khali's attack, smacking Khali with his shillelagh and allowing Hornswoggle to win.

Elsewhere in WWE

January 27: John Cena had been absent from WWE, having torn his pectoral muscle in October 2007. Living up to his motto "Never Give Up," Cena shocked the WWE Universe by being the final entrant in January's 2008 Royal Rumble Match.

Mike Adamle

January 28: A former professional football player, Mike Adamle joined *Monday Night RAW* as an interviewer and commentator. Six months later, he was named the General Manager of *RAW*, making matches and enforcing the rules of in-ring competition. He referred to the matches he made as "Adamle Originals." He resigned from the GM role and left WWE in October of 2008.

World's strongest arm-wrestler

February 4: Randy Orton was set to face John Cena for the WWE Championship in two weeks' time at the *No Way Out* event. Orton enlisted the help of the "World's Strongest Man" Mark Henry to try to reinjure Cena's recently healed torn pectoral muscle and stop him from competing at full strength for the Title. Henry challenged Cena to an arm-wrestling contest, set up so Orton could attack Cena himself. Cena fought off Orton and gave Henry his signature Attitude Adjustment.

January 14: Jeff Hardy dives off the Titan Tron towards Randy Orton.

Fathers and sons

February 11: Mr. McMahon believed Hornswoggle was his son, and for weeks attacked the leprechaun-like Superstar as part of his "parenting workshops" on *RAW*. WWE Superstar Finlay had seen enough of the tough love dished out by McMahon, and saved Hornswoggle from another attack. McMahon was furious, and threatened to fire Finlay. But Finlay stood his ground and protected Hornswoggle. Two weeks later, Mr. McMahon would learn Finlay was actually Hornswoggle's father.

The Money/Big Show showdown

February 18: Big Show tried to make amends to former world champion boxer Floyd "Money" Mayweather for mocking his size at the previous night's *No Way Out* event. Big Show apologized to Mayweather, and extended his hand to him, but Mayweather refused to shake it and walked away. Big Show wasn't done, though. He mocked Mayweather again, and then challenged him to a match at *WrestleMania XXIV*, which Mayweather readily accepted.

February 18: Boxer Floyd "Money" Mayweather stares down Big Show.

One more match

February 25: Ric Flair had been announced as the headlining inductee at 2008's WWE Hall of Fame ceremony during *WrestleMania XXIV* weekend, but Flair also wanted to have a major match at *WrestleMania*. He challenged Shawn Michaels. Michaels was hesitant to accept the challenge because Mr. McMahon had told Flair that he would have to retire following his next loss. Michaels didn't want to cause that loss. But Flair insisted, and the two friends agreed to face each other at *WrestleMania XXIV*.

WrestleMania Rewind

March 10: As the road to *WrestleMania XXIV* began heating up, this episode of *RAW* featured some "*WrestleMania* Rewind" matches: matches from past *WrestleMania* events. WWE legends Barry Windham and Mike Rotunda squared off against their opponents from the very first *WrestleMania*, Nikolai Volkoff and the Iron Sheik, but the match ended before it began when Jillian Hall interrupted it to sing a song. Undertaker faced Mark Henry in a Casket Match—a rematch from their identical encounter at *WrestleMania 22*, with an identical outcome of Undertaker getting the win.

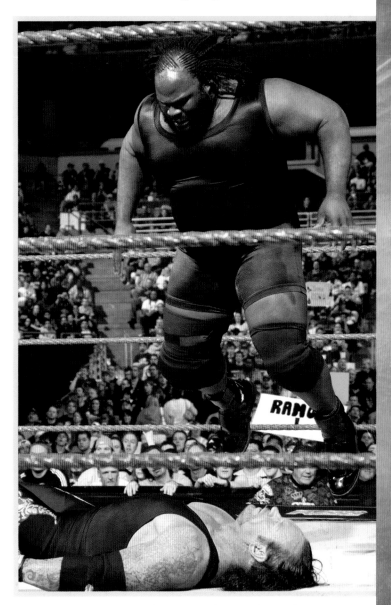

March 10: Mark Henry jumps towards Undertaker in a *WrestleMania* Rewind rematch.

Cena and Orton vs. *RAW*

March 17: Leading to their Triple Threat Match at *WrestleMania XXIV*, Triple H, John Cena, and Randy Orton were each given authority to make matches for a week on *RAW*. To get a competitive advantage over his opponents, Triple H forced the other two into a match where they would team up together and face the entire *RAW* Superstar roster. Cena and Orton fought bravely, but it eventually proved to be too much for them when Triple H entered the match and hit both Superstars with a Pedigree.

March 29–30: Ric Flair experienced the highest of highs and lowest of lows over *WrestleMania XXIV* weekend. He was inducted into the WWE Hall of Fame by Triple H on March 29 and lost his final match to Shawn Michaels the following night, March 30.

Farewell to Flair

March 31: Retiring after losing his match against Shawn Michaels at *WrestleMania XXIV* the night before, Ric Flair addressed the WWE Universe on *RAW*, thanking them for his three-decade-long career. As Flair was finishing up, Triple H walked to the ring and expressed his love for his mentor and Evolution teammate. Soon, many of Flair's other friends and family swarmed the ring until every WWE Superstar and official was surrounding him, giving him a standing ovation for his legendary career. With a tear in his eye, Ric Flair thanked his friends, family, and the WWE Universe for the send-off.

"Rejoice in the fact that I have wrestled in front of more fans, raised more hell, had more fun, and loved all of you every day of my life!"

Ric Flair (March 31, 2008)

March 31: Superstars and Legends gather in the ring to say thank you and goodbye to "Nature Boy" Ric Flair.

April 21: William Regal takes his throne as the new *King of the Ring*.

The Animal and the Heartbreak Kid

April 7: Batista was mad. He was mad that his friend and Evolution teammate Ric Flair was forced to retire. And he was mad at Shawn Michaels for causing it. Batista confronted Shawn Michaels about these issues on Chris Jericho's *Highlight Reel* talk show segment. Michaels tried to make peace with "The Animal" Batista, but it was no use. Batista was determined to exact revenge for losing Flair by challenging Michaels to a match at *Backlash*, the next pay-per-view event, which Michaels accepted.

Of Kings and Presidents

April 21: This edition of *RAW* was a night all about royalty and government leadership. William Regal won an eight-Superstar tournament to be crowned King of the Ring. The proud Brit celebrated his victory by sitting on his throne, promising to rule over WWE for a long time to come. Meanwhile three then-candidates for President of the United States—Barack Obama, Hillary Clinton, and John McCain—appeared in video segments, inviting the WWE Universe to participate in the electoral process by voting in the upcoming election. Later in the evening, actors impersonating Obama, Clinton, and Clinton's husband, former US President Bill Clinton, appeared in the ring for a pretend match between the "candidates." The match ended in a no-contest when Umaga charged the ring and attacked the impersonators.

April 21: Actors portraying Bill and Hillary Clinton appear in the ring.

Regal power

May 5: The newly crowned King of the Ring William Regal had been named as the new *RAW* General Manager, and was abusing his power on those who he felt disrespected him. A week earlier, he ordered the lights turned off during a match between Triple H and Mr. Kennedy. This week, after Triple H complained about the match, Regal ordered Triple H and Kennedy to team up against the entire ECW Superstar roster—much like Triple H had done to Cena and Orton earlier in the year—leading to a loss for Triple H and Kennedy.

May 5: The ECW Superstars attack Triple H in their 2-14 handicap match.

McMahon's millions and Michaels' mistake

June 9: To demonstrate his appreciation to the WWE Universe, Mr. McMahon kicked off a weekly contest where he gave away large amounts of his personal fortune to random winners. Called *McMahon's Millions*, Mr. McMahon would randomly draw an entrant's telephone number and call them live on the air during *RAW*, and inform them of the amount of money they'd won. The WWE Universe watched with eager anticipation, hoping their number would be drawn this week.

Chris Jericho grew up idolizing Shawn Michaels. In fact, Jericho had often said Michaels was his inspiration to become a Superstar. But in the weeks prior to June 9, Michaels had exaggerated an injury, tricking Jericho in a match and causing him to lose that match. Jericho felt lied to and betrayed by his hero. He invited Michaels to appear on his *Highlight Reel* talk show, and viciously attacked his now-former hero, including smashing Michaels into the *Highlight Reel's* massive TV screen.

June 9: Mr. McMahon gives away his fortune in *McMahon's Millions*.

2008

Shakeups

June 23: It was the annual WWE Superstar Draft, where Superstars move between *RAW*, *SmackDown*, and ECW. The roster shakeups between the three brands is often surprising, but perhaps none was more shocking in this edition of the draft than the announcement that Jim Ross, who had been the voice of *Monday Night RAW* for more than a decade, would be moved to *SmackDown*, with Michael Cole replacing him as *RAW*'s lead announcer.

Mr. McMahon had come out to the entrance stage to give away more of his money during *McMahon's Millions*. Suddenly, a light fell from the rafters, crashing next to him. The stage floor gave way, and Mr. McMahon was buried underneath pieces of the *RAW* entrance stage. Superstars like Triple H and John Cena, as well as WWE officials and referees, raced out to help Mr. McMahon. Though he escaped without serious injury, the chaos marked the end of the *McMahon's Millions* giveaway.

Punk cashes in

June 30: World Heavyweight Champion Edge boasted about being drafted to *SmackDown*, leaving *RAW* without a World Champion. He taunted several Superstars, including Batista, about never getting another shot at the World Title. Enraged, Batista attacked Edge, leaving him in a heap. Suddenly, CM Punk raced to the ring, cashing in his Money in the Bank briefcase that allowed him to challenge for a World Championship match whenever he wanted. He hit Edge with his signature GTS move, and pinned him, winning the World Heavyweight Championship and keeping it on *RAW*.

Limo vandals

July 7: John "Bradshaw" Layfield is a very wealthy man, and has always liked to flaunt his wealth and the power it gives him. John Cena views the world a little differently, and sought to knock JBL down a couple of notches, and remind him possessions aren't really all that important. So, with the help of the tag team Cryme Tyme, Cena vandalized JBL's beloved limousine. They smashed windows and mirrors, and left JBL a spray-painted message.

Strange Tag Team Champions

August 4: John Cena and Batista were preparing for a big match against each other at *SummerSlam*. Their rivalry was growing more and more heated, and as such, they were surprised when new *RAW* General Manager Mike Adamle put them in a Tag Team Championship Match against Cody Rhodes and Ted DiBiase. Adamle hoped being forced to compete together would diffuse some of the tension between them. It worked for a moment as Cena and Batista won the match and the Titles, but their reign ended a week later when they lost them back to Rhodes and DiBiase.

INTRODUCING...

Kofi Kingston

June 30: Having debuted in WWE by way of the ECW brand in January, Kofi Kingston joined *Monday Night RAW* as part of June's WWE Supplemental Draft. Kingston's first appearance as a member of the *RAW* roster was on June 30. His high-energy personality and high-flying in-ring offense quickly made him popular with the WWE Universe. He won several championships before becoming one of the longest-reigning WWE Tag Team Champions in history as a member of The New Day.

Kofi Kingston makes a big splash as a member of the *RAW* roster.

Elsewhere in WWE

August 29: The Bella Twins, Brie and Nikki, debut on *SmackDown*. It began a decade-long career that saw them both become household names, win the Divas Championship, and star on WWE's *Total Divas* and *Total Bellas* reality TV series.

July 7: John Cena and Cryme Tyme send a message to JBL by vandalizing his limousine.

September 15: Shawn Michaels challenges Chris Jericho to a Ladder Match.

The Champ is Jericho

September 8: Chris Jericho wasn't scheduled to compete for the World Heavyweight Championship the night before at the *Unforgiven* pay-per-view event, but after the defending champion CM Punk was injured, Jericho replaced him in the match. Jericho defeated four other Superstars to win the Title in a Championship Scramble Match, and boasted about it on *RAW*. Dressed in a new suit and tie, and with a more somber yet arrogant attitude, Jericho declared it was a new era on *RAW*—the era of Chris Jericho.

Ladder Challenge

September 15: Every WWE Superstar wants a shot at the World Championship. It can be a tough decision for a General Manager to make. One week after Jericho won the Title, *RAW* General Manager Mike Adamle announced that the new number-one contender would be Shawn Michaels. Michaels set a ladder up at the entrance stage, and climbed to the top. Sitting atop the ladder, he challenged Jericho to a Ladder Match at the *No Mercy* pay-per-view event the following month.

September 8: Chris Jericho holds his newly won World Heavyweight Championship.

INTRODUCING...

Dolph Ziggler

September 22: Dolph Ziggler debuted on *Monday Night RAW* first by shaking hands backstage with General Manager Mike Adamle and World Heavyweight Champion Chris Jericho. After a few weeks of these introductions, Ziggler competed on *RAW* for the first time on December 1, losing to Batista. Despite this inauspicious beginning, Ziggler would go on to become a two-time World Heavyweight Champion, five-time Intercontinental Champion, one-time United States Champion, and win the Money in the Bank briefcase.

Dolph Ziggler introduces himself to the WWE Universe as part of his first appearance on *RAW*.

Odd couple

September 29: For months, Women's Champion "The Glamazon" Beth Phoenix and Santino Marella had been a romantic couple, called "Glamerella." But as Santino kept needing Phoenix's help to win matches (including winning the Intercontinental Championship) and to save him from uncomfortable situations, tension began to grow between them. Their relationship would only last a few more months, with Phoenix splitting from Marella.

2008

Lumberjacks

October 13: A Lumberjack Match involves two Superstars competing in the ring while a large number of other Superstars, called "Lumberjacks," surround the ring to ensure the action stays inside it. These matches can be difficult because there's no escape. So, it made sense that when Chris Jericho got to pick his future opponent Batista's match, he chose a Lumberjack match against Shawn Michaels. The Lumberjacks attacked Batista and Michaels and the match ended in a no contest, but Jericho believed the Lumberjacks had softened Batista, making him easier to beat later.

Greatest Intercontinental Champions of all time

October 20: After he won the Intercontinental Championship, Santino Marella was determined to become the greatest, longest-reigning champion of all time, unseating the record holder, WWE Legend The Honky Tonk Man. He began tracking his time as champ with a "Honk-O-Meter." Each week he boasted how he was a year or so away from breaking the record. He also dressed up as three of the greatest Intercontinental Champions: Goldust (facepaint), Honky Tonk Man (guitar and wig), and "Rowdy" Roddy Piper (kilt and shirt).

October 20: Santino Marella pays tribute to Intercontinental Champions of the past: Goldust, Honky Tonk Man, and "Rowdy" Roddy Piper.

Shawn Michaels and Triple H reunite as D-Generation X during the 800th episode of *RAW*.

Episode 800

November 3: *Monday Night RAW* celebrated its 800th episode with big matches and exciting appearances. D-Generation X reunited and defeated The Miz and John Morrison. Sixteen women, including WWE Hall of Famer Mae Young, competed in a Tag Team Match. And Chris Jericho defeated Batista for the World Heavyweight Championship inside a steel cage.

November 10: Chris Jericho holds Shawn Michaels in the Walls of Jericho on top of a London taxi in their Last Man Standing Match.

Last Man Standing

November 10: Fresh from his World Heavyweight Championship win the week before, Chris Jericho defended the Title in a Last Man Standing Match against his fiercest rival Shawn Michaels, in London. While the match was a fairly even contest, Shawn Michaels ended up losing the match thanks to an attack from John "Bradshaw" Layfield. While Chris Jericho retained the Championship, Shawn Michaels set his sights on a new target: JBL.

Sibling rivalry

November 24: Mr. McMahon trusted his children Shane and Stephanie to run *Monday Night RAW*, but Shane and Stephanie didn't trust each other. Shane made matches that were subverted by Stephanie. Stephanie claimed Shane's responsibilities included only the corporate side of *RAW*, while she was authorized to make matches. Shane disagreed, stating his sister would destroy *RAW*. It was a classic sibling rivalry.

Legacy

December 1: For months, Cody Rhodes and Ted DiBiase, two second-generation Superstars, had been tag teaming together, but in recent weeks Rhodes had acquired a new second-generation partner, Manu. Randy Orton, a third-generation Superstar, had seen great potential in Rhodes, DiBiase, and Manu, and gathered the young Superstars together, forming a stable called "The Legacy." The Legacy's first act was to attack John Cena following his main-event match against Chris Jericho, leaving Cena unconscious on the arena floor.

December 1: Randy Orton, Cody Rhodes, and Manu (aka the Legacy) attack John Cena post-match.

December 15: JBL makes Shawn Michaels an offer he can't refuse.

Slammy Awards special

December 8: The Slammy Awards were a WWE tradition, given away every few years to WWE Superstars for various achievements in and out of the ring. Often they were presented during a TV special, but beginning in 2008, they were given out during a special episode of *Monday Night RAW*. In this first ever Slammy Awards *RAW*, trophies were given for things like "Most Extreme Moment of the Year," and the most prestigious Slammy, "Superstar of the Year," which Stephanie McMahon presented to World Heavyweight Champion Chris Jericho.

December 8: Matt Hardy and Tiffany present Jeff Hardy with the Slammy Award for Most Extreme Moment of the Year.

JBL's assistant

December 15: Shawn Michaels had fallen on hard financial times, and found himself desperate to provide for his family. Enter John "Bradshaw" Layfield. JBL was known for his tremendous wealth, and was willing to hire Shawn Michaels as his personal assistant. Michaels agreed, even though he knew it meant doing humiliating tasks for JBL—everything from washing his car to helping JBL cheat to win matches. But, Michaels was desperate, and desperate men do desperate things.

December 22, 2008: Trish Stratus makes a triumphant return to the ring partnering with John Cena.

2009

THE WWE UNIVERSE never would have thought that Mr. McMahon would sell *Monday Night RAW,* or that popular game show *The Price Is Right* would be played on *RAW*, but 2009 was nothing if not unpredictable. Donald Trump purchased the brand early in the year, only to sell it back to Mr. McMahon at a big profit. Special guest hosts from the sports and entertainment worlds took on the role of General Manager for much of the year, many of them even competing in the ring. A group of legends came out of retirement to confront Chris Jericho, and D-Generation X found a new mascot.

Viper strikes the boss

January 19: Randy Orton's anger issues had gotten him into a lot of trouble in recent weeks, but nothing was worse than kicking the boss. Mr. McMahon had returned to *RAW* after several months away, and confronted Orton. Orton didn't like what McMahon had to say, and McMahon had to be carried out on a stretcher.

GM Vickie

February 23: Randy Orton's attacks on the McMahon family resulted in a need for an interim General Manager to run things. The WWE Board of Directors selected Vickie Guerrero, who was *SmackDown* GM, widow of WWE Hall of Famer Eddie Guerrero, and current wife of World Heavyweight Champion Edge.

February 23: The widow of WWE Hall of Famer Eddie Guerrero, Vickie, joins *RAW* as the new General Manager.

Michaels eyes Undertaker

March 2: Shawn Michaels was determined to face Undertaker at *WrestleMania 25* and end his undefeated streak. To get that match, Michaels had first to face Vladimir Koslov, who was undefeated in WWE competition. Michaels battled valiantly, winning the match and ending Koslov's streak. The match set, Undertaker appeared on the entrance stage and stared down Michaels.

Homewreckers

March 9: Randy Orton was playing mind games with Triple H and the McMahon family. Orton had attacked Triple H and the McMahons numerous times and now challenged Triple H for the WWE Championship at *WrestleMania*. Triple H had had enough. He traveled to Orton's home and, using his trusty sledgehammer, smashed down the front door. After frightening everyone inside, Triple H found Orton and hurled him through a window. Triple H continued to batter Orton, until arrested by the police.

March 9: "Here's Hunter!" Triple H terrorizes the Orton household.

Meanwhile, Edge and Big Show were set to face off against each other at *WrestleMania 25* with the World Heavyweight Championship on the line. As the two Superstars began signing their contract for the match, under the direction of Edge's wife, *RAW* General Manager Vickie Guerrero, John Cena interrupted and revealed Vickie and Big Show had been romantically involved. This revelation made Edge furious, and got Cena added to the Edge/Big Show match at *WrestleMania*.

March 16: Ric Flair, Ricky Steamboat, Roddy Piper, and Jimmy Snuka surround Jericho, making a challenge for *WrestleMania 25*.

Jericho challenges four of the greats

March 16: Chris Jericho had made a habit out of insulting WWE legends. WWE Hall of Famer Ric Flair was furious and challenged Jericho to face some of these legends at *WrestleMania*. Jericho mocked Flair, but shut up when Flair's legendary friends—Jimmy "Superfly" Snuka, "Rowdy" Roddy Piper, and Ricky "The Dragon" Steamboat—surrounded him in the ring, poised to strike.

Defending Stephanie

March 30: Orton's obsession with the McMahons and Triple H crossed a line one week earlier when he attacked Triple H's family: Vince McMahon, Shane McMahon and Triple H's wife, Stephanie, leaving her unconscious. To a chorus of booing from the audience, Orton boasted about this attack. He had to quickly change his tune when Stephanie's father Mr. McMahon, brother Shane McMahon, and Triple H charged toward the ring. Orton and his Legacy compadres were quickly put to flight, and Triple H proceeded to take his anger out on Orton in the ring.

March 9: John Cena successfully blackmails Vickie Guerrero into making him a part of the main event at *WrestleMania 25*.

March 30: Shane McMahon, Triple H, and Mr. Vince McMahon gather to defend Stephanie McMahon's honor after an attack by Randy Orton.

2009

Elsewhere in WWE

April 4: Stone Cold Steve Austin revolutionized WWE in the late 1990s. His success in the ring and rivalry with Mr. McMahon made *Monday Night RAW* must-see TV. Austin's success earned him an induction into the WWE Hall of Fame the night before *WrestleMania XXV* by his longtime foe, Mr. McMahon.

WrestleMania's All-Stars celebrate

April 6: The night after *WrestleMania XXV*, ten WWE Superstars faced their opponents from the night before in a five-on-five "*WrestleMania* All-Star" Tag Team Match. Ricky "The Dragon" Steamboat, who had been inducted into the WWE Hall of Fame the weekend before, helped his team get the victory when he dove off the top rope on to Edge.

Although not involved in the "All-Star" Tag Team Match, another *WrestleMania* victor, "Santina" Marella (whom everyone knew was Santino Marella), celebrated "her" victory in the previous night's 25 Diva "Miss *WrestleMania*" Battle Royal. Claiming to be Santino's sister, Santina proudly wore the Miss *WrestleMania* sash and tiara as part of the celebration.

April 6: "Santina" Marella celebrates "her" *WrestleMania* win.

April 13: Montel Vontavious Porter joins *RAW* as the number-one Draft Pick in the 2009 Superstar Draft.

MVP of the Draft

April 13: One week after *WrestleMania XXV*, WWE held the annual Superstar Draft where Superstars were moved between *RAW* and *SmackDown*. *RAW*'s number-one pick in this year's draft was United States Champion Montel Vontavious Porter (otherwise known as MVP).

Respect the Dragon

April 20: Prior to competing in the ring at *WrestleMania 25*, Ricky "The Dragon" Steamboat had been retired from in-ring competition for eleven years. Chris Jericho, Steamboat's *WrestleMania* opponent, was jealous of the incredible cheers from the WWE Universe that Steamboat received upon his return to the ring. Jericho challenged Steamboat to one more match at *Backlash 2009*. Steamboat accepted the challenge, setting up his final match ever. Steamboat would put up a brave show, but eventually lose a thrilling encounter on a submission.

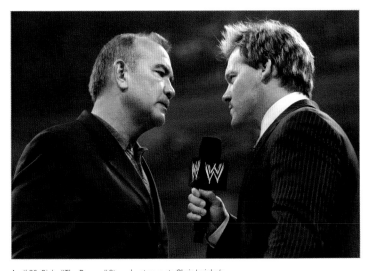

April 20: Ricky "The Dragon" Steamboat accepts Chris Jericho's challenge for a final match at WWE *Backlash*.

April 27: The Bella Twins hide under the ring with Hornswoggle during their *RAW* debut.

The Bellas join *RAW*

April 27: Formerly members of the *SmackDown* roster, Brie and Nikki, The Bella Twins, had joined *RAW* in the draft two weeks earlier, but had yet to appear on the show. Brie debuted as part of an Eight-Diva Tag Team Match, but, before entering the match, hid under the ring. One of Brie's opponents chased after her, looking under the ring and discovering not only Brie, but her sister Nikki and their friend Hornswoggle!

Stars in their eyes

May 11: The Miz fancied himself a major movie star, and was a little jealous of John Cena's Hollywood success. Cena accepted The Miz's challenge for an Exhibition Match, despite having been injured by Big Show in previous weeks. The WWE Universe was shocked when The Miz actually defeated Cena, as Cena was distracted by an on-screen announcement by General Manager Vickie Guerrero stopping the match and saying that Cena would have no chance against Big Show. The Miz claimed that his victory proved he was not only the better Superstar but a bigger movie star.

The Miz is Here!

May 18: Still celebrating his shock victory over John Cena one week earlier, The Miz came to the ring impersonating Cena. The Miz mocked Cena's rap music album, including making a parody of Cena's most popular song "Word Life," which The Miz called "Nerd Life."

May 18: The Miz makes a convincing John Cena impersonator.

Mentor issues

May 25: Although they had both been members of the Superstar faction Evolution, Randy Orton and Ric Flair were no longer friends—far from it. Flair felt that Orton, whom he had previously mentored, had disrespected him in recent weeks, and called him to the ring. Orton contemptibly slapped Flair and continued to insult him. Flair tried to fight back, but was restrained by Batista.

2009

No rules, no referees

June 1: Ric Flair wasn't allowed to compete in the ring since his retirement in 2008, but he'd reached boiling point with Randy Orton. Flair challenged his former protégé to an unsanctioned fight, hoping to teach Orton some respect. The two former Evolution members' relationship crumbled as they battled throughout the arena and parking lot. The brawl ended up inside a steel cage in the ring, where Orton pummeled Flair into submission.

June 1: Ric Flair and Randy Orton take their battle to the arena parking lot.

Trump buys *RAW*

June 15: Mr. McMahon and Donald Trump were both billionaires who'd made their fortunes through savvy business investments. When Trump made McMahon an incredible offer to buy *RAW* and add it to his Trump brand empire, McMahon couldn't refuse. One week later, however, when Trump aired a commercial-free edition, McMahon bought the show back, paying double what he'd received from Trump.

Guest hosts take over

June 29: During his brief ownership of *RAW*, Donald Trump announced that, rather than having a General Manager run the show, he would invite a celebrity Guest Host to be in charge of *RAW* every week. These hosts would be celebrities from the worlds of entertainment, sports, or WWE. The very first Guest Host was injured WWE Superstar Batista.

June 29: Batista returns to *Monday Night RAW*, serving as the show's first Guest Host.

June 15: Billionaire Donald Trump adds *Monday Night RAW* to his portfolio.

Seth Green runs the show

July 13: Celebrity Seth Green, Scott Evil in the *Austin Powers* movies and the voice of Chris Griffin and Neil Goldman in the TV show *Family Guy*, was this week's Guest Host. Green found himself in trouble when he insulted Legacy team members Randy Orton, Ted DiBiase, and Cody Rhodes. Joined by John Cena and Triple H as tag team partners, Green defeated Legacy in the main event.

August 10: The returning Eugene falls to "The Calgary Kid"—The Miz in disguise.

Vegas Birthday Bash

August 24: D-Generation X enjoyed nothing more than making Mr. McMahon's life miserable, so it was no surprise when they threw him a surprise Las Vegas birthday party, complete with an Elvis impersonator and an overweight male exotic dancer springing from a cake. Mr. McMahon's embarrassment and irritation wouldn't last long, however, as Legacy attacked him and DX from behind. For one night only, Mr. McMahon joined DX to face party wreckers Legacy in a match.

July 13: Seth Green celebrates his first match victory with John Cena and Triple H.

Shaq-Fu

July 27: For as long as he could remember, Shaquille O'Neal had been a WWE fan. This made his appearance on *RAW* as a Guest Host extremely exciting for him. The basketball giant was not going be intimidated by the WWE Superstars. When Big Show tried to slam Shaq, Shaq threw Big Show out of the ring with a slam of his own.

"The Calgary Kid"

August 10: One week earlier, The Miz had lost to John Cena, which meant that The Miz was banned. By disguising himself as "The Calgary Kid," The Miz was able to sneak back into WWE. Guest Host Sgt. Slaughter held a "WWE Contract on a Pole Match," where the winner would be the Superstar who grabbed the contract off the pole first. The Miz competed against Eugene, winning the contract and his own WWE return.

August 24: DX throws Mr. McMahon an epic, Vegas-style surprise birthday party.

"You know, Chris, your mother would not be proud of you the way you're behaving… I'm going to have to take you over my knee."

Bob Barker to Chris Jericho (September 7, 2009)

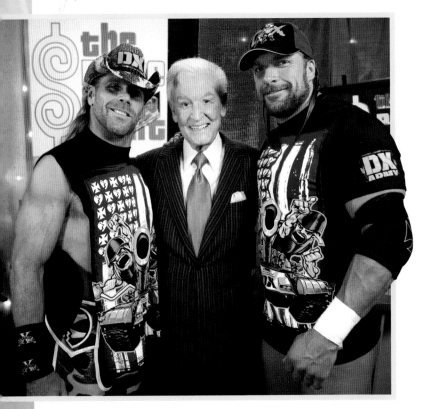

September 7: Celebrity Guest Host and game show legend Bob Barker commemorates his time on *RAW* with DX.

The Price Is RAW

September 7: Guest Host Bob Barker was known the world over as the legendary host of TV game show *The Price Is Right*. Barker brought a version of the game to WWE, calling it *The Price Is RAW*. WWE Superstars, including Santino Marella and Chris Jericho, competed in the game, winning prizes and joking around with Barker. Barker even got in on some of the action, landing a karate chop on Superstar Chavo Guerrero and sending him to the floor.

For one night only

September 14: Trish Stratus, seven-time Women's Champion, returned to WWE for one night only as a Guest Host. Stratus, who had retired from in-ring competition, joined Mark Henry and MVP in a mixed tag team match against Beth Phoenix, Chris Jericho, and Big Show. Stratus won the match by pinning Phoenix.

Legacy maintained

October 19: Randy Orton needed to reassert control over his Legacy teammates Ted DiBiase and Cody Rhodes. DiBiase had pinned Orton in a match a week earlier and it seemed that Legacy might split over the pin. Orton reminded DiBiase who the leader was, and forced him into a match. DiBiase didn't fight back against Orton's offense, succumbing to an RKO to preserve Legacy's unity.

Elsewhere in WWE

October 25: The rivalry between *RAW* and *SmackDown* was the focus of WWE's newest pay-per-view event, *Bragging Rights*. Superstars represented their brands in inter-promotional matches, where the main prize for winning was simply bragging rights.

Kofi destroys Orton's racecar

October 26: To show their appreciation for all he'd done for them, Legacy members Ted DiBiase and Cody Rhodes gave Randy Orton a brand-new racecar. Orton loved the car, and was livid when Kofi Kingston smashed it and covered it in paint.

October 26: Legacy members Randy Orton and Ted DiBiase look on in horror as Kofi Kingston destroys Orton's brand-new racecar.

RAW's got talent

November 2: Ozzy and Sharon Osbourne took over *RAW* as Guest Hosts and held a special talent show featuring the WWE Superstars. Santino Marella bit the head off a bat (a plastic model of Batman), Chris Masters flexed his pecs impressively to Ozzy's classic song "Crazy Train" (prompting Ozzy to shout, "Buy that man a bra!"), and Chavo Guerrero and Jillian threatened to sing a duet. Then Sharon floored Jillian and the whole segment spiraled out of control as Hornswoggle joined the party.

November 2: Ozzy and Sharon Osbourne judge the *RAW* talent show.

Reliving history

November 23: Twelve years earlier, Shawn Michaels and Triple H were involved in a conspiracy to take Bret Hart's WWE Championship away from him. Called "The Montreal Screwjob," the incident had never been forgotten by the WWE Universe, DX, or the Hart family. Bret's niece Natalya and nephews David Hart Smith and Tyson Kidd had formed the Hart Dynasty tag team, and had the chance to face DX and avenge the screwjob over a decade later. DX won the match, but showed respect to the Hart Dynasty.

Sheamus won a Battle Royal earlier in the evening to become the number-one contender for John Cena's WWE Championship at the upcoming *TLC* pay-per-view. Guest Host WWE Hall of Famer and former governor of Minnesota Jesse "The Body" Ventura conducted a contract signing for that match, where Sheamus attacked Cena, slamming him through the signing table.

November 23: Triple H hits Tyson Kidd with a brutal knee.

Sheamus spikes Cuban

December 7: Guest Host Mark Cuban, the billionaire owner of basketball's Dallas Mavericks, set up face-to-face confrontation between WWE Champion John Cena and number-one contender Sheamus. When the confrontation turned physical, Cuban tried to get between Sheamus and Cena. Sheamus smashed Cuban through a table for his trouble.

December 7: Sheamus drives the Guest Host, billionaire Mark Cuban, through a table.

D-Generation X's new mascot

December 21: After weeks of being teased by DX, Hornswoggle sued Shawn Michaels and Triple H. DX appeared in "Little People's Court," but left the courtroom before the judge could make her ruling. DX apologized to Hornswoggle and invited him to become D-Generation X's official mascot, which Hornswoggle excitedly accepted, putting an end to his lawsuit and bringing the curtain down on a tumultuous year.

December 21: Hornswoggle joins D-Generation X as their new mascot.

2010

2010 BEGAN WITH THE RETURN of Bret "Hit Man" Hart and ended with the unexpected coronation of The Miz. In between, WWE lost one of its greatest all-time Superstars when Shawn Michaels risked his storied career against Undertaker's incredible *WrestleMania* streak. Another former World Champion, Batista, then shockingly quit a few months later. However, nothing rocked *RAW* and WWE like the arrival of the Nexus, a group of brash rookies that ran roughshod over WWE throughout the latter half of the year.

January 4: Bret "Hit Man" Hart and Shawn Michaels finally put their animosity in the past.

January 11: The WWE Universe loved seeing guest GM Mike Tyson pose with D-Generation X to close the show.

The return of the Hit Man

January 4: More than 12 years after the infamous "Montreal Screwjob," Bret "Hit Man" Hart returned to *RAW* as the guest General Manager. Hart was looking for closure from the Montreal incident, first with his longtime rival Shawn Michaels, and the two buried the hatchet. Mr. McMahon, however, would not play along, kicking the Hit Man in the gut.

The baddest General Manager on the planet

January 11: Former boxing champion Mike Tyson served as guest General Manager on the January 11 episode of *RAW*. There could have been trouble—as Chris Jericho's tag team partner, Tyson challenged D-Generation X for the night's main event, repeating tension from *WrestleMania XIV*. But Tyson double-crossed Jericho, posing and celebrating with DX at the end of the show.

The Animal aligns with the Chairman

February 1: Bret "Hit Man" Hart returned to *RAW*, looking for a little payback against the Chairman, Mr. McMahon. However, the Chairman of WWE got the upper hand once again when he arranged for "The Animal" Batista to ambush Hart and deal out even more physical punishment.

New unified Tag Team Champions

February 8: In the main event, D-Generation X (Shawn Michaels and Triple H) defended the Unified Tag Team Championships in a Triple Threat Match against the teams of Sho-Miz (Big Show and The Miz) and CM Punk and Luke Gallows. Sho-Miz won the Championships for the first time together.

February 8: The pairing of Big Show and The Miz take the Unified Tag Team Championships from D-Generation X and hold the Title for more than two months.

Divas Champion once again

February 22: Melina was injured in January 2010, forcing her to vacate the WWE Divas Championship. Over the next few weeks, a tournament was held to crown a new champion. Maryse defeated Brie Bella, Eve Torres, and finally Gail Kim to become the first two-time champion in the Title's history.

February 22: Maryse defeats Brie Bella, Eve Torres, and Gail Kim (a trio that collectively won five championships in their careers) to capture her second Divas Championship.

Elsewhere in WWE...

February 23: NXT debuted, a show designed to find the next big WWE Superstar. Eight men would compete for a WWE contract and Championship opportunity. Little did the WWE Universe know of the impact all eight would make on *RAW* before the year was over.

One last match for DX

March 1: Trying to regain the Unified Tag Team Championships, D-Generation X challenged Sho-Miz to a match. The outrageous duo was unsuccessful and would never compete together again, making this the last match for D-Generation X.

2010

A shock for Mr. McMahon

March 15: Stone Cold Steve Austin hosted *RAW* on March 15, overseeing the *WrestleMania* contract signing between Mr. McMahon and Bret "Hit Man" Hart. Mr. McMahon was confident about the match, but was in for a rude awakening when Bret revealed that he was not actually injured.

March 15: Mr. McMahon learns that Bret Hart had been faking his injury ahead of their *WrestleMania* match.

> "...for the longest time, this ring, and all of you, was the only thing I had in my life."

Shawn Michaels says goodbye to the WWE Universe (March 29, 2010)

An emotional parting

March 29: Shawn Michaels bid farewell to the WWE Universe after losing the career-ending match to Undertaker at *WrestleMania XXVI*. The rest of the *RAW* locker room paid tribute to the "Heartbreak Kid." Even Undertaker, his opponent from the night before, came to the stage and gave Michaels a silent salute.

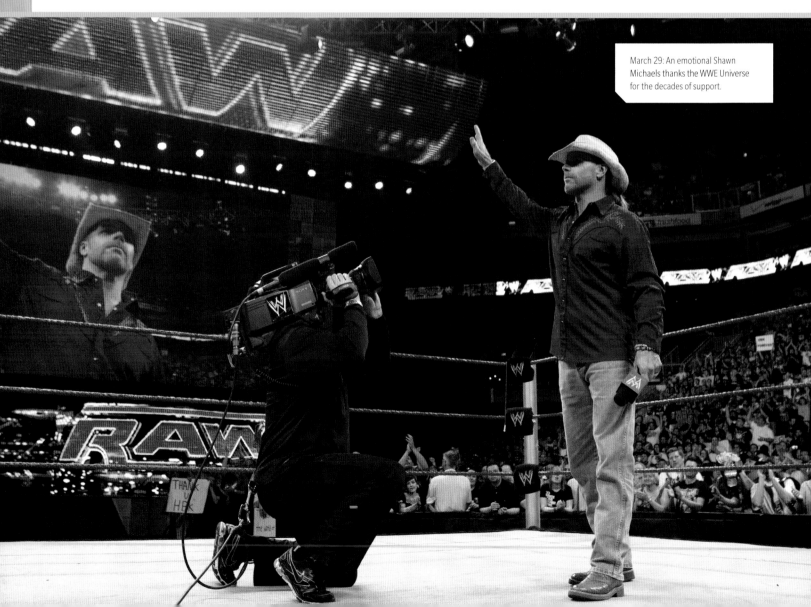

March 29: An emotional Shawn Michaels thanks the WWE Universe for the decades of support.

Unlikely partners

April 5: NXT Rookie and guest General Manager David Otunga forced bitter rivals John Cena and Batista to team together to fight for the Unified Tag Team Championships. However, the duo could not get along, so Otunga made Cena challenge the champs a second time with a different partner—Otunga himself! Both times, Sho-Miz retained their Championship.

Championship Eve

April 12: Eve Torres defeated Maryse for the WWE Divas Championship in London, England. It was the first Championship reign for Torres, who would go on to hold the Title on three separate occasions.

Superstars stranded

April 19: Due to the eruption of an Icelandic volcano, Superstars were stranded in Europe, unable to make *RAW*. *SmackDown* Superstars took over, with a main event featuring Triple H, Edge, and Rey Mysterio vs. Chris Jericho, CM Punk, and Luke Gallows.

The 2010 WWE Draft

April 26: The rosters of *RAW* and *SmackDown* were shaken up in the 2010 WWE Draft. While *RAW* may have lost Big Show, Kelly Kelly, Kofi Kingston, and Christian to *SmackDown*, the show gained Edge, Chris Jericho, John Morrison, and R-Truth.

April 26: Following the draft, Edge shakes up the main event picture on *RAW*, spearing Randy Orton and costing him a shot at the WWE Championship.

The excellence of execution

May 17: Bret "Hit Man" Hart was able to recapture Championship magic one last time in his career, winning the United States Championship from The Miz. Locking The Miz in the Sharpshooter and forcing him to submit, the Hit Man began his fifth career reign with the Title.

Batista bids goodbye, Hart becomes GM

May 24: After his brutal "I Quit" Match with John Cena the night before, Batista quit WWE when new *RAW* General Manager Bret "Hit Man" Hart tried to make "The Animal" compete in a match. It would be years before the WWE Universe would see Batista compete again.

After Bret "Hit Man" Hart won the United States Championship, he decided to relinquish the Title and focus on being a General Manager. He set a match between former champion The Miz and R-Truth. R-Truth won the Title for the first time in his career.

May 24: Angry at how he felt he was being treated by WWE management, Batista quits the company the night after his "I Quit" Match against John Cena.

INTRODUCING...

The Uso brothers and Tamina

May 24: Looking to make an immediate impact on the WWE Universe, the Uso brothers and their cousin Tamina attacked the Hart Dynasty on their first episode of *RAW*. The identical twin brothers would become a dominant force in WWE, winning five Tag Team Championships. Tamina continues to chase her championship dreams as well.

Cousins the Usos and Tamina have made an incredible impact since they joined WWE, competing in the tag team division and women's division respectively.

2010

A destructive debut

June 7: The main event featured John Cena and CM Punk, but their match ended in a no contest when the eight rookies from the first season of NXT swarmed the ring. Now known as the Nexus, they overwhelmed the two competitors, ring officials, and announcers, and even destroyed the ring itself!

Fatal Four-Way for the United States Championship

June 14: The Miz was able to regain the United States Championship for the second time in his career, winning a Fatal Four-Way Match over John Morrison, Zack Ryder, and current champion R-Truth. The Miz would go on to hold the Championship for more than three months.

Under new, anonymous management

June 21: Mr. McMahon fired Bret Hart as *RAW* General Manager and replaced him with the Anonymous General Manager, a leader who sent missives to a ringside laptop computer. The Chairman soon regretted this decision, however, as the new GM awarded all the Nexus contracts—they proceeded to attack Mr. McMahon himself at the end of the night.

June 21: The Nexus is willing to target anyone in their way—including the Chairman of WWE, Mr. McMahon.

June 7: The NXT Season 1 rookies wreaked havoc on WWE, targeting the biggest Superstars in the company, including the WWE Champion, John Cena.

Lady Luck takes brutal turn

September 13: A spin of the wheel determined match stipulations during the latest installment of *RAW Roulette*. The WWE Universe was treated to Submission Matches, a Song & Dance Contest, a Steel Cage Match, and, in an incredible main event, a Tables Match between longtime rivals John Cena and Randy Orton.

A new, reluctant member of the group

October 4: One night earlier, John Cena lost a match to Nexus leader Wade Barrett at *Hell in a Cell*, forcing Cena to join the Nexus. On *RAW*, Cena was officially inducted into the group, and as his first assignment, helped Barrett win a 20-man Battle Royal to become the number-one contender for the WWE Championship.

October 4: The WWE Universe is shocked to see John Cena wearing the "N" armband of his bitter rivals, the Nexus.

SummerSlam preview

July 26: The WWE Universe was looking forward to finally seeing the Nexus in a fair fight, as the *SummerSlam 2010* main event was going to be a 7-on-7 Elimination Tag Team Match. The Nexus had a warm-up match on *RAW*, which must have made their *SummerSlam* opponents worried, as they swept the match 7-0.

The enemy of my enemy

August 9: Charged with putting together a team of WWE Superstars to face the Nexus at *SummerSlam*, Bret "Hit Man" Hart reached out to his former rivals Chris Jericho and Edge. He was able to convince his fellow Canadians to see the bigger picture and agree to join his all-star squad.

August 9: Bret "Hit Man" Hart is looking to build the strongest team possible to take on the Nexus at *SummerSlam*, and that includes both Chris Jericho and Edge.

2010

Double duty for Cena

October 25: John Cena competed twice in the same show, with mixed results. He opened the show defending the World Tag Team Championships, but he and partner David Otunga lost to fellow Nexus members Heath Slater and Justin Gabriel. In the main event, Cena beat Randy Orton, allowing Nexus leader Wade Barrett to pick the guest referee for his Title match at that year's *Survivor Series*.

I know you're the guest host, but what am I?

November 1: Star of television, film, and Broadway, Pee Wee Herman brought an absurd sense of humor to *RAW* as Guest Host of the night. While the WWE Universe was happy to see Pee Wee, The Miz and his apprentice, Alex Riley, did not enjoy his antics and confronted him in the ring. When Pee Wee needed back-up, he got it from his distant relative—Big Show!

November 1: Pee Wee Herman and the Big Show showing a family resemblance—at least in dress sense.

November 22: Seizing on a downed Randy Orton, The Miz cashes in his Money in the Bank opportunity and becomes WWE Champion for the first time in his career.

An unexpected firing and a new WWE Champion

November 22: Wade Barrett had threatened to fire reluctant Nexus member, "John Cena," from WWE if he didn't help Barrett win the WWE Championship at *Survivor Series 2010*. After Randy Orton retained the Title, Barrett made good on his promise on the following evening's *RAW*, terminating Cena's employment.

After Randy Orton was left beaten in the ring after a vicious attack by the Nexus, The Miz seized his chance and cashed in his Money in the Bank opportunity on a wounded Champion. Winning the match, "The Awesome One" gained his first WWE Championship and cut short Orton's reign.

All hail the Irish King

November 29: After defeating Kofi Kingston in the quarterfinals, the "Celtic Warrior" Sheamus received a bye into the finals. By then beating John Morrison in the finals, Sheamus became the latest WWE King of the Ring, the 19th man to hold the Title.

November 29: Sheamus takes the throne as the WWE's 19th *King of the Ring*.

A mismatched Championship pair

December 6: WWE Tag Team Champions Heath Slater and Justin Gabriel were forced to defend their Titles in a Fatal Four-Way Elimination Match. They managed to eliminate Mark Henry and Yoshi Tatsu, but the unlikely duo of Santino Marella and Vladimir Kozlov eliminated The Usos and the champions to win the Tag Team Championships.

December 6: The odd tag team pairing of Santino Marella and Vladimir Kozlov pays off handsomely, with the duo capturing the WWE Tag Team Championships.

The Slammy Awards and Cena's comeback

December 13: The WWE Universe was able to relive some of the wildest and most amazing moments of the year, thanks to the Slammy Awards. Honorees included the debut of the Nexus, the *WrestleMania* bout between Shawn Michaels and Undertaker, CM Punk's evil behavior, Michelle McCool, and John Cena.

The only person who could rehire John Cena was Nexus leader Wade Barrett. While Barrett was sure he'd never do that, Cena's guerrilla attacks on other members of The Nexus spurred the rest of the group to demand that Barratt bring Cena back, which he did.

December 13: Lay-Cool both won Slammys in 2010—the Knucklehead Moment of the Year for losing a match to 87-year-old Hall of Famer Mae Young!

December 13: Wade Barrett thought he had gotten rid of John Cena permanently, but his fellow Nexus members force him to hire Cena back.

2011

THIS YEAR CAN BE DIVIDED into two halves, BPB and APB—Before and After Pipe Bomb. CM Punk's explosive promo at the end of June fundamentally changed the landscape of WWE and *Monday Night RAW*. His war with the McMahons and WWE management spilled over into title matches against John Cena and Alberto Del Rio. Punk wasn't Cena's only rival—he battled with The Miz for the WWE Championship in the first half of the year and he waged a war of words with the returning Rock.

January 10: After CM Punk takes control of Nexus, David Otunga has to confront the "World's Largest Athlete," Big Show, in order to prove his loyalty to the group.

January 3: In pursuit of the WWE Championship, John Morrison executes a high-flying, risky dive in an attempt to neutralize both The Miz and his protégé Alex Riley.

An "Awesome" start to the year
January 3: The first edition of 2011 had a big-match feel. The Miz was forced to defend the WWE Championship in a Falls Count Anywhere Match—no countouts and no disqualifications— against his former tag team partner John Morrison. "The Awesome One" won a thrilling, seesaw contest by pinning Morrison.

A Nexus coup
January 10: Convincing the members of the Nexus that they'd go even further under his leadership, CM Punk grabbed control of the group from Wade Barrett. He initiated the members back into the Nexus by making them sacrifice themselves in and out of the ring.

The King challenges for another throne
January 31: To select The Miz's WWE Championship challenger at *Elimination Chamber 2011*, *RAW* held a 7-Man *RAW* Rumble. Overcoming a field featuring four past and future World Champions, Jerry "The King" Lawler eliminated John Cena and Sheamus to earn the Championship opportunity.

The Rock is back!
February 14: After "seven long years," The Rock, the "Most Electrifying Man in All of Entertainment," returned to WWE. He made a blockbuster announcement—he was returning to host *WrestleMania*. With the big news out of the way, "The Great One" took time to delight the WWE Universe by cutting John Cena down to size with some pointed verbal jabs.

An unspoken agreement and a war of words

February 21: After lengthy absences, both Undertaker and Triple H returned to *RAW*. Confronting each other in the ring, no words were spoken between the two, but their shared interest was clear— they meant to face each other at *WrestleMania XXVII*.

All week the WWE Universe had wondered whether John Cena would respond to The Rock's previous taunts on *RAW*. Now Cena fired back at "The Great One" with a stinging freestyle promo that both questioned The Rock's commitment to WWE and poured scorn on his movie career.

Announce-team rivalry

March 7: The *RAW* announcer team was fractured in 2011, with Michael Cole and Jerry Lawler ready to clash at *WrestleMania*. Stone Cold Steve Austin appointed himself the special guest official for their match at the contract signing.

Crossing a personal line

March 21: The bitter rivalry between CM Punk and "The Viper" Randy Orton was already intense in the ring, but Punk made his *WrestleMania* match with Orton extra personal by implying that he was set to attack Orton's wife, Samantha, and then ambushing Orton in the parking lot.

February 21: There is no need for words when Triple H and Undertaker meet face-to-face. Both want an epic *WrestleMania* confrontation with the other.

February 14: The Rock promises the WWE Universe that he is "never going away" before ribbing WWE Champion The Miz and making fun of John Cena.

2011

Ramping up the trash talk

March 28: In the last *RAW* before *WrestleMania XXVII*, Shawn Michaels found himself caught in the middle of the Triple H–Undertaker rivalry, when he expressed doubts about his best friend's ability to end Undertaker's streak. The same night, The Miz, John Cena, and The Rock all tossed verbal barbs at each other, heading into the WWE Championship Match.

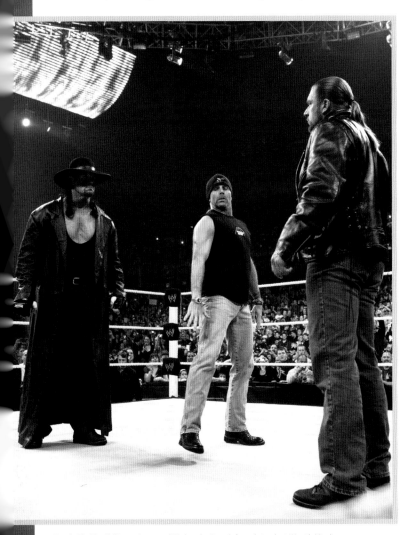

March 28: After failing twice to end Undertaker's undefeated streak at *WrestleMania*, Shawn Michaels is not sure that his best friend, Triple H, will fare any better.

Elsewhere in WWE...

April 4: *Tough Enough* returned to the USA Network after a seven-year break. On *RAW*, Stone Cold Steve Austin introduced the new show's cast to the WWE Universe, and contestants made their case as to why they would win the competition and become the next WWE Superstar.

A match one year in the making

April 4: Claiming that The Rock had cost him his title shot at *WrestleMania XXVII*, John Cena called out "The Great One." The two agreed that the time for talk was over and that they needed to settle matters in the ring. They also agreed that the match should be on the biggest stage of all—*WrestleMania XXVIII*—one year later.

INTRODUCING...

Sin Cara

April 4: A new masked Mexican Superstar debuted on the April 4 episode of *RAW*. Sin Cara thrilled the WWE Universe with his exciting brand of high-flying luchador action when he saved Daniel Bryan from an attack by Sheamus. In addition to significant success as a singles competitor, Sin Cara also partnered with Kalisto, and the duo won the NXT Tag Team Championships.

With a name that translates as "without face," Sin Cara leaves stunned looks on the faces of the WWE Universe with his high-risk aerial maneuvers.

Bittersweet farewell to the Ultimate Opportunist

April 11: The WWE Universe was shocked that the reigning World Heavyweight Champion Edge was forced to retire due to a career-ending injury. Over a storied career, Edge won 17 singles titles and 14 Tag Team Championships (with an incredible six different partners!) and would be inducted into the WWE Hall of Fame a year later.

April 11: Despite the pain of being forced into an early retirement, Edge manages to be all smiles for the WWE Universe.

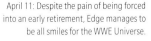

April 4: The Rock and John Cena know that the only way to settle their differences is in the ring. They also know that *WrestleMania* is the only place for such a titanic encounter.

Double draft

April 25: The 2011 WWE Draft once again saw some crazy Superstar movement—*RAW* gained Alberto Del Rio, Rey Mysterio, and Big Show, while losing Randy Orton, Sin Cara, and Mark Henry. *RAW* almost lost one of its most popular Superstars when John Cena was drafted to *SmackDown* early in the night. However, *RAW* scored the final draft pick of the night and claimed back Cena.

Happy birthday to The Great One

May 2: *RAW* featured a birthday celebration, when stars of screen, sports, and more came out to honor The Rock on his special day. Even Mr. McMahon got in on the act, sharing a video tribute with the WWE Universe. John Cena informed The Rock that his gift would be making their *WrestleMania* match a WWE Championship bout, although Cena was not able to keep that promise.

April 25: After being drafted to *SmackDown*, John Cena competes against his former championship rival The Miz in an intrabrand match that eventually leads to Cena returning to *RAW*.

June 27: With his contract ending, no topics are off limits when CM Punk decides to tell the WWE Universe what he really thinks of WWE management and its top star, John Cena.

The People's Championship choice

June 20: This was a special "Power to the People" episode of *RAW*, in which the WWE Universe got to select match opponents and stipulate the rules. They certainly got the challenger to the Divas Championship right. Kelly Kelly received 53 per cent of the votes and she used her title shot to beat Brie Bella and win her first Divas Championship.

The Pipe Bomb

June 27: It was the promo heard around the world, forever known as the Pipe Bomb. CM Punk lambasted everything about WWE, promising to leave the company with the WWE Championship when his contract expired immediately after *Money in the Bank*.

A shock for Mr. McMahon

July 18: Mr. McMahon had told John Cena that Cena would be fired if CM Punk won the WWE Championship at *Money in the Bank 2011*. Punk duly won, and the Chairman was set to deliver on his threat. Then Triple H arrived with shocking news—the WWE Board of Directors had decided to relieve Mr. McMahon of his duties.

June 20: Kelly Kelly proudly displays the Divas Championship, the first, and only, title she won in her career.

July 18: On behalf of the Board of Directors, Triple H is forced to relieve Mr. McMahon of his duties after the Chairman attempts to fire John Cena.

"There's one thing you're better at than I am, and that's kissing Vince McMahon's ass!"

CM Punk to John Cena (June 27, 2011)

September 5: "The Game" puts business ahead of friendship when he fires Kevin Nash for his actions after the main event of *SummerSlam*.

Two WWE Champions

July 25: After CM Punk won the WWE Championship and left WWE, a tournament was run across two episodes of *RAW* to crown a new champion. While Rey Mysterio won the Title, John Cena cashed in his rematch clause to take the Title on the same night. Instead of having a new champion, *RAW* suddenly had two, when CM Punk returned with his WWE Title.

First title defense for Del Rio

August 15: One night after cashing in his Money in the Bank opportunity and winning the WWE Championship at *SummerSlam 2011*, Alberto Del Rio made his first successful Title defense against longtime rival Rey Mysterio. Del Rio literally added injury to insult by hurting Mysterio in the match to the point that Mysterio required surgery.

Air Boom for the Win

August 22: The new Superstar pairing of Evan Bourne and Kofi Kingston, collectively known as Air Boom, proved to be highly successful, winning numerous matches. They reached the pinnacle of tag team competition by defeating David Otunga and Michael McGillicutty and becoming WWE Tag Team Champions.

Terminating Big Sexy

September 5: Finding out that Kevin Nash had been lying to him and the WWE Universe about who ordered Nash to attack CM Punk after his WWE Championship victory at *SummerSlam 2011*, WWE Chief Operating Officer Triple H fired his former Kliq buddy.

July 25: Two men—CM Punk and John Cena—both claim to be WWE Champion, and each has a Championship Title to back up his claim.

2011

Hollywood backup for Ryder

September 19: Celebrity Guest Host of *RAW* and star of stage and screen Hugh Jackman was in Zack Ryder's corner when Ryder defeated United States Champion Dolph Ziggler in a non-title match. Jackman even landed a thunderous punch on Ziggler!

Superstars on strike

October 10: After replacing Mr. McMahon as *RAW*'s primary authority figure, Triple H ran into some significant problems when most of the roster went on strike. Together with John Cena, Sheamus, and CM Punk, he tried to keep the show going. However, the WWE Board of Directors once again decided to make a change and installed John Laurinaitis as Interim General Manger.

Big Sexy's revenge

October 24: Just six weeks after being fired by Triple H, Kevin Nash exacted brutal payback by returning to *RAW* and attacking his former friend. In a cruel twist, Nash used a sledgehammer, Triple H's weapon of choice, to do most of the damage.

October 10: Convinced that Triple H has lost control of the locker room, WWE's Board of Directors turns to John Laurinaitis for a new leadership direction.

October 31: Jack Swagger and Vickie Guerrero object to Miss Piggy and Kermit's appearance on *RAW*. Kermit tries to calm the situation, saying, "Mr. Swagger... We don't want any trouble from you—or your mother!"

Who doesn't love The Muppets?

October 31: The WWE Universe was excited to see The Muppets appear on *RAW* as special guests. However, not everyone appreciated having them around. Vickie Guerrero and her client Jack Swagger decided to mix it up with Kermit and Miss Piggy.

September 19: Guest Host Hugh Jackman decides to get involved in the action, landing a powerful punch on Dolph Ziggler.

November 14: The Rock shows his lack of appreciation for Mick Foley's tribute to John Cena by laying out his former tag team partner with his signature Rock Bottom side slam.

History doesn't repeat itself

November 14: The most electrifying tag team in history—John Cena and The Rock—was set to partner up at *Survivor Series 2011*. Mick Foley tried to join the action by recapping John Cena's career with some special guests in an update to his 1999 "This Is Your Life" tribute to The Rock. Things didn't go so well, and Foley received a Rock Bottom from his old Rock 'n' Sock Connection partner.

One final match

November 28: Former tag team partners John Morrison and The Miz had been bitter foes for the past few years, but their rivalry came to a decisive end when, with his Skull-Crushing Finale facebuster, The Miz injured Morrison in a Falls Count Anywhere Match; Morrison has not been seen in WWE since.

The annual awards tradition continues

December 12: Once again, the Slammies returned to *RAW*; CM Punk took home the top honor—Superstar of the Year. Snooki snagged the Guest Star of the Year, and The Rock, Undertaker, Zack Ryder, Jim Ross, Big Show, and Kelly Kelly also won awards.

Kane vs. Cena

December 26: After being away from WWE for months, Kane returned to WWE in December 2011. He explained his return by viciously attacking John Cena over several weeks on *RAW*. He finally announced his reasons—he was unhappy with John Cena's "Rise Above Hate" slogan because he felt that all people hate.

December 26: "The Big Red Monster" Kane claims that he will prove that John Cena is incapable of rising above hate.

2012

FOR THE FIRST TIME in a quarter-century, a single individual held the WWE Championship for an entire calendar year. CM Punk began 2012 as the Champion and he managed to defeat every challenger for the Title. Despite this championship stability, *RAW* still saw its fair share of mayhem. Several people battled for control of the show, including John Laurinaitis, AJ Lee, and Mr. McMahon. 2012 was also a year of celebration, as *RAW* reached a milestone few television shows could claim—1,000 episodes! And its momentum continued to build toward 2,000.

February 27: After The Rock has had his say, John Cena makes it abundantly clear that he will take care of business at *WrestleMania* and pin "The Great One."

The meaning behind the code
January 2: After weeks of speculation, the WWE Universe finally learned the reason behind the 1-2-12 announcements they had been seeing. Chris Jericho was returning to *RAW*. Decked out in a spectacular light-up jacket, Jericho entered to cheers, but the WWE Universe quickly became frustrated when Jericho refused to speak.

The All-American United States Champion
January 16: A few months after partnering with Vickie Guerrero, Jack Swagger impressed his new manager by defeating Zack Ryder and winning the United States Championship for the first time in his career. The "All-American American" would go on to hold the Title for just under two months.

Review interrupted
January 30: Triple H decided to grade Interim General Manager John Laurinaitis' performance, and it seemed like "The Game" was set to steal his father-in-law's "You're fired!" catchphrase. The review was interrupted by Undertaker, who clearly indicated that he wanted to face Triple H at *WrestleMania XXVIII*. However, "The Game" refused the challenge and left the ring.

Jericho gets a shot at Punk
February 20: A 10-man Battle Royal decided who would challenge CM Punk for the WWE Championship at *WrestleMania XXVIII*. Chris Jericho eliminated longtime rival Kofi Kingston, but it looked like he would fall victim to Big Show. Outside interference by Cody Rhodes allowed Jericho to win the match and the Title shot.

January 2: While Chris Jericho is all smiles on his return, his bizarre behavior soon leaves the WWE Universe more puzzled than happy.

One year in the making

February 27: After almost a year, the WWE Universe got to watch The Rock and John Cena ratchet up the tension for their *WrestleMania XXVIII* encounter. They pulled no verbal punches in advance of their epic bout. The WWE Universe clearly seemed to be on The Rock's side, cheering the insults he aimed at Cena.

> ## "I don't want to talk to you—I would much rather slap your lying face with a piece of Kung Pao chicken!"

The Rock, addressing John Cena (February 27, 2012)

Hell in a Cell

March 19: Triple H agreed to face Undertaker at *WrestleMania* again, but only in a Hell in a Cell Match. The intrigue increased when Shawn Michaels—Triple H's best friend and the man forced to retire by Undertaker two years earlier—was announced as the guest referee. Triple H later came agonizingly close to ending Undertaker's streak at *WrestleMania*, but Undertaker prevailed.

March 19: For the second year running, Triple H and Undertaker battle at *WrestleMania*— this time in a Hell in a Cell, with Shawn Michaels as the guest referee.

2012

INTRODUCING...

Lord Tensai

April 2: The night after *WrestleMania XXVIII*, Lord Tensai made his WWE debut, crushing Alex Riley. Tensai used his imposing size and incredible strength to begin his career with an impressive winning streak, including victories over John Cena and CM Punk. However, he was never able to capture a singles championship in his career.

Few Superstars stood much of a chance against Lord Tensai's devastating array of power moves.

Return of the Beast

April 2: John Cena was looking for a new direction after losing his Once in a Lifetime Match to The Rock. He got it when Brock Lesnar returned to WWE for the first time in eight years and brutally attacked Cena. The two would meet at *Extreme Rules 2012*.

The power of twin magic

April 23: Nikki Bella defeated Beth Phoenix in a Lumberjill Match to capture the WWE Divas Championship. It was the first Divas Championship reign for Nikki and it came a little over a year after her twin sister Brie's first Title reign.

A violent renegotiation

April 30: As one half of the Air Boom tag team, Kofi Kingston lost the WWE Tag Team Championships to Primo & Epico in January 2012. He managed to recapture the Titles with a new partner, R-Truth, making him a two-time champion.

Also in this episode, Brock Lesnar thought he was getting a new, renegotiated contract to stay in WWE, after facing John Cena (who had defeated him with his Attitude Adjustment) at *Extreme Rules 2012*. WWE Chief Operating Officer Triple H said that Lesnar could only stay in WWE under the original terms of his contract. Enraged, Lesnar seemingly broke Triple H's arm!

People Power overcomes the Champ

May 21: John Cena improbably lost a bout with *RAW* General Manager John Laurinaitis at *Over the Limit 2012,* thanks to interference by Big Show. In this *RAW* episode, Cena was looking for payback against either man, but fell victim to the duo of Laurinaitis and Show once again in a 2-on-1 Handicap Match.

Slater versus the Legends

June 11: Throughout June and July, Heath Slater tried to make a name for himself at the expense of WWE Legends. It did not go well. He ran afoul of Vader in this episode, and would not have any more success in subsequent weeks against "Rowdy" Roddy Piper, Sycho Sid, Bob Backlund, Rikishi, and Lita.

Foley tries out for GM

June 18: With John Laurinaitis fired a week earlier, Mick Foley was given a chance to impress the WWE Board of Directors by running *RAW*. He certainly impressed the WWE Universe, creating a match that pitted CM Punk and Sheamus versus Daniel Bryan and Kane—a match that Sheamus and the WWE Champion won.

April 2: "The Beast Incarnate" Brock Lesnar announces his return to WWE with an exclamation point— taking out John Cena.

June 11: Vader had not competed in a WWE ring for some time, but he proves to be more muscle than Heath Slater can handle.

AJ complicates the Championship chase

July 2: While CM Punk and Daniel Bryan continued their WWE Championship rivalry in the tag team main event, it was AJ who stole the show. She planted a surprising kiss on CM Punk and then sent him crashing through a table that Daniel Bryan was prone on, further baffling both men as to whom she was supporting.

Revealed: the Anonymous GM

July 9: For one week only, the Anonymous *RAW* General Manager returned to run the show. Santino managed to answer the question that had plagued the WWE Universe for years—the identity of the Anonymous GM. Incredibly, it turned out to be Hornswoggle! The diminutive Superstar had been running things in secret, but was now exposed.

July 2: Things are looking good for CM Punk when AJ kisses him, but they quickly and painfully take a turn for the worse (inset right).

An incredible episodic milestone

July 23: *Monday Night RAW* reached a remarkable milestone on this day—1000 episodes! Packed with Superstars past and present, the show featured many memorable moments, including a DX reunion, the wedding of AJ and Daniel Bryan (with Slick acting as reverend), epic appearances by The Rock and Brock Lesnar, as well as Undertaker and Kane teaming up as the Brothers of Destruction.

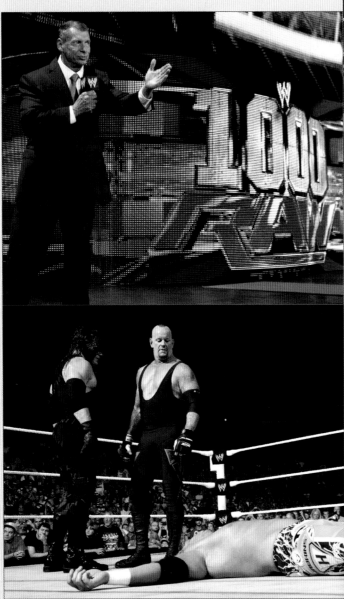

Perhaps the most action-packed instalment in its history, the 1,000th episode of *RAW* featured (clockwise from top) Mr. McMahon choosing a new GM; CM Punk ambushing The Rock; AJ leaving a stunned Daniel Bryan at the altar, having said yes to another man; D-Generation X appearing together; Kane and Undertaker wreaking havoc.

AJ crowdsources a contender

August 6: New *RAW* General Manager AJ Lee gave power to the WWE Universe, allowing the crowd to choose WWE Champion CM Punk's opponent for his match. They chose Rey Mysterio, but the masked luchador was unable to defeat Punk.

A *SummerSlam* sneak peek?

August 13: Looking to send a message to Triple H before their *SummerSlam* encounter, Brock Lesnar dragged Triple H's best friend, Shawn Michaels, to the ring. He punished him with an F5 Facebuster, and seized his arm in a brutal Kimura Lock.

The briefcase versus the job

August 20: Chris Jericho faced Dolph Ziggler with some extreme stipulations—if Jericho won, he would receive Ziggler's Money in the Bank opportunity. A Ziggler win, however, would terminate Jericho's WWE employment. Ziggler won and Jericho was forced to leave the company.

Dr. Shelby's worst nightmare

September 3: Attempting to function better as a tag team, Daniel Bryan and Kane attended anger management classes. It was pretty clear that therapist Dr. Shelby had never had patients like this deranged duo, but he did what he could to help them to trust each other and work better together.

Miz TV debuts

September 17: Already an accomplished champion, having won the WWE, Intercontinental, United States, and Tag Team championships, The Miz added talkshow host to his awesome resume with the launch of Miz TV. The historic first episode featured WWE Hall of Famer and *SmackDown* General Manager Booker T as his first guest.

August 13: Shawn Michaels is retired from in-ring competition, but Brock Lesnar doesn't care, putting the former champion in a painful Kimura Lock submission hold.

The Chairman challenges the Champion

October 8: After delivering a state of the WWE address to the WWE Universe, Mr. McMahon tried to teach WWE Champion CM Punk some respect by challenging him to a match. Punk decided to gain the upper hand with a sneak attack before the match even started.

September 17: With all the glitz and glamor of a Hollywood A-lister, the Miz makes his talk show segment Miz TV a must-see segment of *RAW*, particularly with guests like *SmackDown* General Manager Booker T.

2012

Punk Shell Shocked

October 15: With an impressive winning streak to the start of his WWE career, it was no surprise that Ryback would eventually earn himself a WWE Championship opportunity. On *RAW*, he signed a contract to face CM Punk for the title in the main event of *Hell in a Cell 2012*. Ryback celebrated the opportunity by delivering a thunderous Shell Shock to the champion.

No beating Hell No

October 22: Cody Rhodes and Damien Sandow, collectively known as Team Rhodes Scholars, defeated Rey Mysterio and Sin Cara, winning a multi-week tournament to select the number-one contenders for Team Hell No's Tag Team Championships. Unfortunately for Rhodes and Sandow, their championship pursuit at *Hell in a Cell 2012* failed. Team Hell No would hold the Titles through May 2013, when The Shield stable ended their reign.

Ryback's revenge

November 12: Disgraced former official Brad Maddox helped CM Punk win his match at *Hell in a Cell* because Maddox wanted to become a WWE Superstar and he thought doing something controversial would help him stand out. Mr. McMahon decided to give Maddox a shot—if Maddox beat Ryback in a match, Maddox would earn a WWE contract. It was not to be—the monstrous Ryback destroyed the crooked referee.

October 15: Ryback gives CM Punk a sample of his raw power when he drops the WWE Champion with a Shell Shock.

Elsewhere in WWE

November 18: Through the years, *Survivor Series* has seen some historic debuts, including Undertaker, The Rock, and Kurt Angle. The 2012 edition added the names of three future World Champions to that list. Seth Rollins, Dean Ambrose, and Roman Reigns—collectively known as The Shield—emerged from the crowd to attack Ryback and help CM Punk retain the WWE Championship.

No matter the size of the opponent, when The Shield targets an opponent for their Triple Powerbomb, even someone like Ryback won't be getting back up.

INTRODUCING...

Big E Langston

December 17: Big E Langston made quite a first impression on *RAW*, aligning himself with AJ Lee and Dolph Ziggler, serving as their muscle and attacking John Cena. A former NXT Champion, Langston would go on to win the Intercontinental Championship from Curtis Axel. The WWE Universe came to love Big E when he joined forces with Kofi Kingston and Xavier Woods to form the New Day, a trio that set a WWE record for the longest tag team reign in history, for one of the group's four Tag Team Championships.

Big E came to WWE with a championship pedigree, having held the NXT Title for almost six months.

Diva of the Year

December 17: AJ Lee may have lost her job as General Manager of *RAW*, but she did capture the Slammy for Diva of the Year. Other winners included John Cena (Superstar of the Year), Ryback (Newcomer of the Year), Jerry Lawler (Comeback of the Year), and Daniel Bryan (Upset of the Year). Ryback's "Feed me more," was Crowd Chant of the Year. Booker T awarded Kofi Kingston's elimination-avoiding handstand at the *Royal Rumble* the moment of the year, and the spectacular Hell in a Cell Match at *WrestleMania XXVIII* between Undertaker and Triple H that saw Undertaker's streak go to 20-0 was chosen as the Match of the Year.

A vehicular attack on St. Nick

December 24: It was almost a Christmas Eve tragedy when Alberto Del Rio struck Santa Claus with his car. Luckily, medical personnel made sure Santa was able to keep all his holiday appointments. Before leaving, St. Nick gave the WWE Universe a special present—*RAW*'s main event would be a Miracle on 34th Street Fight between Alberto Del Rio and John Cena. When Cena won the match with assistance from Santa, the two celebrated in the ring together.

New year, new champion

December 31: The last *RAW* of 2012 was a special Champion's Choice episode in which all current title holders would be defending their titles against the opponents of their choice. Intercontinental Champion Kofi Kingston undoubtedly regretted his choice, as Wade Barrett took advantage of a mistake and nailed the Champion with his signature Bull Hammer move to win the Title. It was the second Intercontinental Title win in Barrett's career, and it would be the longest of his five championship reigns.

December 24: Christmas Eve almost ends in tragedy when Alberto Del Rio hits Santa with his car.

2013

WHO SAYS the number 13 is unlucky? The year 2013 certainly wasn't for *RAW*'s Superstars. In addition to *RAW*'s 20th anniversary, the first quarter of 2013 saw an eighth WWE Championship reign by The Rock when he ended CM Punk's incredible 434-day Title run, and the year closed with an exciting Title Unification Match that led to the WWE and World Heavyweight championships being combined into one Title. The most unlikely success story of the year was the ascension of Daniel Bryan to a main-event Superstar. But Triple H and Stephanie McMahon did everything they could to derail Bryan's success.

January 7: CM Punk needed help to defeat Ryback, but at the end of the match, he stands tall at the top of a ladder, still WWE Champion.

Overcoming Ryback and TLC

January 7: CM Punk was forced to defend his WWE Championship against the monstrous Superstar Ryback in a TLC Match. At first it seemed like Punk was unlikely to retain his Championship, but thanks to some assistance from The Shield, Punk managed to keep hold of his Title. Punk's win set him up for a showdown with The Rock at the *Royal Rumble*.

20th Anniversary title change

January 14: Kaitlyn marked *RAW*'s 20th Anniversary by defeating Eve and capturing her first Divas Championship. Unlike typical title matches, Eve was told she would lose her title if she was counted out or disqualified. Refusing to tap out to Eve's painful submission move, Kaitlyn turned the tide of the match with an Inverted DDT and a massive Spear move that kept Eve down for the three-count.

Advocating for the advocate

January 28: Mr. McMahon was about to terminate CM Punk's manager Paul Heyman during a performance appraisal when Heyman's other client, Brock Lesnar, altered the Chairman's plans. Appearing in WWE for the first time since *SummerSlam 2012*, Lesnar decimated Mr. McMahon by dropping him with his F5 slam.

INTRODUCING...

Zeb Colter

February 11: Zeb Colter accompanied Jack Swagger to the ring for Swagger's return match. Colter became Swagger's manager for the next few years, and also managed Antonio Cesaro and Alberto Del Rio. Colter never managed to guide his charges to championship gold. He left WWE in late 2015.

Zeb Colter had a singular talent for riling up the WWE Universe with his "We the People" rhetoric.

Finally beating Punk

February 25: By reminding John Cena that he hadn't beaten him in a meaningful match, CM Punk convinced Cena to put his *WrestleMania* Title shot against The Rock on the line for a match. Punk's efforts went unrewarded; Cena pinned Punk, his longtime nemesis, and kept his spot in the *WrestleMania* main event.

Timeless brawl

March 4: This *Old School RAW* episode featured throwback announcers, graphics, and Superstars. It also featured an unexpected brawl between Alberto Del Rio and his *WrestleMania* challenger for the World Heavyweight Championship, Jack Swagger.

A disrespectful interruption

March 11: Undertaker attempted to pay tribute to his longtime manager Paul Bearer, who had recently passed away. But his upcoming *WrestleMania* opponent CM Punk ruined the ceremony by coming out and mocking the Undertaker's former mentor.

Grilling the champion and challenger

March 25: A panel of WWE legends, including Dusty Rhodes, Booker T, Mick Foley, and Bret "Hit Man" Hart asked John Cena and The Rock some pointed questions in advance of their *WrestleMania* title match. The verbal confrontation between Rock and Cena turned physical when The Rock dropped his challenger with a Rock Bottom move.

March 25: Words only go so far, so WWE Champion Rock uses a Rock Bottom to make his point against his *WrestleMania* challenger John Cena.

2013

Moral support from Michaels

April 1: Shawn Michaels made a rare appearance to announce that he would be in Triple H's corner for his career-threatening *WrestleMania* match against Brock Lesnar. His appearance led to a confrontation with all three competitors in the ring.

April 1: Shawn Michaels reminds Triple H that his *WrestleMania* opponent, Brock Lesnar, broke both of their arms the previous year, while a snarling Lesnar and his advocate, Paul Heyman, look on from the entrance ramp (top right inset).

April 8: Feeding off the incredible energy of the post-*WrestleMania* crowd, Dolph Ziggler cashes in his *Money in the Bank* opportunity and gaines the World Heavyweight Championship.

Taking advantage of the moment

April 8: Taking advantage of a weary Alberto Del Rio, who had just fought in a two-on-one match, Dolph Ziggler cashed in his *Money in the Bank* opportunity to capture the World Heavyweight Championship. The win was his second World Title in an illustrious career.

Bringing the boom to the United States Championship

April 15: In an entertaining clash of styles, Kofi Kingston used his high-flying aerial moves to overcome the technical prowess of Antonio Cesaro and capture the United States Championship. The win was Kingston's third reign with the Title in his career.

Battling The Shield

April 22: In a rare *RAW* appearance, Undertaker teamed with his fellow Brother of Destruction, Kane, and Daniel Bryan to take on their common enemy—the three members of The Shield. Despite the incredible talent Bryan, Undertaker, and Kane represented, they were beaten when Dean Ambrose pinned Daniel Bryan.

Advocating for a Third Man

May 20: Already counting CM Punk and Brock Lesnar among his client base, Paul Heyman added a third Superstar to his stable: Curtis Axel. The newest "Paul Heyman Guy" made quite the first impression, fighting Triple H to a standstill that night with neither party winning.

Saving "The Game" from himself

June 3: An intervention is not something you typically see on *Monday Night RAW*, but the McMahon family felt they had to step in when Triple H continued to compete against doctor's orders. Triple H said he would fight on the June 10 episode of *RAW* against Curtis Axel, but Mr. McMahon blocked his son-in-law's intention by declaring the first match over by disqualification and the second by forfeit.

Return of Captain Charisma

June 17: The WWE Universe was treated to an exciting surprise—the return after almost a year of "Captain Charisma," Christian. The two-time World Heavyweight Champion had been sidelined since August 2012 with a shoulder injury but hardly missed a beat on his return. He defeated the former Intercontinental Champion Wade Barrett in his first match.

It looked like the end of a historic career when Mark Henry, "The World's Strongest Man," interrupted John Cena to tearfully announce he was retiring. But it was all just a ruse. Cena, who was about to show his sympathy, was caught completely off guard when Henry attacked him.

June 17: Mark Henry looks down on John Cena after tricking him with a phony retirement announcement and slamming him to the mat.

INTRODUCING...

The Wyatt Family

July 8: After weeks of vignettes announcing their impending arrival, The Wyatt Family debuted in WWE by attacking the "Big Red Monster" Kane. Bray Wyatt was the leader of the group and other members over the years have included Luke Harper, Erick Rowan, and Braun Strowman. The family also recruited other Superstars like Daniel Bryan and Randy Orton, and has held the WWE Championship and the *SmackDown* Tag Team Titles.

Wyatt Family leader Bray Wyatt would often sit at ringside and enjoy the destruction wrought by his disciples Luke Harper and Erick Rowan.

A much-wanted *SummerSlam* match

July 8: Mr. McMahon shocked the world by naming Brad Maddox the new General Manager of *RAW*. The following week, Maddox kicked off his first episode in charge of *RAW* by announcing that WWE Champion John Cena could select his own opponent for *SummerSlam*. Cena gave the WWE Universe what they wanted —a title shot for Daniel Bryan.

One of a kind once again

July 15: The night after appearing at *Money in the Bank 2013*, Rob Van Dam competed on *RAW* for the first time in six years. Van Dam faced Chris Jericho and hit his signature moves, including Roundhouse Kicks, Standing Moonsaults, and the Five-Star Frog Splash, which earned him a three-count for a glorious victory.

Elsewhere in WWE

July 28: The WWE Universe got to see another side of the female Superstars of WWE when the new show, *Total Divas*, debuted on the E! Network. The personal and professional lives of some of WWE's most popular female Superstars were highlighted in the show. The program has so far produced seven seasons and a spinoff program, *Total Bellas*.

July 8: John Cena gives Daniel Bryan just want he wants—a chance to battle him for the WWE Championship.

Getting hands on Heyman

August 12: *SummerSlam* was set to feature a bout between a current and former Paul Heyman client: Brock Lesnar and CM Punk. But first, Punk attempted to get revenge on Paul Heyman for his betrayal of Punk at *Money in the Bank 2013*, which ended up costing Punk a title shot. Punk, dressed as a cameraman, surprised Lesnar and Heyman, then floored Lesnar while Heyman escaped.

August 12: CM Punk surprises Brock Lesnar by disguising himself as a cameraman and attacking him with recording equipment.

"I hope you understand that my husband Triple H… He was just doing what was best for business."

Stephanie McMahon (August 19, 2013)

Explaining an inexplicable act

August 19: Triple H appointed himself special guest official for the WWE Championship Match at *SummerSlam* to ensure it was fair. However, after Daniel Bryan won the bout, Triple H Pedigreed Bryan, allowing Randy Orton to cash in his *Money in the Bank* opportunity and take the Title. The next night, on *RAW*, Triple H, Stephanie McMahon, and Mr. McMahon explained that betraying Bryan was "best for business."

Pipe bomb part deux

August 26: A few years after CM Punk delivered his famous "pipe bomb" promo on *RAW*, Divas Champion AJ Lee launched into a similar tirade, running down the Superstars who feature in the *Total Divas* reality show with some biting words. Lee made it known that the cast were nowhere near her league athletically.

Stripped of the title

September 16: Believing he wasn't a main-event talent, Triple H continued to stack the deck against Daniel Bryan in Bryan's dogged pursuit of the WWE Championship. Bryan defeated Orton for the title at *Night of Champions 2013,* but on the next night's episode of *RAW*, Triple H stripped Bryan of the title for what he called a fast count by the official.

August 26: In a vicious interview, WWE Divas Champion AJ Lee blasts her challengers for the Divas Championship with a tirade full of withering insults.

2013

Big Show's last stand
October 7: Stephanie McMahon decided to fire Big Show for insubordination, but her decision had unfortunate consequences for her husband, Triple H. With nothing left to lose, Big Show, "The World's Largest Athlete," KO'ed Triple H at the end of the night.

The Rhodes Brothers capture gold
October 14: Cody Rhodes and his brother Goldust managed to defeat Seth Rollins and Roman Reigns of The Shield to capture the WWE Tag Team Championships. The win ended The Shield's Title reign at just under five months.

Championship opportunity failure
October 28: One night after John Cena won the World Heavyweight Championship at *Hell in a Cell,* Damien Sandow tried to cash in his *Money in the Bank* opportunity. Unfortunately for Sandow, he became only the second Superstar in history (joining, oddly enough, John Cena) to fail to turn a *Money in the Bank* opportunity into a World Championship win.

An unlikely ally for Punk
November 4: After CM Punk defeated Wyatt Family member Luke Harper, all three members of the family tried to beat down the former WWE Champion. But Punk got some help from an unlikely source—former rival Daniel Bryan.

October 14: Brothers Cody Rhodes and Goldust celebrate after beating The Shield and capturing the WWE Tag Team Championships.

November 18: Rey Mysterio makes a dramatic return after an eight-month injury hiatus to aid CM Punk, Daniel Bryan, The Usos, and the Rhodes brothers.

A massive main event

November 18: The main event of *RAW* was a chaotic 12-man brawl featuring The Shield and The Wyatt Family teaming up to face Goldust and Cody Rhodes, The Usos, CM Punk, and Daniel Bryan in a 6-on-6 Tag Match. Ironically, three more Superstars got involved post-match. The Real Americans tried to tip the scales against The Usos and The Rhodes by making it 8-on-6, but an exciting return by Rey Mysterio helped even the odds.

Title unification

November 25: The night after *Survivor Series 2013*, John Cena and Randy Orton agreed to unify both the WWE and World Heavyweight championships. The unification happened in a devastating Tables, Ladders, and Chairs Match to be held at *TLC 2013*.

An awkward presentation

December 9: 2013 Slammy Award presenter Shawn Michaels was forced to hand Daniel Bryan the trophy for Superstar of the Year. The tense exchange happened less than two months after Michaels double-crossed Bryan for the WWE Championship.

Keeping his title through the end of the year

December 30: The final episode of *RAW* in 2013 saw Big E Langston successfully defend his WWE Intercontinental Championship against the number one contender Fandango. Fandango tried to use his silky smooth moves to take out Big E, but the Champion's power proved to be too much for Fandango. Big E retained his title by hitting Fandango with a Big Ending and securing the three-count.

December 30: Intercontinental Champion Big E Langston drops his challenger Fandango with a powerful shoulder block.

March 11, 2013: Kneeling to the signature urn that Paul Bearer used to carry to the ring for his matches, Undertaker paid tribute to his longtime manager after his passing.

2014

THE MOTTO FOR *RAW* in 2014 was "What's best for business." But that really meant whatever WWE management, Stephanie McMahon and Triple H, thought was best for business. The duo and their lackeys, collectively known as The Authority, ruled over WWE with an iron fist. Any Superstars who did not fall in line suffered their wrath. The Authority's enemies included Daniel Bryan, John Cena, and The Shield stable. The destruction of the latter was particularly insidious, when The Authority convinced Seth Rollins to betray the other two members of The Shield in exchange for being anointed "The future of WWE."

Why, Daniel, why?
January 6: Seeing Daniel Bryan as a member of his bitter rivals The Wyatt Family was shocking to the WWE Universe. But Bryan put aside differences and teamed up with Luke Harper and Erick Rowan in a losing effort against Rey Mysterio and The Usos.

The return of "The Animal"
January 20: Every Superstar was gunning for the World Champion, Randy Orton. But Orton's list of foes got a significant addition on *RAW* when his former Evolution stablemate, Batista, returned to WWE after a four-year absence. "The Animal" Batista told the WWE Universe he was back to win the *Royal Rumble* and capture the WWE Championship at *WrestleMania 30,* and there wasn't a thing that Orton could do about it.

Win and you're in
January 27: In a Six-Man Tag Team Match where the winning team would earn three spots in the *RAW* Elimination Chamber Match, the makeshift team of John Cena, Sheamus, and Daniel Bryan defeated The Shield stable. Their win secured their positions in the unforgiving steel structure.

Tag team steel cage title defense
February 3: The New Age Outlaws successfully defended the Tag Team Championships in a Steel Cage Match against the Rhodes Brothers on *RAW*. Cody Rhodes almost recorded a pinfall, so he decided to finish off Road Dogg with a spectacular Moonsault move off the top of the cage. He missed the move and was pinned by Billy Gunn.

An explosive announcement
February 24: Hulk Hogan returned to WWE to celebrate the launch of the WWE Network and addressed the WWE Universe for the first time in years. Not only did Hogan tell the Universe about the new streaming network, he also announced that he would be the guest host of *WrestleMania 30*.

Brock Lesnar was furious that he had not been given the opportunity to compete for the WWE Championship at *WrestleMania 30*. But Undertaker appeared on *RAW* to give him an even bigger opportunity. Undertaker agreed to put his undefeated streak on the line to battle Lesnar at the Showcase of the Immortals.

Elsewhere in WWE

February 27: The newly created WWE Network gave the NXT brand a chance to shine. One of the first events to air live on the Network was *NXT Takeover: Arrival*. The debut episode saw Adrian Neville capture the NXT Championship from Bo Dallas in an exciting main event.

January 20: Randy Orton isn't pleased to see his old partner and occasional rival Batista back in WWE for the first time in four years.

February 24: Hulk Hogan pumps up the WWE Universe talking about the launch of the WWE Network and his hosting role at *WrestleMania 30*.

First taste of gold for The Usos

March 3: In a battle between tag teams of the past and the future, The Usos defeated The New Age Outlaws to become the WWE Tag Team Champions on *RAW*. It was the first Title reign of Jimmy and Jey Uso and it ended the sixth and final Tag Team Championships reign of the Road Dogg and "Bad Ass" Billy Gunn.

The people take over *RAW*

March 10: Tired of being marginalized by The Authority and denied a match with Triple H at *WrestleMania*, Daniel Bryan staged a massive sit-in with the WWE Universe. The WWE Universe stormed the ring wearing "YES" T-shirts in support of Bryan, and refused to leave until Triple H agreed to face Bryan at *WrestleMania* and give Bryan a spot in the Title match if he won.

March 10: The WWE Universe storm the ring and refuse to leave in support of Daniel Bryan.

> "...We hate to say we told you so... But ladies and gentlemen, WE TOLD YOU SO!"
>
> **Paul Heyman, bragging about Brock Lesnar ending Undertaker's undefeated streak (April 7)**

2014

April 7: Two nights after his induction into the WWE Hall of Fame, The Ultimate Warrior returns to *RAW* and speaks to fans about his incredible career.

An ultimate farewell

April 7: After a stunning *WrestleMania* result that saw his client Brock Lesner do the unthinkable—end the *WrestleMania* streak of the Undertaker—Paul Heyman emerged to gleefully antagonize a still-reeling WWE Universe. Later in the show, The Ultimate Warrior addressed the crowd. His emotional speech had additional impact when the Warrior tragically passed away the next day.

INTRODUCING...

Paige

April 7: After defeating the entire Divas division at *WrestleMania 30*, AJ Lee thought she had no more challengers. Enter Paige, the NXT Women's Champion. Paige shocked the world by defeating AJ Lee for the Divas Championship in her WWE debut match on April 7th and went on to hold the Title twice in 2014.

Paige holds up the Divas Championship in triumph after beating AJ Lee in her debut match.

Evolution reunited

April 21: Although all three men were after the WWE Championship, Triple H, Randy Orton, and Batista decided to put their differences aside and reform the Evolution stable for the first time in almost a decade to battle a common foe—The Shield.

A creepy children's choir

April 28: John Cena defeated Bray Wyatt at *WrestleMania 30*, but The Wyatt Family wasn't done with Cena yet. Attempting to unnerve his rival in advance of their Steel Cage Match at *Extreme Rules* 2014, Wyatt gatecrashed Cena's speech on *RAW* with a group of children dressed in black cloaks. The creepy choir surrounded the ring with Cena inside it and serenaded him with a spine-chilling rendition of "He's Got the Whole World in His Hands."

April 28: A group of children cloaked in black robes and wearing masks create a creepy atmosphere to unsettle John Cena.

April 21: For the first time in almost a decade, Triple H, Randy Orton, and Batista come together as the dominating group known as Evolution.

Setting the odds against Ambrose
May 6: Triple H forced Dean Ambrose to defend his United States Championship in a 20-Man Battle Royale. Ambrose made the final two, but lost his Championship to Sheamus, ending his Title reign at just under a year.

A painful end to the *RAW* GM
May 26: Brad Maddox's tenure as *RAW* General Manager ended live on the show. Stephanie McMahon had The Authority's Director of Operations, Kane, chokeslam Maddox before informing him that he was fired.

The end of Evolution and The Shield
June 2: At *Payback* the night before, The Shield stable had handed Evolution a second straight pay-per-view loss. A frustrated Batista quit WWE again, much like he did in 2010, when he wasn't granted a title match against Daniel Bryan. But The Shield had problems of its own—Seth Rollins shockingly turned on his brothers and aligned himself with The Authority to get more power in WWE.

June 2: Rollins shocks the WWE Universe when he betrayed Ambrose and Reigns, beating them with steel chairs before joining up with Triple H.

Reluctantly relinquishing the Championship
June 9: Suffering from an injury from which doctors refused to clear him to compete, WWE Champion Daniel Bryan was forced to relinquish his Title to Stephanie McMahon. Stephanie then ruled that a Money in the Bank Match would be used to determine the next Champion.

A unique duo
June 16: Goldust finally found a tag team partner who was as bizarre as him—his brother! Cody Rhodes was reintroduced to WWE under a quirky new alter ego, Stardust. The new duo displayed their connection immediately, dispatching Ryback and Curtis Axel that same night.

Stephanie into the muck
June 23: Stephanie McMahon decided to fire *SmackDown* General Manager Vickie Guerrero for not following orders. But to further humiliate her, she challenged her to a Job-Saving Match where the loser would be tossed into a disgusting pool of filth. Guerrero lost the match, but she gained a measure of revenge by tossing Stephanie into the pool as well.

June 23: Stephanie McMahon's Job-Saving Match with Vickie Guerrero has a messy ending.

Taking the Title back from Paige
June 30: Less than three months after she stunningly lost the Title to Paige in a post-*WrestleMania* upset, AJ Lee reclaimed the Divas Championship on *RAW*. Paige and Lee's rivalry for the Title continued throughout the year; Paige took the title back at *SummerSlam* and Lee won the title a third time at *Night of Champions*.

The enemy of my enemy
July 21: Unhappy that John Cena, the WWE Champion, would not work with The Authority, Triple H made a deal with the devil, or more specifically, The Beast. Putting his checkered past with Brock Lesnar behind him, Triple H introduced Lesnar as John Cena's WWE Championship *SummerSlam* challenger.

2014

Brie's revenge
July 28: Stephanie McMahon fired Daniel Bryan's wife, Brie Bella, in an attempt to torment him. But when Stephanie slapped Brie, she was charged with assault and was forced to re-hire Brie to make the charges go away. To make matters worse, she also had to agree to face the disgruntled Bella in a match at *SummerSlam*.

Happy birthday to the Hulkster
August 11: The original members of nWo returned to *RAW*, along with a number of former WWE Legends, to wish the "Immortal" Hulk Hogan a happy birthday. Brock Lesnar and Paul Heyman tried to crash the party, but John Cena saved Hogan from certain destruction at the hands of the gatecrashers.

August 11: More than 10,000 guests in Portland, Oregon, and millions of viewers around the world celebrate Hulk Hogan's birthday.

Curb-stomping Ambrose
August 18: The idea of a Shield reunion died when Seth Rollins curb-stomped former ally and "Hounds of Justice" member Dean Ambrose through a pile of cinder blocks. The devastating attack knocked Ambrose out of action for a month.

Steel cage clash
September 8: Chris Jericho faced Bray Wyatt in a Steel Cage Match, hoping to keep other members of the Wyatt Family from interfering. Jericho gave the WWE Universe an incredible and indelible memory when he leapt off the top of the cage onto Wyatt in the ring below.

Short title reign
September 22: One night after losing the Intercontinental Championship to The Miz at *Night of Champions*, Dolph Ziggler regained the Title by overcoming both The Miz and his stunt double, Damian Mizdow. The Miz trapped Ziggler in a finishing move by pulling on his tights, but Ziggler flipped the move and grabbed The Miz's tights to take the Title a third time in his career.

Rocking Rusev
October 6: Rusev and Lana decided to taunt the WWE Universe by boasting about the superiority of Russia. But the WWE Universe exploded with delight when The Rock made a surprise appearance and put Rusev in his place both verbally and physically. He insulted Rusev and Lana before leaping at Rusev and dumping him out of the ring.

Fighting for the right to face Rollins

October 13: Two of Seth Rollins' rivals, John Cena and Dean Ambrose, were itching to get Rollins inside Hell in a Cell. The Authority stable took advantage of the situation, forcing them to face each other in a Contract on a Pole Match. Seth Rollins and The Authority involved themselves in the match, but in the chaos, Dean Ambrose managed to grab the contract and the right to face his former Shield teammate Rollins in the demonic structure.

Survivor Series stakes

November 3: The Authority stable finally began to see cracks in their unity. The show opened with Mr. McMahon returning to television for the first time in almost a year and dropping a bombshell—if Team Authority lost to Team Cena at *Survivor Series*, The Authority would no longer be in power. The Authority then parted ways with member Randy Orton, brutally attacking him ringside when he wouldn't fall in line.

Championship quid pro quo

November 17: Siding with The Authority has its advantages. After joining Team Authority for the stable's *Survivor Series* match, Luke Harper was granted an Intercontinental Championship title shot against Dolph Ziggler on *RAW*. Harper went on to win the match and the Title.

October 6: The Rock made a surprising return to WWE to confront Rusev after tiring of his anti-American rhetoric.

An award-winning shocking debut

December 8: The "This is Awesome!" moment of the year was awarded at the 2014 Slammy Award ceremony on *RAW*. The winning moment was when Team Cena overcame Team Authority at *Survivor Series*, despite The Authority cheating and Big Show's betrayal. The moment was heightened further when Cena's team got some unexpected help when Sting made his first-ever appearance in a WWE ring.

December 8: No one ever imagined that they would see Sting appear in a WWE Ring, so it was no surprise that the moment won a WWE Slammy.

Reinstating The Authority

December 29: WWE wasn't without The Authority for very long. After The Authority's November 3 loss to Team Cena, Seth Rollins forced John Cena to repeal the match stipulation by threatening to hurt his ally Edge. Then the newly reinstated Authority members taunted Cena further by celebrating with his upcoming *Royal Rumble* opponent, Brock Lesnar.

2015

THE WWE UNIVERSE geared up for Roman Reigns' opportunity to capture the WWE Championship from Brock Lesnar at *WrestleMania 31*. However, Reigns' former Shield teammate Seth Rollins successfully cashed in his Money in the Bank opportunity and reigned for half the year as WWE Heavyweight Champion. Reigns did eventually capture the championship in November, but had to fight off the McMahons, Triple H, and the rest of The Authority in the process.

From bad to worse

January 5: The Authority had regained their power in WWE and wanted to show their strength. They targeted former adversary Dolph Ziggler, forcing him to defend his Intercontinental Championship against Wade Barrett. When Ziggler pinned Barrett, The Authority decided it wasn't over and changed the rules, making the bout a 2-out-of-3 Falls Match. Barrett won the next two falls and the title. But things got worse for Ziggler later that night when he, as well as Ryback and Erick Rowan, were fired for standing up to The Authority.

Royal Rumble panel

January 19: A trio of legendary Superstars weighed in on the 2015 *Royal Rumble* match when three former winners of the match—Hulk Hogan, Ric Flair, and Shawn Michaels—all spoke about their experiences in Rumble matches and each selected who they thought would win. Michaels selected Bray Wyatt, Flair picked Dean Ambrose, and Hogan thought Daniel Bryan would be the overall winner.

Snow *RAW*

January 26: It is rare that Mother Nature interferes with *RAW*, but a massive snowstorm led to the cancellation of the January 26 episode. Instead, a special episode aired from WWE Headquarters in Connecticut, featuring an intense confrontation between WWE Champion Brock Lesnar and his *WrestleMania* opponent, Royal Rumble winner Roman Reigns.

Two Superstars hit the wall

February 9: John Cena and Rusev took their rivalry for the United States Championship to a heated level in February 2015 on *RAW*. On February 9th, Rusev drove Cena into the LED screen on the *RAW* entrance ramp, and a week later, on February 16th, Cena returned the favor.

Jon Stewart vs. Seth Rollins

March 2: Comedian and talk show host Jon Stewart made an appearance after Seth Rollins invaded an episode of *The Daily Show* the previous week. Stewart confronted Rollins with a verbal assault and managed to escape physical retribution when Randy Orton arrived and distracted Rollins.

Daniel Bryan returns

March 16: After being forced to relinquish the WWE Championship due to injury in June 2014, Daniel Bryan returned to the ring and entered the seven-man Ladder Match for the Intercontinental Championship at *WrestleMania 31*.

The Authority, including Big Show and Kane, seemed to have Randy Orton vastly outnumbered before Orton's match with Seth Rollins. But Sting made a surprise appearance and evened the odds with his trusty baseball bat, much to the chagrin of Triple H.

January 26: The night after winning the *Royal Rumble* and a title shot at *WrestleMania*, Roman Reigns gets right in the face of champion Brock Lesnar.

March 2: Jon Stewart is on the opposite side of his usual spot at the interviewer's desk and in the crosshairs of an angry host when he confronts Seth Rollins.

The Beast suspended

March 30: Seth Rollins stunned the WWE Universe by cashing in his Money in the Bank opportunity and stealing the WWE Championship at *WrestleMania 31*. The next night at *RAW*, Brock Lesnar came looking for revenge—but the rematch never got off the ground because Lesnar attacked much of the ringside crew and The Authority, leading Stephanie McMahon to suspend Lesnar.

Home country advantage for Barrett

April 13: To honor the United States Championship he won at *WrestleMania 31*, John Cena instituted the United States Open Challenge, where he would face anyone willing to step up for the opportunity each week on *RAW*. On April 13, Cena overcame British Superstar Wade Barrett's home-country advantage and retained the title in London, England.

Crowning a new king

April 27: It was time to crown a new King of the Ring in 2015. For the first time ever, the semifinals and finals were contested on a WWE Network special, but the quarterfinals aired on *RAW*. Wade Barrett, R-Truth, Sheamus, and Neville advanced to the final four in the match, but British Superstar Barrett ultimately earned the crown by overcoming his fellow countryman Neville.

Axelmania and Mandow Madness!

May 11: Much like the two Superstars they were imitating, Hulk Hogan and Randy Savage, it was a modern-day "Mega Powers Explode" showdown when Axelmania (Curtis Axel) took on Macho Mandow (Damian Sandow). If the WWE Universe didn't look too closely, they may have thought it was the Hulkster and the Macho Man in the ring. However, The Ascension tag team interrupted the bout, forcing Axel and Sandow to work together to dispatch their foes.

April 13: Wade Barrett uses his Wasteland finishing move to defeat Neville and become King of the Ring.

2015

June 1: It didn't matter that Roman Reigns had to compete three times in one night—on each occasion he had his hand raised in victory.

INTRODUCING...

Kevin Owens

May 18th: John Cena's United States Championship Open Challenge received a surprising response when NXT Champion Kevin Owens came out. While he wasn't looking to fight for the title, he cemented his villainous image with a sneaky Pop-Up Powerbomb move on Cena and declared his title was better than Cena's. Owens would further back up his words by defeating Cena at *Elimination Chamber 2015*, Owens' WWE in-ring debut.

Kevin Owens adds insult to injury after hitting him with a Powerbomb move by taunting Cena with his own "You Can't See Me" gesture.

You want unfair?

May 25: The New Day tried to argue that defending their Tag Team Championship against five other teams in an Elimination Chamber was completely unfair. The Authority's Director of Operations Kane showed them the true meaning of unfair when he put them in a 10-on-3 match against all five other teams on *RAW*. The trio understandably succumbed to their opponents.

Three matches in one night

June 1: The Authority was not happy that Roman Reigns helped Dean Ambrose steal Seth Rollins' Championship Title. To punish Reigns, they placed him in three matches on *RAW*, with the stipulation that if he lost any of the matches, he would be removed from the upcoming *Money in the Bank* match. It was a brutal chain of Superstars to face, but Reigns took out King Barrett, Mark Henry, and Bray Wyatt.

Farewell to the Dream and Lesnar returns

June 15: To open *RAW*, WWE paid tribute to Hall of Famer "The American Dream" Dusty Rhodes, who had passed away a few days earlier. The Dream made an indelible mark on sports entertainment—he was a three-time NWA World Champion, the father of Goldust and Cody Rhodes, and one of the brains behind NXT.

Looking to do "what's best for business," The Authority ended Brock Lesnar's indefinite suspension on *RAW* and made him Seth Rollins' Title challenger at *Battleground 2015*. First, though, Lesnar was also required to issue some apologies to the innocent bystanders who had felt his wrath on March 30, including announcers Michael Cole and JBL.

Elsewhere in WWE

July 5: What better way to celebrate WWE's status as a global entertainment property than to hold a live event on Independence Day halfway across the world in Japan? The special, titled *The Beast in the East*, aired live on the WWE Network, and featured Brock Lesnar, Chris Jericho, John Cena, and an NXT Championship match where Finn Bálor took the Title from Kevin Owens.

Finn Bálor finishes off NXT Champion Kevin Owens with his Coup de Grâce move, leaping off the top rope and stomping on Owens' chest.

May 25: Tired of hearing The New Day complain, Kane makes them face five other tag teams in a single match.

August 24: The Authority is excited to show Seth Rollins his statue, but instead, they got a return of their old rival, Sting.

INTRODUCING...

Charlotte Flair, Sasha Banks and Becky Lynch

July 13: Stephanie McMahon planned to bring about a Divas Revolution in *RAW* by bringing in a new wave of athletic female Superstars from NXT to the WWE roster. She added Charlotte Flair, Sasha Banks, and Becky Lynch to the roster. These three former NXT Superstars dominated competition over the next few years, combining to win numerous championships on both *RAW* and *SmackDown*.

With four reigns as the *RAW* Women's Champion, Charlotte helped usher in a new era for female Superstars in WWE.

Another tragic loss

August 3: Less than two months after losing one of the WWE greats, Hall of Famer Dusty Rhodes, sports entertainment lost another iconic figure in WWE. *RAW* opened with a ten-bell salute to "Rowdy" Roddy Piper, who had passed away on July 31.

Where's my statue?

August 24: Seth Rollins thought he was getting a statue erected to honor his *SummerSlam* victory over John Cena and becoming the first Superstar to hold the WWE and United States Championships simultaneously. The unveiling of the statue was marred when, instead of revealing his statue, he got Sting (a future challenger for his Title) instead.

> ## "Now that is an injustice, because Seth is a legend in his own mind!"
>
> **Sting, responding to the idea that Seth Rollins is one of the all-time greats (August 31, 2015)**

Revenge of the Deadman

July 20: Undertaker appeared on *RAW* to explain why he cost Brock Lesnar his WWE Championship opportunity at *Battleground*. He wanted revenge for Lesnar ending his streak, or more accurately, revenge for Paul Heyman's incessant gloating over Lesnar ending the streak. To settle their issues, the two planned to battle it out at *SummerSlam 2015,* but their upcoming match didn't stop them from trying to attack each other that night.

The Champion challenges for another championship

July 27: John Cena successfully defended the United States Championship against an unlikely challenger—WWE Champion Seth Rollins—on *RAW*. Cena wanted to fight for Rollins' Title, but The Authority decided that Cena's Championship should be on the line instead.

July 20: It literally took the entire WWE locker room to keep Brock Lesnar and Undertaker apart in advance of their *SummerSlam* clash.

2015

Prelude to Hell
October 19: With Undertaker's controversial victory over Brock Lesnar at *SummerSlam*, it seemed like the only way to settle their rivalry was in a Hell in a Cell Match. Six days before their epic bout, the two exchanged words face to face in a summit hosted by Stone Cold Steve Austin.

October 19: In advance of their Hell in a Cell Match, Undertaker claimed he'd be sending Brock Lesnar's soul straight to hell.

September 21: Demon Kane takes drastic action against the WWE Champion Seth Rollins.

Back to Dudleyville
August 31: A blast from the past appeared to challenge The New Day after they recaptured the Tag Team Championship at *SummerSlam 2015*. The Dudley Boyz competed in a *RAW* ring for the first time in a decade and beat The New Day in a non-title match.

Dealing with the Demon
September 21: Seth Rollins assumed that The Authority's Director of Operations, Kane, was on his side. What Rollins (and the rest of the WWE Universe) did not know is that there were two Kanes—the suit-wearing member of The Authority and an untamed creature named the Demon. The latter pulled Seth Rollins into the depths of Hell after Rollins' match with John Cena for the United States Championship in the main event.

Adding allies to the fight
October 5: An intense rivalry between Roman Reigns and Bray Wyatt expanded to numerous other Superstars when *RAW* featured a Six-Man Tag Match with Reigns, Ambrose, and Orton against the Wyatt Family. The match was won by Reigns and his allies.

A Championship void creates an opportunity

November 9: When Seth Rollins was injured during a Title defense and needed to relinquish the Championship, WWE was left without a WWE Champion. The Authority announced a tournament to crown a new Champion. Triple H gave Roman Reigns an interesting proposition—either enter the tournament like everyone else or agree to work with The Authority and receive a preferential treatment—including a spot in the tournament final. Reigns rejected the offer and chose to maintain his integrity.

The Wyatt Family kidnapped both Undertaker and Kane with Bray Wyatt claiming that he had stolen their souls and powers. Not quite. During Bray's eulogy for the two brothers, Undertaker and Kane reemerged and made their way to the ring. After getting their revenge, they announced that they would face any two members of The Wyatt Family at *Survivor Series 2015*.

Sheamus cashes in

November 30: Roman Reigns finally won the WWE Championship at *Survivor Series,* but his celebration was short-lived. Sheamus immediately cashed in his *Money in the Bank* opportunity and took the title from Reigns. Reigns tried to defeat Sheamus on *RAW*, but he didn't stand a chance. Sheamus received aid from his new group—the League of Nations, which included Alberto Del Rio, King Barrett, and Rusev.

New WWE Champion

December 14: Roman Reigns finally overcame the League of Nations and beat Sheamus for the WWE Championship. He became Champion for the second time in less than a month, further angering The Authority.

A frame job foiled

December 28: Mr. McMahon provoked Roman Reigns into putting his hands on him and then tried to get the police at the show to arrest Reigns. When the officers refused to act as the McMahon's personal security detail, Mr McMahon got angry and grabbed an officer, leading to him being arrested instead!

December 14: Despite outside interference by the other members of the League of Nations, Roman Reigns pins Sheamus to become a two-time WWE World Heavyweight Champion.

2016

FOR THE FIRST TIME in five years, the roster of WWE Superstars was divided into two groups as part of a brand split between *RAW* and *SmackDown*. A draft took place in July, with *RAW*'s Superstars selected by Commissioner Stephanie McMahon and General Manager Mick Foley. The pair chose well—the roster included established Superstars like Brock Lesnar, Seth Rollins, and Roman Reigns, and incredible new blood such as Charlotte Flair, Finn Bálor, and Sasha Banks. The split was due to a McMahon family rivalry precipitated by the return of Shane McMahon to WWE. Another incredible return happened later in the year when Goldberg came back to *RAW* after 12 years away from WWE.

Knocking out the Chairman

January 4: Trying to relieve Roman Reigns of the WWE Championship on *RAW*, Mr. McMahon served as the special guest referee for Reigns' Title Match. Reigns KO'ed the crooked Chairman, which may have saved his Title in the short term, but would cost him so much more; Mr. McMahon told Reigns that he would have to defend the WWE against 29 competitors in the Royal Rumble Match.

First taste of gold

January 11: Kalisto defeated Alberto Del Rio to win the United States Championship, his first Championship in WWE. Del Rio would take the title back later in the week on *SmackDown*, but Kalisto beat Del Rio for the Title again at the *Royal Rumble*, and held the Championship for four months.

January 4: Overcoming Mr. McMahon's best efforts to relieve him of the title, Roman Reigns stands tall as the WWE World Heavyweight Champion.

January 11: Kalisto employs a dizzying array of high-flying moves to overcome the United States Champion Alberto Del Rio and win the first title in the masked luchador's career.

INTRODUCING...

AJ Styles

January 25: AJ Styles stunned the WWE Universe with his shocking debut in the *2016 Royal Rumble*, and he made it clear it wasn't a one-time appearance by appearing the next night on *RAW* where he defeated Chris Jericho in an intense match. Styles has become a main event mainstay in WWE, and he captured the WWE Championship within a year of being on the roster.

In his first year in WWE, in addition to winning the WWE Championship, AJ Styles also managed to beat John Cena in some epic matches.

"And by damn, I have one more night to feel this energy, and feel this crowd!"

Daniel Bryan announcing his retirement due to injury (February 8, 2016)

Bryan bids farewell

February 8: Twice in the past two years, Daniel Bryan was forced to vacate championships due to injuries. When his health did not get any better, Bryan finally decided to retire due to long-term medical concerns. *RAW* was in Bryan's home state of Washington, so he took the time to explain the decision to the WWE Universe in an emotional farewell speech.

The best of five

February 15: Kevin Owens won a Fatal Five-Way Match over Dolph Ziggler, Stardust, Tyler Breeze, and current Champion Dean Ambrose to capture the Intercontinental Championship on *RAW*. It was Owens' second reign with the Title, and he would hold it until *WrestleMania 32*.

Here comes the money

February 22: The Chairman, Vince McMahon, created the Vincent J. McMahon Legacy of Excellence Award and announced that Stephanie McMahon was the first recipient of the honor. However, before she could begin her acceptance speech, she was interrupted by a blast from her past—her brother Shane McMahon, returning to *RAW* for the first time in almost six years.

February 22: The McMahon family decided to air out their dirty laundry in public to the entertainment of the WWE Universe.

Triple threat announced for the Divas Championship

March 7: A match on the previous week's *RAW* between Becky Lynch and Sasha Banks resulted in a double pin and no clear winner. Without a clear contender for Charlotte's WWE Divas Championship, both were awarded a shot at the Title at *WrestleMania* in a Triple Threat Match.

Ready for *WrestleMania*

March 21: Roman Reigns attacked Triple H in the parking lot of the arena to send a clear message to the WWE Champion less than two weeks before their match at *WrestleMania*.

February 8: While enjoying the outpouring of love shown him by the WWE Universe, Daniel Bryan shares the sobering news that his in-ring career is over.

177

2016

One-Day Champ

April 4: Zack Ryder finally had his moment at *WrestleMania 32* when he won the Intercontinental Championship. But his reign lasted less than 24 hours. Defending his new championship against The Miz, Ryder was distracted by a ringside altercation between The Miz's wife Maryse and Ryder's father. The Miz took advantage, hitting the champion with a Skull-Crushing Finale to capture the Title.

Fighting a common foe

April 11: Is the enemy of an enemy a viable tag team partner? Roman Reigns and Bray Wyatt had to face this problem when they both had issues with the League of Nations stable. The formerly bitter rivals teamed up to face Sheamus and Alberto Del Rio in the main event of *RAW*. Almost in unison, Wyatt hit Alberto Del Rio with his Sister Abigail move while Reigns floored Sheamus with his Spear maneuver to win the match.

April 11: Bitter foes Roman Reigns and Bray Wyatt come together to function effectively as a tag team against their shared foes.

Sibling rivalry becomes sibling partnership

May 2: Even though Shane McMahon lost his *WrestleMania 32* match to Undertaker, Mr. McMahon still gave him an opportunity to run *RAW*. Eventually Stephanie and Shane thought the Chairman would pick one to run the show, but at *Payback 2016*, Mr. McMahon decided to put them both in charge. The May 2 *RAW* was the first episode the two ran together, and despite some initial fits and starts, the show was a success.

A prized possession destroyed

May 9: Chris Jericho couldn't be blamed for holding a long-term grudge against The Lunatic Fringe, Dean Ambrose, after he destroyed Jericho's $15,000 jacket during his match with Big Cass. Ambrose, angry that Jericho had ruined his favorite potted plant, decided to cut up Jericho's bold fashion choice and stomp on its lighting apparatus.

May 9: Dean Ambrose destroys Chris Jericho's beloved jacket in an act of sweet revenge.

Rollins' angry return

May 23: Seth Rollins was supposed to be recovering from a devastating injury that forced him to vacate the WWE Championship and undergo months of gruelling rehabilitation. But the Superstar shocked the WWE Universe by returning and attacking WWE Champion Roman Reigns at *Extreme Rules*. Rollins opened the next night's episode of *RAW* by explaining that, since he never lost the title, he wanted to make a big statement on his return. Shane McMahon then granted Rollins a title match at *Money in the Bank 2016*.

Cena interrupted

May 30: John Cena returned to WWE following an injury that sidelined him for five months. Before he could properly address the WWE Universe, AJ Styles came out to face him. While it initially seemed like Styles was paying respect to Cena, it quickly descended into a war of words. The argument then escalated to a physical battle when Styles' Club partners Gallows and Anderson helped beat down Cena.

A night of Shield champions

June 20: At *Money in the Bank 2016*, all three members of The Shield stable held the WWE Championship in one night. Seth Rollins pinned the reigning Champion Roman Reigns for the WWE Title. But Dean Ambrose then cashed in his Money in the Bank opportunity and took the title from Rollins. The next night on *RAW*, Reigns and Rollins fought in the main event for the right to challenge Ambrose for the title. The match ended as a double countout, so all three members fought in a Triple Threat Match for the Title at *WWE Battleground*.

General Manager tryouts

June 27: News broke of an upcoming brand split between *RAW* and *SmackDown*—with Stephanie running one show and Shane the other. A number of former authority figures in WWE showed up on *RAW* in order to throw their hats into the ring for the General Manager positions on the two shows. Superstars eager to be considered included Teddy Long, John Laurinaitis, Corporate Kane, and Vickie Guerrero.

May 30: Former Club members AJ Styles, Karl Anderson, and Luke Gallows come together to decimate a common enemy: John Cena.

2016

USA vs. The World

July 4: To celebrate Independence Day, a 16-Man Elimination Tag Match pitted a team of American Superstars that included Kane, Big Show, Mark Henry, and The Dudley Boyz against an alliance of competitors from around the world. They defeated the team led by Kevin Owens, Alberto Del Rio, Chris Jericho, and the Lucha Dragons.

July 4: The United States team manages to hold off the International team in a 16-man match on Independence Day.

Elsewhere in WWE

July 19: Stephanie McMahon (and her General Manager Mick Foley) had taken over *RAW* and Shane McMahon (and his General Manager Daniel Bryan) had taken over *SmackDown Live*. Their final task was to divide up the roster of Superstars in the WWE Draft on a special July 19 episode of *SmackDown Live*. Stephanie selected Seth Rollins for *RAW*, while Dean Ambrose, holder of the WWE Championship, was *SmackDown Live's* first choice.

Showing off the draft picks

July 25: The first *RAW* after the WWE Draft highlighted the wisdom of the picks made by Stephanie McMahon and Mick Foley. Their first-round pick Finn Bálor won a pair of matches to earn a shot at *RAW's* newly created Universal Championship. Their top two female Superstars, Charlotte and Sasha Banks, met in a Title Match where Banks captured the *RAW* Women's Title for the first time in her career.

July 25: Sasha Banks becomes the first Superstar to win a title on *RAW* after the 2016 brand split, defeating Charlotte for the *RAW* Women's Championship.

Roman Reigns, wedding crasher

August 8: Roman Reigns spoiled the wedding celebration of Rusev and Lana by crashing the reception. Reigns offered an insult-filled toast to the newlyweds before ending up in a tussle with Rusev, which resulted in Lana being covered in her own wedding cake.

Fighting for a job

August 15: After not being drafted to *RAW* or *SmackDown*, Heath Slater hoped to impress management and earn a contract for *RAW* by winning his next match. Unfortunately for Slater, his opponent was "The Beast" Brock Lesnar. And while there was always the possibility that Lesnar would underestimate Slater's ability while concentrating on his *SummerSlam* competitor Randy Orton, it did not happen. Instead, Lesnar sent a clear message to Orton by demolishing Slater, denying him a *RAW* contract in the process.

Abdicating the Title

August 29: The first Universal Championship reign will go down as one of the shortest reigns in the Title's history. While Finn Bálor defeated Seth Rollins for the Championship at *SummerSlam*, he suffered an injury to his shoulder that forced him to vacate the title. *RAW*'s main event was a Fatal 4-Way Elimination Match to crown the next Universal Champion. The final showdown came down to Kevin Owens and Seth Rollins, but Rollins' former mentor Triple H appeared and helped Owens win the Title.

Best of seven

September 12: *RAW* General Manager Mick Foley challenged two of his *RAW* Superstars, Sheamus and Cesaro, to do something unique to impress him. He then went on to put them in a best-of-seven series of matches with the winner being guaranteed a Championship opportunity. It looked like the battle was over when Sheamus captured the first three decisions, meaning that he only had to win one more, but Cesaro fought back. Cesaro won the fourth match and then, on September 12, captured the decision to make it three wins for Sheamus to two for Cesaro.

Rage in the cage

September 19: As General Manager of *RAW*, Mick Foley tried to give the WWE Universe as much excitement as possible. The main event featured a non-title Steel Cage Match between WWE Universal Champion Kevin Owens and Roman Reigns. Both Reigns and Owens fought well, but a Superman Punch from a height floored Owens. As Reigns clambered over the top of the cage, Owens made his way to the cage door to exit the ring. Reigns managed to leap over the cage and win the match, only to encounter Owens' ally Rusev. Seth Rollins arrived to help his friend and drew the battle to a close by leaping from the top of the cage to flatten Rusev and Owens.

August 29: Taking advantage of Finn Bálor's injury and the support of Triple H, Kevin Owens captures the WWE Universal Championship.

September 19: Roman Reigns lets everyone know that he should be the number-one contender for the Universal Championship by beating Kevin Owens in a Steel Cage Match.

Stepping up to the spotlight

October 3: For the first time in more than a decade, the main event of *RAW* featured a Women's Championship Match. Sasha Banks made the most of the bright spotlight, beating Charlotte for the Title. It seemed like Charlotte had the match in hand when she targeted Banks' previously injured back and came close to pinning the challenger several times. Banks dug deep and kept fighting back, eventually forcing Charlotte to tap out of her painful Bank Statement move.

Lesnar's next!

October 17: Goldberg made an exciting return following his 12-year break from WWE, in his first *RAW* appearance in more than a decade. He arrived specifically to address the insulting remarks Paul Heyman had made on behalf of Heyman's client Brock Lesnar, who was trying to goad Goldberg back into the ring. To the delight of the WWE Universe, Goldberg accepted the challenge!

Representing *RAW*

November 7: Heading into *Survivor Series 2016, SmackDown's* Dolph Ziggler issued an open challenge to anyone on the *RAW* roster to face him for the Intercontinental Championship. Mick Foley wanted Sami Zayn to grab the opportunity, but Stephanie McMahon thought Rusev was the man for the job. So Zayn and Rusev met in a match to earn the title shot on *RAW*. Zayn took the win when he nailed Rusev with a Helluva Kick move, as Rusev tried to leap at him from the top rope. Rusev was floored, giving Zayn the three-count and the Title shot.

Security detail

November 14: Brock Lesnar attempted to intimidate Goldberg ahead of their *Survivor Series* clash by questioning whether Goldberg was ready for a match with Lesnar at Survivor Series. But Goldberg would not back down. This led to a mass of security entering the ring and separating the two Superstars in an attempt to keep the war of words from escalating into a physical confrontation.

November 14: *RAW* management puts a wall of security between Goldberg and Brock Lesnar to keep them apart until their *Survivor Series* clash.

December 12: The New Day's celebrations for their record-breaking Championship reign turns sour when they accidentally spray champagne all over Stephanie McMahon.

Undercover interference

November 21: Kevin Owens was forced by General Manager Mick Foley to defend the Universal Championship against Seth Rollins. Chris Jericho would try and help Owens win matches via outside illegal interference. As a friend of Rollins, Reigns would try to counteract Jericho. To ensure that the fight was settled fairly, both Jericho and Reigns were banned from ringside. During the match, Rollins was accosted by a fan in the front row wearing a Sin Cara mask. Rollins unmasked the fan and revealed it was really Chris Jericho! The distraction was enough to help Owens win the match and retain the Title.

A third Championship reign

November 28: For the third time in 2016, Sasha Banks defeated Charlotte Flair for the *RAW* Women's Championship on *RAW*. The two bitter rivals fought in a Falls Count Anywhere Match to cap their intense 2016 rivalry. The action spilled out of the ring, and Charlotte almost won with a Moonsault maneuver off the announcing table. But Banks kicked out and eventually put the champion in a Bank Statement hold through the guard rail and Flair was forced to submit.

A record-breaking reign

December 12: The New Day only needed to win their tag team match on *RAW* to surpass Demolition's all-time tag team record of 478 days. They managed to defeat the teams of Gallows and Anderson and Cesaro and Sheamus in a Triple Threat Match to hold on to their Title and beat the 478-day record. However, during their backstage celebration, they spilled champagne over Stephanie McMahon, and the vengeful Commissioner forced them to defend their Titles in a second Triple Threat Match that would have cost them the record. Luckily the trio defeated Jeri-KO and Rollins and Reigns to keep hold of the Titles.

A not-so-merry Christmas

December 19: Because of his failure to win against Sami Zayn the night before, Braun Strowman entered the ring in a foul mood during Sin Cara and Titus O'Neil's match. He took out his anger on Sin Cara and O'Neil, but Sin Cara got the worst treatment. Strowman launched the masked Superstar off the stage into a Christmas tree and a pile of presents.

2017

ON *MONDAY NIGHT RAW*, everything in 2017 was larger than life, even by WWE's massive standards. While Kevin Owens started the year holding *RAW*'s top title, Universal Champion, Goldberg was next—until he lost the title in a titanic clash with the "Beast," Brock Lesnar. Lesnar would face monstrous challengers throughout the year, including Braun Strowman. Strowman created a number of viral video moments on *RAW* with feats of strength designed to wreck his rival Roman Reigns. Power on *RAW* also came in smaller packages. Alexa Bliss jumped from *SmackDown* to *RAW* and dominated the *RAW* Women's Championship, but the entire Women's division was put on notice when the undefeated Asuka arrived from NXT.

INTRODUCING...

Samoa Joe

January 30: Former two-time NXT Champion Samoa Joe made his *RAW* debut when he attacked Seth Rollins, who was on his way to the ring to confront Triple H for his betrayal. The brawl continued in the ring, where Joe demolished Rollins, aligning himself with Triple H, and making a statement to the WWE Universe and the rest of the locker room. Joe would quickly become a main-event mainstay, challenging Brock Lesnar for the WWE Universal Championship in July and August.

With steely determination, Samoa Joe had the upper hand throughout his *RAW* debut match against Seth Rollins.

The Festival of Friendship and a new Champion

February 13: To honor his close bond with Universal Champion Kevin Owens, Chris Jericho created the first ever Festival of Friendship. The Champ appeared unimpressed with the artistic gifts and hired entertainment, but did seem somewhat moved by Jericho's heartfelt speech. Then Owens gave Jericho a gift as well—a new list. But it turned out to be the List of Owens and Jericho was the only name on it. Jericho also received an unwanted extra gift—a vicious beatdown from the Champion.

That same night, Bayley captured her first WWE *RAW* Women's Championship when she defeated Charlotte with the help of Sasha Banks. Bayley would hold on to the Championship for more than two months, successfully defending it against Charlotte, Sasha Banks, and Nia Jax in a Fatal 4-Way Elimination Match.

One final new Championship

January 9: Chris Jericho had won almost every major championship in WWE history with one exception: he had never captured the United States Championship. On *RAW*, Jericho and his best friend Kevin Owens faced United States champion Roman Reigns and beat him in a 2-on-1 Handicap Match to award Jericho his first-ever reign as United States Champion.

January 9: Chris Jericho celebrates winning his first ever United States Championship with Kevin Owens.

February 13: Bayley drops a top-rope elbow on Charlotte en route to defeating the Queen and winning the *RAW* Women's Championship.

Putting the Champ on alert

March 6: Brock Lesnar and Goldberg were already set for a titanic clash at *WrestleMania 33*. Then Goldberg won the WWE Universal Championship at *Fastlane*, and the match became a Championship bout. On *RAW*, Lesnar made sure that the Champ knew their *WrestleMania* match would be different than their previous encounters, driving Goldberg to the mat with an F5 maneuver.

End of the Foley era

March 20: For months Mick Foley had been on thin ice in his position as General Manager of *RAW*. Refusing to fire a Superstar despite Stephanie's order to do so, and putting Triple H in his painful Socko claw hold the week before did not help matters. Stephanie fired Foley on the March 20 episode of the show.

Claiming Reigns' soul

March 27: The mind games between Undertaker and Roman Reigns continued throughout the month leading up to their *WrestleMania* encounter, reaching a crescendo on the final episode of *RAW* before *WrestleMania 33*. As Reigns stood in the ring, assuring the WWE Universe that he'd win at *WrestleMania*, Undertaker appeared on the Titan Tron with a clear message: a fresh new tombstone with Reigns' name on it.

March 20: *RAW* General Manager Mick Foley stands up to Stephanie McMahon and her husband Triple H, but the defiance ends up costing him his job.

March 27: Claiming that the ring is "his yard," Roman Reigns challenges Undertaker to an epic *WrestleMania* encounter.

2017

A new GM and new tag team blood

April 3: With Mick Foley's departure, *RAW* had a need for a new General Manager. On this edition of *RAW*, the position was filled by recent Hall of Fame inductee Kurt Angle. It's odd to say that a massive "You suck" chant would be the ultimate sign of love and affection, but the WWE Universe used it to tell the Olympic athlete that they were happy to see him back home again.

The *RAW* after *WrestleMania* 33 featured two tag teams that had not been with the brand the week before: the Hardys and The Revival. The Hardys made their return to WWE at *WrestleMania* 33, winning the WWE *RAW* Tag Team Championships, while former NXT standout pair The Revival answered an open challenge from former champions The New Day, stunning them with a pinfall victory.

April 3: Making a dramatic return to *RAW* for the first time in more than a decade, Kurt Angle becomes the second *RAW* General Manager since the 2016 brand split.

April 10: Jumping from *SmackDown* to *RAW* in the Superstar Shakeup, Alexa Bliss would capture the *RAW* Women's Championship within a month.

Superstar Shakeup

April 10: *RAW* featured the Superstar Shakeup—talent moving from *SmackDown* to *RAW* and vice versa. *RAW* added some incredible talent from their rival brand, including former WWE Champions Dean Ambrose (also the reigning Intercontinental Champion), The Miz, and Bray Wyatt. *RAW* also gained two former Women's Champions, Alexa Bliss and Mickie James.

You'd have to excuse Roman Reigns if he wished Braun Strowman had been sent to *SmackDown* in the Shakeup. Later on the same episode, Strowman ambushed Reigns and beat the Big Dog so badly, he had to be taken from the arena in an ambulance. Strowman had not finished punishing Reigns however—once Reigns was loaded into the ambulance, Strowman came back and flipped the vehicle on its side.

April 10: In case anyone doubted that Braun Strowman was a Monster Among Men, they get a powerful reminder when Strowman flips over an ambulance with his rival Roman Reigns in it.

A pair of unqualified GMs

May 8: *RAW* General Manager Kurt Angle could not make this episode of *RAW* held in London, England, so bitter rivals Dean Ambrose and The Miz were appointed as co-General Managers for the night. With the two in charge, chaos reigned. Ambrose forced The Miz to face Finn Bálor and The Miz pitted Ambrose against Bray Wyatt in the night's main event.

Not on the same page

May 29: Despite having common enemies in Samoa Joe and Bray Wyatt, former Shield stablemates Seth Rollins and Roman Reigns could not come together to beat them in a tag team match on the previous week's *RAW*. Their continuing problems led Kurt Angle to pit them against each other in a singles match, a closely fought affair that Reigns eventually prevailed in.

Choking out the advocate

June 12: On the previous week's *RAW*, the newly minted number-one contender to the Universal Championship, Samoa Joe, had sent Brock Lesnar a message by putting Lesnar's advocate Paul Heyman in the Coquina Clutch. On June 12, a steamed Lesnar came to *RAW* looking to put the hurt on Joe, but Samoa Joe was ready and it took the entire locker room to keep the two separated.

May 29: Roman Reigns delivers a vicious Spear maneuver to his former Shield partner Seth Rollins in a match on *RAW*, a bout won by Reigns.

June 12: Several *RAW* Superstars strain to hold back Samoa Joe when WWE Universal Champion Brock Lesnar turns up on *RAW*, looking for him.

2017

The Big Baller Brand represents

June 26: The Miz TV segment emanating from Los Angeles had one of the bigger sports stories of the year covered when the Awesome One interviewed Los Angeles Laker first-round pick Lonzo Ball, as well as his brother LaMelo and his father LaVar. The Miz thought the Ball family would want to work with him, but instead they aligned themselves with The Miz's rival Dean Ambrose.

June 26: A chaotic Miz TV segment featured NBA parent LaVar Ball and his talented sons taking over the show and confronting The Miz.

A family reunion and other surprises

July 17: Kurt Angle was tormented with a secret from his past. Rather than let the secret destroy him, his career, and his family, Angle decided to tell the world. He admitted that in college he had fathered a child, one he did not know about until recently. This child had clearly inherited Angle's athletic ability, as he was a WWE Superstar—American Alpha member Jason Jordan. Angle invited Jordan to *RAW* and the two had an emotional reunion.

Both Roman Reigns and Samoa Joe thought they deserved the *SummerSlam* shot at Brock Lesnar's Universal Championship. To decide, Kurt Angle had the two meet in the main event of *RAW*. The match ended as a No Contest when Braun Strowman interfered in the match to stake his claim as the top contender. The following week, Angle decided that all three would face Lesnar in a Fatal 4-Way match for the title.

A brutal *SummerSlam* preview

August 7: With three challengers for his Universal Championship at *SummerSlam*, the deck seemed stacked against Brock Lesnar. But the Beast decided to use a Miz TV segment on *RAW* to show the WWE Universe his version of *SummerSlam*. Lesnar used the Miz and his two-man Miztourage as substitutes for his three challengers, and destroyed everyone in sight.

August 7: Instead of sticking to an interview, Brock Lesnar decides to use Miz TV as a warmup for his Fatal 4-Way Match at *SummerSlam*, decimating the Miztourage.

August 14: It took several weeks to get there, but the WWE Universe roars with delight when Dean Ambrose and Seth Rollins joins fists like they did when they were in the Shield.

Finally reunited

August 14: Both Seth Rollins and Dean Ambrose had their share of problems with the WWE *RAW* Tag Team Champions Seamus and Cesaro. But they could not agree to work together as a team until they had aired out their differences over two years of battles and betrayal. They finally came together on *RAW*, earning a *SummerSlam* shot at the *RAW* Tag Team Titles.

The Champ returns to RAW

August 21: *RAW* General Manager Kurt Angle pulled off quite the free agent coup, when he stole 16-time World Champion John Cena from *SmackDown*. The Champ returned to *RAW* with one target in mind—Roman Reigns. Although the two teamed together in the main event of the night, it was clear an intense rivalry would begin over the next few months between the two polarizing figures.

Elsewhere in WWE

August 28: The Women's Revolution in WWE reached dizzying heights in the summer of 2017. The Mae Young Classic was a tournament featuring 32 incredible competitors from around the world fighting in a single-elimination tournament. After four grueling rounds of competition, it came down to Kairi Sane from Japan and the United States' Shayna Baszler, with Sane claiming the first ever Mae Young Classic.

August 21: Despite teaming up for a victorious tag team match, John Cena and Roman Reigns are on a collision course for a one-on-one encounter.

2017

#undersiege

October 23: *Survivor Series 2017* was set to pit the best of the *RAW* roster against *SmackDown Live*'s finest Superstars. *SmackDown* commissioner Shane McMahon decided to strike first, leading an invasion of *SmackDown* Superstars into *RAW* where they ambushed much of the *RAW* locker room backstage, taking them out with superior numbers. McMahon told *RAW* General Manager Kurt Angle that *RAW* was #underseige and that his brand would finish the job at *Survivor Series*.

Re-raising the bar

November 6: Challenging Seth Rollins and Dean Ambrose for the *RAW* Tag Team Championships, The Bar (aka Cesaro and Sheamus) received an unexpected assist when the New Day entered the arena. With the New Day threatening another *SmackDown* siege of *RAW*, Sheamus took advantage of the resulting chaos, nailing Rollins with a Brogue Kick and allowing The Bar to win the Tag Team Championships.

October 23: Shane McMahon declares war on *RAW*, bringing a cadre of *SmackDown* Superstars in through the audience to attack an unsuspecting *RAW* roster.

November 6: The Bar, Sheamus and Cesaro, pose on the rampway with their WWE Tag Team Championship titles, clearly mocking their downed opponents, Seth Rollins and Dean Ambrose.

December 18: All the female Superstars of *RAW* celebrate with Stephanie McMahon after the Commissioner's historic announcement of the first-ever Women's Royal Rumble Match.

Trios under fire

December 11: For weeks, Paige, Mandy Rose, and Sonya Deville, the trio known as Absolution, had looked to make their presence felt and to shake up the Women's Division by picking off their competitors one by one. The women of *RAW* had had enough. Putting their own differences aside, they attacked the trio in the ring and overwhelmed them with superior numbers.

Samoa Joe and Tag Team Champions the Bar had been taking the competition to the Shield in recent weeks, so *RAW* General Manager Kurt Angle set up three one-on-one matches where all other allies were banned from ringside. In the first two matches, members of the The Shield triumphed: Seth Rollins defeated Sheamus and Roman Reigns retained the Intercontinental Title against Cesaro. Dean Ambrose could not make it a clean sweep, as Samoa Joe took him out with the Coquina Clutch to win the match.

The Women's revolution goes royal

December 18: *RAW* commissioner Stephanie McMahon stunned the female Superstars of *RAW* and *SmackDown Live* when she announced that, for the first time in history, there would be a Women's Royal Rumble Match. At *Royal Rumble 2018*, 30 women would compete to be the last woman standing and earn the right to compete for a championship at *WrestleMania 34*.

> ## "What do you say ladies? You make history once again!"
>
> ### Stephanie McMahon (December 18, 2017)

A Championship present

December 25: The WWE Universe received an unexpected gift Christmas day—new Tag Team Champions! Competing in their first-ever match as a pair, Seth Rollins and Jason Jordan were able to work together and defeat The Bar for the Titles when Jordan pinned Cesaro while Rollins kept Sheamus outside the ring, preventing him from breaking up the pinfall.

December 11: Seth Rollins drops Sheamus to the mat en route to a one-on-one victory over the Celtic Warrior.

2018

AS THE NEW YEAR BEGAN, WWE celebrated 25 years and 1,287 episodes of *Monday Night RAW*. A spectacular super show was held on January 22 in two locations in New York City: The Manhattan Center, which was the location of the very first *Monday Night RAW* broadcast in January 1993, and The Barclays Center in Brooklyn that has been the home of WWE's annual *SummerSlam* event each August for the past three years. Legends returned to commemorate *RAW*'s anniversary. In the weeks leading up to the 25th anniversary edition of *RAW*, the WWE Superstars were focused on the upcoming *Royal Rumble* with its first-ever Women's Royal Rumble Match, and the chance that both the male and female Superstars had at gaining a Championship Match at *WrestleMania 34* in April.

January 1: It takes the entire *RAW* locker room to pull apart Kane and Brock Lesnar after incendiary comments from Lesnar's advocate Paul Heyman.

The Bálor Club vs. the Champions Club
January 8: For years, Finn Bálor together with Karl Anderson and Luke Gallows formed a club of Superstars who dominated sports entertainment in Japan. After reforming as "The Bálor Club" a week earlier on *RAW*, the talented trio battled Intercontinental Champion Roman Reigns and Tag Team Champions Seth Rollins and Jason Jordan. Jordan had arrogantly named their team the "Champions Club," irritating Reigns and Rollins. Jordan angered his teammates further after costing them the win by distracting the referee and causing Rollins to feel The Bálor Club's wrath.

The Devil's favorite
January 1: Brock Lesnar was set to defend his Universal Championship against challengers Kane and Braun Strowman at the *Royal Rumble* event taking place four weeks after this edition of *RAW*. Lesnar's advocate Paul Heyman addressed the WWE Universe in the ring, dismissing Kane's claims of being the Devil's chosen WWE Superstar and declaring that Brock Lesnar was actually the Devil's favorite. This caused Kane to run to the ring and attack Lesnar, requiring numerous Superstars to pull the two combatants apart.

January 8: Finn Bálor reunites with his longtime friends Gallows and Anderson to form The Bálor Club, throwing up their signature hand gesture called the "Too Sweet."

Firing and rehiring a monster

January 15: For the last several weeks, Braun Strowman had attacked Brock Lesnar and Kane anywhere he could find them. One week earlier on *RAW*, Strowman launched into a devastating attack backstage, almost permanently injuring Lesnar and Kane. As a consequence, General Manager Kurt Angle fired Strowman in this week's episode. Strowman snapped, destroying the backstage area, threatening WWE production staff, and tipping over a production truck. Following Strowman's nearly hour-long rampage, *RAW* Commissioner Stephanie McMahon phoned Angle, ordering him to rehire Strowman.

Elsewhere in WWE

January 16: Always at the forefront of entertainment, WWE began a new series called the "Mixed Match Challenge" that aired exclusively on Facebook. The Superstars of both *Monday Night RAW* and *SmackDown Live* competed in a 12-week, mixed tag team (one male and one female Superstar per team) tournament where the winning team won $100,000 for charity.

January 15: An enraged Braun Strowman lets his anger out on a WWE television production truck.

Monday Night RAW: the 25th Anniversary Special

January 22: Beginning with a special one-hour pre-show, aired exclusively on the WWE Network, the WWE Universe celebrated the 25th anniversary of the longest running episodic series in television history with a special episode of *Monday Night RAW*. Held at two locations—the Barclays Center in Brooklyn, and the Manhattan Center in New York City—the special episode featured returns of legendary Superstars, celebrity guests, and incredible in-ring action.

Stone Cold Steve Austin celebrates 25 years of *RAW* by hitting Mr. McMahon with his trademark Stunner.

Undertaker, who competed in the ring against Damien Demento on the very first episode of *RAW*, returned to the Manhattan Center for the anniversary special. Standing in the middle of the ring, which he described as the "sacred ground of evil," he warned his fallen opponents of the past to rest in peace.

The WWE Hall of Fame announce team—Jerry "The King" Lawler and Jim Ross—called all the action from the Manhattan Center.

Flanked by his children, Shane and Stephanie, WWE Chairman Vince McMahon returned to *RAW*, welcoming the WWE Universe to the show, and congratulating himself for *RAW* celebrating its 25th anniversary. His self-celebration was cut short when his greatest rival in *RAW* history, Stone Cold Steve Austin, stormed the ring and once again hit both Shane and Vince with a Stone Cold Stunner.

Undertaker poses in the middle of the ring to address fans and past and present Superstars.

2018

Returning to *RAW* from filming a movie, The Miz made history of his own on this historic night by defeating Roman Reigns for his eighth Intercontinental Championship. He was supported by his Miztourage cohorts, Bo Dallas and Curtis Axel.

Chris Jericho, DX, Razor Ramon, The APA, The Dudley Boyz, former *RAW* General Manager Eric Bischoff, Brother Love, The Godfather, Trish Stratus, and countless other WWE Legends appeared on *RAW*, joining in the festivities at both locations.

Triple H, along with the rest of the reunited D-Generation X , welcomes fellow Kliq member Razor Ramon to the ring to celebrate their collective history on *RAW*.

The Miz levels Roman Reigns in a match that would lead him to capture the Intercontinental Championship for the eighth time.

For weeks the trio of Brock Lesnar, Braun Strowman, and Kane attacked each other in anticipation of their WWE Universal Championship match at the *Royal Rumble* event six days later. *RAW* General Manager Kurt Angle didn't want the chaos of previous weeks' events to put a damper on the celebratory night, so he directed every WWE Superstar and legend in Brooklyn to surround the ring during a confrontation between the three combatants. But it wasn't enough as Strowman, Kane, and Lesnar resumed their battle, with Strowman ending the memorable night standing tall over a fallen Lesnar and Kane.

Another physical battle is waged between Brock Lesnar, Braun Strowman, and Kane, ending in victory for Strowman, as WWE Superstars and legends look on.

The Manhattan Center, which played host to the first episode of *Monday Night RAW*, co-hosts the 25th Anniversary episode.

An excited crowd fills The Barclays Center, home to the 25th anniversary episode of *Monday Night RAW*.

GLOSSARY

10-BELL SALUTE: A gesture of respect given to a person who has passed away.

ATTITUDE ADJUSTMENT: John Cena raises his opponent onto his shoulders in a fireman's lift and then slams him down on the mat.

BANK STATEMENT: Sasha Banks flips her opponent over her body, grips them in a facelock and pulls back, causing a submission.

BATISTA BOMB: Batista locks his opponent's head between his legs, spins them up onto his shoulders, and slams them down onto the mat.

BIG ENDING: Big E holds his opponent over his shoulder by the waist and slams them down to the mat.

BOILER ROOM BRAWL: A battle between Superstars where the first person to leave the boiler room wins.

BULL HAMMER: Wade Barrett smashes his elbow into his opponent.

CAMEL CLUTCH SUBMISSION HOLD: Iron Sheik sits on his opponent's back and pulls their head and shoulders back in a painful submission move.

CASH IN (A MONEY IN THE BANK OPPORTUNITY): By winning the "Money in the Bank" ladder match, a Superstar is guaranteed a Championship match whenever they want it. They get that opportunity by presenting a referee with the Money in the Bank briefcase which contains the match contract.

COQUINA CLUTCH: Samoa Joe grips his opponent around the neck and head and uses his other arm to apply pressure.

COUNT OUT: When a Superstar exits the ring and the referee counts to ten before the Superstar returns resulting in a disqualification.

COUP DE GRÂCE: Finn Bálor leaps from the top rope and lands feet first on his opponent's chest.

CROSSFACE CHICKEN WING: Bob Backlund twists his arms under his opponent's shoulders and in front of their face, forcing them to submit.

DOUBLE PIN: Rare incident where a Superstar pins the shoulders of two competitors to the mat at the same time.

ECW: Abbreviation for Extreme Championship Wrestling, a popular sports entertainment promotion in the 1990s and early 2000s, which rapidly built a loyal fanbase. ECW was known for its unique and intense matches.

F5: Brock Lesnar hoists his opponent up onto his shoulders, then lifts and twists, slamming them chest down onto the mat.

G.T.S (GO TO SLEEP): Hideo Itami hoists his opponent onto his shoulders then drops them down onto his raised knee.

HELLUVA KICK: Sami Zayn rams his foot into his opponent.

KIMURA LOCK: Brock Lesnar grips his opponent's arm across his body, falls to the mat and pulls back.

LAYING [THE] BOOTS: The act of giving someone a kicking – using boots or not!

LUCHADOR: The name given to those who compete in Lucha Libre wrestling in Mexico.

MANDIBLE CLAW: Mick Foley pushes two fingers into his opponent's mouth beneath the tongue and pushes down, leading to a submission.

MASTERLOCK: Chris Masters places his arms under his opponent's arms and grips the back of his head, forcing him to submit.

MOONSAULT: Lita balances on the top rope, then backflips onto her prone or standing opponent for the pin.

NO CONTEST: An match ending where there is no clear winner because of outside interference or because both competitors are disqualified.

PEDIGREE: Triple H hooks his bent-over opponent by his arms and jumps, slamming him down into the mat. Also used occasionally by Seth Rollins.

PERFECT-PLEX: "Mr. Perfect" Curt Henning hooks his opponent by the arm and leg, then flips them over his head into a pin.

PINFALL VICTORY: A Superstar holds his or her opponent's shoulders to the mat for a three count.

POSE-DOWN: When Superstars compete for the most powerful physique.

RKO: Randy Orton applies a facelock and dives onto his back, bringing his opponent down face-first onto the mat.

October 19, 1998: Superstars including The Rock, "Bad Ass" Billy Gunn, Chyna, Edge, Jeff Jarrett, Mankind, The New Age Outlaws, "Road Dogg" Jesse James, and X-Pac pose for a ring portrait on *RAW*.

ROCK BOTTOM: The Rock holds his opponent with his arm outstretched, connects with his opponent's upper body and falls forward, slamming their body onto the mat.

ROLLING THUNDER: Rob Van Dam does a standing somersault before landing on his opponent.

ROUNDHOUSE KICKS: A Superstar twists and delivers a high kick to his or her opponent.

SKULL-CRUSHING FINALE: The Miz grabs his opponent behind the head and drives them face-first to the mat.

SHARPSHOOTER: Bret "Hit Man" Hart wraps his opponent's legs around his own leg, turns his opponent onto their stomach and leans back.

SHELL SHOCK: Ryback hoists his opponent onto his shoulders, then falls backward, bringing his opponent onto the mat.

SISTER ABIGAIL: Bray Wyatt leans his opponent's back over his knee, and twisting, whips the opponent over, slamming them onto the ground.

STONE COLD STUNNER: Stone Cold Steve Austin holds his opponent in a three-quarter facelock, falls to a sitting position onto the mat, bouncing them backward.

SWANTON DIVE: Jeff Hardy launches himself of the top rope, flips in the air and lands back-first on his opponent.

SWEET CHIN MUSIC: Shawn Michaels runs across the ring and delivers a kick to his opponent's chin.

TOMBSTONE: Undertaker holds his opponent upside down then drops to his knees, driving him to the mat.

TADPOLE SPLASH: Like Eddie Guerrero's Frog Splash, Hornswoggle leaps from the top rope and "flattens" his opponent.

TITAN TRON: The large screen above the entrance stage on *Monday Night RAW*, *SmackDown Live*, and pay-per-view events.

VADER BOMB: Vader jumps from the second rope, crashing on top of his opponent.

WALLS OF JERICHO: Chris Jericho grabs his opponent's legs while they are on their back, hooks them over his knees, turns them over, and leans back.

WCW: Abbreviation for World Championship Wrestling, a national sports entertainment promotion that competed with WWE for television ratings supremacy for years before the company went out of business in early 2001.

INDEX

Page numbers in **bold** refer to Introducing... boxes.

1-2-3 Kid 6, 8, 12, 15
8-Ball 32

A

The Acolytes 47
Adamle, Mike 112, 116, 117
Adams, Brian *see* Crush
Air Boom 143, 148
Akebono 14
Albano, "Captain" Lou 13
Albert 59
The Alliance 62, 63, 65
Ambrose, Dean 152, 157, 167, 168, 169, 170, 172, 174, 177, 178, 179, 186, 187, 188, 189
American Alpha 188
American Badass *see* Undertaker
Anderson, Arn 61, 67
Anderson, Karl 179, 183
Andre the Giant 7, 11
Angle, Kurt 50, 52, 55, 56, 57, 58, 59, 60, 61, 62, 63, 64, 65, 70, 89, 91, 94, 95, 96, 152, 186, 187, 188, 189
Animal 34, 36
APA 47
Apollo, Phil 6
The Ascension 171
Attitude Era 6, 11, 18, 24, 28, 36, 44, 51, 53
Austin, Stone Cold Steve 11, 24, 26, 28, 29, 30, 31, 32, 33, 35, 36, 37, 38, 39, 40, 41, 44, 45, 46, 47, 52, 56, 57, 58, 59, 60, 61, 62, 63, 64, 65, 68, 69, 74, 75, 76, 78, 80, 81, 84, 85, 96, 107, 110, 111, 124, 132, 139, 140, 174
The Authority 164, 165, 167, 169, 170, 171, 172, 173, 174, 175
Awesome, Mike 62
Axel, Curtis 152, 157, 167, 171

B

Backlash 100, 108, 115, 124
Backlund, Bob 12, 16, 17, 148
Bagwell, Buff 61
Ball, Lonzo 188
Bálor, Finn 176, 180, 181, 187
Banks, Sacha **173**, 176, 177, 180, 182, 183, 184
Barker, Bob 128
Barrett, Wade 135, 136, 137, 138, 153, 157, 170, 171, 172, 175
Bartlett, Rob 6
Baszler, Shayna 189
Batista ("The Animal") 74, 81, 85, 87, 91, 94, 112, 115, 116, 118, 125, 126, 130, 131, 133, 164, 166, 167
Battleground 172, 173, 179
Bayley 184
Bearer, Paul 15, 32, 85, 155, 162
Bella, Brie 112, 116, 125, 131, 142, 148,168
Bella, Nikki 112, 116, 126, 148
Bella Twins 112, 116, 125
Benjamin, Shelton 98, 110
Benoit, Chris 53
Big Bad Booty Daddy *see* Steiner, Scott
Big Cass 178, 187
Big Show 7, 14, 44, 46, 48, 50, 52, 53, 68, 70, 99, 100, 104, 113, 123, 125, 127, 128, 131, 133, 136, 141, 145, 146, 148, 160, 169, 170, 180
Bigelow, Bam Bam ("The Beast from the East") 15, 19, 20

Bischoff, Eric 34, **70**, 71, 72, 73, 76, 80, 81, 85, 86, 87, 92, 93, 96, 97, 105, 107
Blayze, Alundra 23
Bliss, Alexa 186
Blu Brothers 21
Bodydonnas 20
Booger, Bastion 11
Booker T 58, 61, 62, 65, 74, 85, 104, 109, 110, 151, 153, 155
Borga, Ludvig 6, 11
Bossman, Big 40, 50
Bourne, Evan 143
Bragging Rights 128
Brawl for All 39
Breeze, Tyler 177
Brisco, Gerald 37, 38, 39, 55
British Bulldog 17, 22, 23, 24, 26, 28, 31, 32, 33, 49
Brothers of Destruction 42–3, 150, 157
Brown, D'Lo 39, 40, 48
Brutus "The Barber" Beefcake 6
Bryan, Daniel 140, 148, 149, 150, 151, 153, 154, 157, 158, 159, 160, 161, 164, 165, 167, 168, 170, 177, 180
Bundy, King Kong 12, 17, 20

C

Cactus Jack 25, 33, 36
    see also Foley, Mick
Cade, Lance 104
Candido, Chris 20
Cara, Sin **140**, 141, 152, 183
Carlito 94, 110
Cena, John 31, 70, 86, 90, 91, 92, 93, 95, 96, 97, 98, 99, 101, 102, 103, 104, 105, 106, 108, 109, 110, 112, 113, 115, 116, 119, 120–1, 123, 125, 127, 129, 133, 134, 135, 136, 137, 138, 139, 140, 141, 142, 143, 144, 145, 147, 148, 152, 153, 155, 157, 158, 160, 164, 166, 167, 168, 169, 170, 171, 172, 173, 179, 189
Cesaro, Antonio 154, 157, 181, 183, 189
Chainsaw Charlie 36
Charlotte *see* Flair, Charlotte
Christian 56, 59, 63, 67, 72, 77, 84, 86, 133, 157
Christopher, Brian 58
Chyna 34, 36, 37, 44, 53
Clinton, Bill 115
Clinton, Hillary 115
Coachman, Jonathan 80, 99, 110
Cole, Michael 139, 172
Coleman, Gary 92
Colter, Zeb **154**
Cornette, Jim 9, 18, 21, 26, 27, 28
The Corporation 36, 41, 44, 45, 46
Credible, Justin 58
Crush 10, 11, 13, 28, 32
Cryme Tyme 116
Crystal, John 20
Cuban, Mark 129

D

D-Generation X 17, 20, 30, 34, 36, 37, 38, 39, 41, 44, 46, 52, 69, 71, 98, 102, 103, 104, 105, 111, 118, 122, 127, 129, 131, 150
Daivari **89**
Dallas, Bo 164
Deadman *see* Undertaker
Dean, Simon 88
Del Rio, Alberto 138, 141, 143, 153, 154, 155, 157, 175, 176, 178, 180
Demento, Damien 6

Demolition 183
DiBiase, Ted 12, 15, 19, 24, 111, 116, 119, 127, 128
Diesel, "Big Daddy Cool" **8**, 12, 13, 14, 15, 18, 19, 20, 22, 23, 24, 29
Dink 16
Disciples of the Apocalypse 28, 32
Diva Search 84, 88, 95
Divas Championship 100, 116, 131, 133, 142, 148, 154, 159, 166, 167, 177
Doink 16, 19
Double J. 48
Douglas, Dean 23
Douglas, Shane 21
Dreamer, Tommy 62, 71, 101
Dudley, D-Von 59, 62
Dudley, Spike 59, 72
Dudley Boyz 59, 62, 64, 73, 174, 180

E

Earthquake 14
ECW 31, 33, 58, 62, 102, 127
Edge 56, 59, 63, 88, 90, 92, 94, 95, 96, 97, 98, 99, 101, 102, 103, 104, 105, 106, 109, 116, 122, 123, 133, 135, 140, 169
Elimination Chamber 72, 138, 164, 172
The Eliminators 31
Estrada, Armando Alejandro 106
Eugene **86**, 87, 95, 127
European Championship 31, 37, 48, 53, 58, 71
Eve 154
Evolution 74, 76, 77, 78, 79, 85, 87, 88, 91, 114, 115, 125, 126, 164, 166, 167
Extreme Championship Wrestling *see* ECW
Extreme Rules 148, 166, 179

F

Fandango 161
Farooq 29, 40
Fatu 13
Faye, Bertha 23
Federline, Kevin 104
Finkel, Howard "The Fink" 17, 71
Finlay 104, 112, 113
Flair, Charlotte **173**, 176, 177, 180, 182, 183, 184
Flair, David 67
Flair, Ric 6, 65, 66, 67, 68, 69, 74, 77, 79, 85, 87, 96, 97, 98, 102, 105, 111, 112, 113, 114, 115, 123, 125, 126, 170
Foley, Mick 25, 33, 36, 40, 44, 50, 51, 52, 53, 55, 57, 60, 78, 81, 84, 85, 97, 99, 101, 102, 107, 111, 145, 148, 155, 176, 180, 181, 182, 183, 185, 186
Fuji, Mr. 9, 10, 11, 21
Funk, Terry 101

G

Gabriel, Justin 136, 137
Gallows, Luke 131, 133, 179, 183
The Game *see* Triple H
Garcia, Lillian 71
Gianfriddo, Lou 16
Giant Gonzales 7
Glamerella 117
The Godfather 50
Godwinn, Henry 21
The Godwinns 20, 34
Gold Rush Tournament 92
Goldberg **76**, 79, 80, 81, 82–3, 84, 176, 182, 185
Goldust 21, 23, 25, 26, 27, 32, 33, 70, 74, 109, 118, 160, 161, 167, 172
Green, Seth 127
Guerrero, Chavo 95, 97, 128, 129
Guerrero, Eddie 53, 58, 68, 90, 97
Guerrero, Vickie 122, 123, 125, 144, 146, 167, 179

Gunn, "Bad Ass" Billy 17, 53, 164, 165
Gunn, Bart 39

H

Hall, Jillian 113, 129
Hall, Scott 67
Hardcore Championship 55, 71, 78, 101
Hardy, Jeff 47, 59, 60, 71, 72, 112
Hardy, Matt 47, 59, 60, 86, 87, 88, 90, 94, 95, 96
The Hardy Boyz 47, 59, 108, 186
Harper, Luke 158, 160, 164, 169
Hart, Bret "Hit Man" 7, 11, 12, 13, 14, 15, 17, 18, 19, 22, 23, 24, 25, 26, 30, 31, 33, 34, 35, 79, 129, 130, 131, 132, 133, 134, 135, 155
Hart, Bruce 11
Hart, Jimmy 6
Hart, Keith 11
Hart, Owen 9, 11, 12, 17, 19, 20, 22, 23, 27, 28, 31, 32, 33, 35, 37, 40, 47
Hart Dynasty 129, 133
Hart Foundation 17, 31, 32, 33, 34, 35
Hart-Smith, Diana 26
Hassan, Muhammad 89, 90
Hawk 34, 36
Hayes, Michael 47, 97
The Headshrinkers 13, 14
Heenan, Bobby "The Brain" 6, 7, 9, 11, 18
Hell in a Cell 25, 135, 147, 152, 153, 160, 169, 174
Helmsley, Hunter Hearst *see* Triple H
Hemme, Christy 88, 90
Hennig, Curt *see* Perfect, Mr.
Henry, Mark 40, 41, 112, 113, 128, 137, 141, 157, 172, 180
Herman, Pee Wee 136
Heyman, Paul 59, 62, 65, 67, 92, 101, 154, 156, 157, 158, 165, 168, 173, 182, 187
Highlight Reel 76, 77, 91, 115
Hogan, Hulk 6, 7, 11, 17, 27, 67, 68, 94, 95, 103, 111, 164, 165, 168, 170, 171
Holly, Bob 11, 33
Holly, Crash 55
The Honky Tonk Man 118
Hornswoggle 110, 112, 113, 125, 129, 149
Hounds of Justice 168
Hudson, Scott 61
The Hurricane 72

I

In Your House 20, 21, 27, 28, 30, 32
Intercontinental Championship 6, 10, 15, 17, 23, 26, 29, 33, 35, 60, 63, 68, 71, 108, 117, 118, 152, 153, 161, 168, 169, 170, 171, 178, 182
USS Intrepid 9
Iron Sheik 113
IRS 21
Italy, *RAW* broadcast from 108
Ivory 49

J

Jackman, Hugh 144–5
Jacqueline 40
Jacques and Pierre 9
Jamal 71
James, Brian *see* Road Dogg
James, Mickie **96**, 100, 105, 186
Jannetty, Marty 8, 12, 21, 91
Japan, *RAW* broadcast from 91
Jarrett, Jeff 17, 34, 48
Jax, Nia 184
JBL 97, 116, 118, 119, 172
Jericho, Chris 44, **48**, 53, 55, 58, 62, 64, 65, 67, 72, 76, 77, 79, 80, 84, 86, 91, 92, 95, 111, 115, 117, 118, 119, 122, 123, 124, 128, 131, 133, 135, 146, 151, 158, 168, 177, 178, 180, 183, 184

Johnson, Ahmed 23, 27, 32
Jordan, Jason 188
Judgment Day 54, 68

K

Kaitlyn 154
Kalisto 176
Kane 30, 32, 36, 37, 39, 40, 42–3, 54, 56, 62, 65, 72, 77, 78, 79, 84, 85, 86, 87, 88, 90, 92, 94, 100, 101, 145, 148, 150, 151, 157, 158, 167, 170, 172, 174, 175, 179, 180
Kanellis, Maria 90
Kanyon, Chris 63
Keibler, Stacy 61, 64
Kelly, Kelly 133, 142, 145
Kelly, Kevin 18, 29
Kennedy, Mr. 109, 112, 115
Khali, The Great 89, 108, 110, 112
Kidd, Tyson 129
Kim, Gail 78, 131
King Booker *see* Booker T
King of the Ring 21, 25, 27, 39, 55, 61, 63, 104, 109, 115, 137, 171
Kingston, Kofi 112, **116**, 128, 133, 137, 143, 146, 148, 152, 153, 157
Kozlov, Vladimir 122, 137
Kronus, John 31

L

Lana 168
Langston, Big E **152**, 161
Lashley, Bobby 107, 108, 109
Laurinaitis, John 144, 146, 148, 179
Lawler, Jerry "The King" 13, 14, 16, 18, 21, 22, 27, 31, 55, 59, 73, 80, 84, 99, 100, 109, 110, 138, 139, 153
Layfield, John Bradshaw 47, 116, 118, 119
The League of Nations 175, 178
Lee, AJ 146, 149, 150, 151, 152, 153, 159, 166, 167
The Legacy 109, 119, 123, 127, 128
Legion of Doom 34, 36, 74, 77
Lesnar, Brock **67**, 69, 71, 72, 76, 84, 85, 148, 150, 151, 154, 156, 157, 158, 159, 164, 165, 167, 168, 169, 170, 171, 172, 173, 174, 176, 180, 182, 184, 185, 188
Lita 55, 56, 60, 84, 86, 87, 88, 89, 90, 92, 94, 95, 98, 103, 105, 148
Little Beaver 17
Long, Teddy 84, 179
Lothario, Jose 30
Lothario, Pete 30
Love, Dude 25, 33, 37
    see also Foley, Mick
The Lucha Dragons 180
Luger, Lex 9, 11, 12, 13, 15, 17, 19, 21, 22
Lumberjacks 118
The Lunatic Fringe 178
Lynch, Becky **173**, 177

M

Mabel and Mo ("Men on a Mission") 22
McCain, John 115
McCool, Michelle 137
McDaniel, "Chief" Wahoo 13
McGillicutty, Michael 143
McMahon, Linda 57, 59, 79, 96
McMahon, Mr. 6, 11, 12, 15, 16, 23, 24, 25, 30, 33, 34, 35, 36, 37, 38, 39, 40, 41, 44, 45, 46, 47, 49, 50, 52, 53, 54, 55, 57, 59, 60, 61, 62, 65, 66, 67, 68, 69, 70, 79, 85, 89, 92, 96, 97, 98, 99, 100, 102, 106, 107, 108, 109, 110, 111, 113, 115, 116, 118, 122, 123, 124, 126, 127, 131, 132, 134, 141, 142, 143, 144, 146, 150, 151, 152, 154, 157, 158, 159, 169, 175, 176, 177, 178

McMahon, Shane 41, 45, 48, 53, 54, 59, 60, 61, 62, 65, 79, 100, 102, 107, 118, 123, 176, 177, 178, 179, 180

McMahon, Stephanie 45, 46, 50, 52, 53, 55, 56, 57, 59, 60, 62, 64, 65, 66, 67, 71, 118, 119, 123, 154, 159, 160, 164, 167, 168, 171, 173, 176, 177, 178, 179, 180, 182, 183, 185

McMahon, Vince see McMahon, Mr.

McMahon family 58, 96, 102, 103, 111, 122, 123, 138, 157, 170, 176

Maddox, Brad 152, 158, 167

Mae Young Classic 189

Maivia, Rocky see The Rock

Malenko, Dean 53

Manhattan Center (New York) 6

Mankind 25, 33, 39, 40, 44, 46, 48, 49, 50, 51

see also Foley, Mick

Mantaur 21

Manu 119

Marella, Santino 108, 110, 117, 118, 124, 129, 137, 149

Maria 105

Marshall, Debra 48

Martel, Rick 10

Martel, Sherri 7

Maryse 131, 133, 178, 189

Massaro, Ashley 95

Masters, Chris 92, 107, 129

Maven 67

Mayweather, Floyd "Money" 113

Melina 131

Mero, Marc 29, 40

Michaels, Shawn ("The Heartbreak Kid") 6, 8, 10, 11, 12, 13, 14, 15, 18, 19, 20, 21, 22, 23, 24, 25, 26, 27, 28, 30, 31, 32, 33, 34, 35, 36, 37, 41, 54, 55, 69, 71, 72, 73, 79, 82–3, 88, 90, 91, 94, 95, 96, 97, 99, 100, 102, 103, 105, 106, 108, 110, 113, 114, 115, 117, 118, 119, 122, 129, 130, 131, 132, 137, 140, 147, 151, 156, 161, 170

Million Dollar Corporation 12, 15, 17, 19, 20

Million Dollar Man see DiBiase, Ted

Ministry of Darkness 45, 46, 47

The Miz 98, 101, 118, 125, 127, 130, 131, 133, 134, 136, 138, 140, 145, 151, 168, 178, 186, 187, 188, 189

Mizdow, Damien 168

Monday Night RAW

15th anniversary celebrations 111

20th anniversary 154

100th episode 19

800th episode 112, 118

1000th episode 146, 150

brand split between *RAW* and *SmackDown* 176, 179, 180

cancelled by snowstorm 170

debut 6, 96

Trump buys 122, 126

Monday Night Wars 18, 22, 35, 36, 37, 38, 44, 49, 58, 60, 85

Money in the Bank 92, 97, 98, 101, 109, 116, 117, 136, 142, 143, 151, 157, 158, 159, 160, 167, 170, 171, 172, 175, 179

Money Inc. 6

Monsoon, Gorilla 11, 18, 19, 24, 26, 29

Montreal Screwjob 14, 30, 33, 34, 79, 129, 131

Moolah, Fabulous 49, 71

Moon, Max 6

Morrison, John 118, 133, 134, 138, 145

The Mountie 11

The Muppets 144

Murdoch, Trevor 104

MVP see Porter, Montel Vontavious

Mysterio, Rey 96, 133, 141, 143, 151, 152, 161, 164

N

Nash, Kevin 29, 67, 69, 76, 79, 143, 144

Natalya 129

Nation of Domination 28, 32, 36, 39, 40, 104

Neidhart, Jim "The Anvil" 17

Neville, Adrian 164, 171

New Age Outlaws 17, 36, 37, 39, 50, 164, 165

The New Day 116, 152, 172, 174, 183, 186

"New Generation" 12

New World Order see nWo

The Nexus 130, 134, 135, 136, 137, 138

Nicky 99, 105

see also Ziggler, Dolph

Nielsen, Leslie 15

Night of Champions 159, 167, 168

Nitro 7, 18, 22, 35, 37, 38, 60, 70

nWo 8, 27, 46, 67, 69, 168

NXT Takeover Arrival 164

O

Obama, Barack 115

One Night Stand 31, 90, 93, 96, 101, 102

O'Neill, Shaquille 127

O'Neill, Titus 183

Orton, Randy ("The Viper") 72, 74, 79, 81, 84, 85, 87, 88, 91, 92, 103, 104, 105, 106, 109, 110, 111, 112, 113, 115, 119, 122, 123, 125, 126, 127, 128, 135, 136, 139, 141, 158, 159, 164, 166, 169, 170, 174, 180

Osbourne, Ozzy 129

Osbourne, Sharon 129

Otunga, David 133, 136, 143

Owens, Kevin 172, 177, 180, 181, 183, 184

P

Page, Diamond Dallas 61, 67

Paige 166, 167

The Patriot 33

Patterson, Pat 37, 38, 55

Payback 178

Payton, Walter 15

The Peep Show 77

Perfect, Mr. 6, 8, 29

Phoenix, Beth 98, 100, 117, 128, 148

Pillman, Brian 17, 27, 29, 33

Pipe Bomb 138, 142, 159

Piper, "Rowdy" Roddy 13, 24, 25, 95, 105, 118, 123, 148, 173

Polo, Johnny (Raven) 9, 12, 13

Porter, Montel Vontavious 124, 128

The Price Is Right 122, 128

Prime Time Wrestling 6

Primo & Epico 148

Punk, CM 102, 116, 117, 131, 133, 134, 137, 138, 139, 142, 143, 144, 145, 146, 148, 149, 150, 151, 152, 154, 155, 157, 158, 159, 160, 161

Q

"Quebec Province Rules" 9

Quebecers 12, 13, 14

R

R-Truth 133, 134, 148, 171

The Radicalz 53

Ramon, Razor "The Bad Guy" 6, 8, 10, 11, 12, 13, 15, 21, 23, 24, 29

Rated RKO 104, 105

Raven 55, 62

see also Polo, Johnny

RAW Roulette 72, 81, 135

Ray, Bubba 62, 72

Regal, William 58, 60, 64, 68, 73, 86, 87, 91, 104, 110, 115

Reigns, Roman 152, 160, 170, 172, 174,

175, 176, 177, 178, 179, 180, 181, 183, 185, 186, 187, 188, 189

The Revival 186

Rhodes, Cody 109, 116, 119, 127, 128, 146, 152, 160, 161, 164, 167, 172

Rhodes, Dusty 21, 105, 109, 155, 172, 173

Rhodes Brothers 164

Rhyno 59

Richards, Steven 72

Rikishi 55, 57, 60, 148

Riley, Alex 136, 148

Road Dogg 17, 39, 53, 164, 165

Road Warrior Animal 77

Road Warrior Hawk 77

Roberts, Jake "The Snake" 91

Robinson, Charles 64

The Rock 24, 29, 30, 35, 36, 40, 41, 44, 45, 46, 48, 49, 50, 51, 52, 53, 54, 55, 56, 57, 59, 60, 62, 64, 65, 67, 68, 69, 74, 75, 76, 77, 85, 87, 107, 138, 139, 140, 141, 145, 147, 150, 152, 154, 155, 168

The Rockers 90, 91

Rollins, Seth 152, 160, 164, 167, 168, 169, 170, 171, 172, 173, 174, 175, 176, 179, 181, 183, 184, 187, 189

Rosey 71

Ross, Jim 18, 19, 29, 31, 35, 55, 59, 65, 72, 73, 79, 80, 96, 116, 145

Rotunda, Mike 113

Rowan, Erick 158, 164, 170

Royal Rumble 12, 18, 20, 23, 30, 36, 44, 52, 66, 106, 112, 153, 154, 164, 169, 170, 176, 177

Rude, Ravishing Rick 34, 69

Rusev 168, 170, 175, 180, 181, 182

Ryback 152, 153, 154, 167, 170

Ryder, Zack 134, 144, 145, 146, 178

S

Sable 29, 40

Samoa Joe 184, 187, 188

Samu 13

The Sandman 110

Sandow, Damien 152, 160, 171

Sane, Kairi 189

Santo, Larry 19

Saturn, Perry 31, 53, 59

Savage, Randy "Macho Man" 6, 10, 13, 15, 17, 171

Shamrock, Ken 31, 32, 45, 46

Shatner, William 18

Sheamus 127, 129, 137, 138, 140, 144, 148, 164, 167, 171, 175, 178, 181, 183, 189

Shelby, Dr. 151

The Shield 152, 154, 157, 160, 161, 164, 166, 167, 168, 169, 170, 179

Sho-Miz 131, 133

Sid, Sycho 18, 19, 20, 21, 23, 24, 27, 30, 32, 148

Simmons, Ron 47

Sincere, Salvatore 29

Skip 20

Skull 32

Slammy Awards 100, 119, 137, 145, 153, 161, 169

Slater, Heath 136, 137, 148, 149, 180

Slaughter, Sgt. 33, 39, 90, 127

Slick 150

SmackDown 49, 56, 60, 63, 68, 70, 71, 72, 84, 86, 88, 90, 91, 92, 93, 94, 96, 101, 104, 109, 116, 122, 124, 125, 127, 128, 133, 141, 151, 158, 167, 173, 176, 179, 180, 186, 189

Smith, Davey Boy see British Bulldog

Smith, David Hart 129

The Smoking Gunns 20, 22, 28

Snitsky 88, 89, 90

Snooki 145

Snow, Al 67, 80

Snuka, Jimmy "Superfly" 123

Socko, Mr. 40, 48, 49, 85

175, 176, 177, 178, 179, 180, 181, 183, 185, 186, 187, 188, 189

Spike TV 96

Spirit Squad 99, 100, 102, 105

Stardust 167, 177

see also Rhodes, Cody

Steamboat, Ricky "The Dragon" 123, 124

steel cage matches 17, 22, 54, 60, 90, 104, 118, 126, 135, 164, 166, 168, 181

Steiner, Scott 73, 74

Steiner Brothers 9, 11

Stewart, Jon 170, 171

Stiller, Ben 48

Sting 170, 173

Storm, Lance 62, 63, 73

Stratus, Trish 55, 84, 86, 89, 90, 96, 100, 103, 105, 120–1, 128

Strongbow, "Chief" Jay 13

Strowman, Braun 158, 183, 186, 188

Styles, AJ 177, 179

Styles, Joey 96, 100

SummerSlam 9, 15, 20, 21, 23, 33, 47, 48, 49, 88, 102, 103, 110, 135, 143, 151, 158, 159, 167, 168, 173, 174, 180, 181, 188

Sumo wrestling 14

Sunny 20, 29

Survivor Series 11, 14, 18, 20, 23, 24, 29, 34, 35, 41, 52, 64, 65, 72, 73, 105, 145, 152, 161, 169, 175, 182

Swagger, Jack 144, 146, 154, 155

T

Tajiri 63, 91

Tamina 133

Tatanka 6, 13, 15, 17, 19, 21

Tatsu, Yoshi 137

Taylor, Lawrence 19

Tazz 55, 62

Team Hell No 152

Team Rhodes Scholars 152

Tensai, Lord 148

Test 46, 50, 51, 58

Three Minute Warning 71

Tomko, Tyson 86

Too Cold Scorpio 38

Torres, Eve 131, 133

Total Bellas 116, 158

Total Divas 116, 158, 159

Tough Enough 140

Tribute to the Troops 97

Triple H 11, 20, 26, 29, 30, 33, 34, 36, 37, 39, 41, 46, 48, 50, 52, 53, 54, 55, 56, 57, 58, 59, 60, 66, 67, 71, 72, 73, 74, 75, 76, 77, 78, 79, 86, 87, 88, 89, 91, 94, 96, 97, 99, 102, 103, 105, 110, 113, 114, 115, 116, 122, 123, 127, 129, 131, 133, 140, 142, 143, 144, 146, 147, 148, 151, 153, 154, 156, 157, 159, 160, 164, 165, 166, 167, 170, 175, 177, 181, 185

Trump, Donald 106, 107, 109, 122, 126

Tunney, Jack 12, 16

Turner, Ted 49

Tyson, Mike 36, 37, 130, 131

U

The Ultimate Warrior 24, 26, 27, 166

Umaga 105, 106, 107, 108

Undertaker 6, 7, 11, 12, 15, 18, 22, 24, 28, 30, 32, 36, 37, 39, 40, 42–3, 44, 45, 46, 47, 48, 52, 54, 55, 56, 61, 62, 65, 67, 68, 84, 85, 92, 111, 113, 122, 130, 132, 137, 139, 140, 145, 146, 147, 150, 153, 155, 157, 162–3, 164, 165, 173, 174, 175, 185

Unforgiven 49, 56, 88, 103, 105, 117

Unified Tag Team Championship 131, 133

The Union 46

United Kingdom, *RAW* first broadcast in 84, 88

United States Championship 63, 117, 133, 134, 146, 157, 167, 170, 171, 172, 173, 174, 176, 184

USA Network 96

Uso, Jey 165

Uso, Jimmy 165

Uso Brothers 133, 137, 161, 164, 165

V

Vachon, Luna 7

Vader 9, 24, 27, 28, 30, 31, 32, 35, 148, 149

Van Dam, Rob 31, 58, 62, 64, 65, 68, 71, 72, 73, 77, 78, 85, 94, 98, 99, 101, 102, 111, 158

Vega, Savio 26, 29

Venis, Val 38

Ventura, Jesse "The Body" 129

Victoria 78

Volkoff, Nikolai 15, 113

W

WCW

join forces with ECW against WWE 62

launch Nitro 18

WWE dominate in ratings 52

WWE overtake in ratings 36, 37

WWE purchased 58

see also Monday Night Wars; Nitro

White, Kerwin see Guerrero, Chavo

Windham, Barry 113

Wippleman, Harvey 17, 23

Women's Championship 23, 40, 49, 56, 78, 89, 96, 100, 103, 105, 166, 173, 180, 182, 183, 184, 186

Woods, Xavier 152

World Heavyweight Championship 20, 38, 72, 73, 74, 76, 77, 79, 80, 87, 88, 89, 91, 92, 104, 116, 117, 118, 123, 154, 155, 157, 160, 161

WrestleMania 6, 7, 11, 12, 13, 14, 15, 17, 18, 19, 20, 24, 25, 26, 30, 32, 37, 39, 41, 44, 53, 58, 59, 60, 67, 74, 75, 84, 87, 91, 92, 96, 99, 100, 101, 106, 107, 108, 109, 113, 114, 123, 124, 130, 131, 132, 137, 138, 139, 140, 146, 147, 148, 153, 155, 156, 164, 165, 166, 167, 170, 171, 177, 178, 185, 186

Wright, Paul see Big Show

WWE Championship 12, 18, 20, 23, 24, 25, 32, 34, 37, 38, 39, 44, 47, 48, 52, 54, 57, 64, 68, 72, 98, 102, 110, 112, 136, 138, 143, 146, 149, 152, 154, 170, 171, 175, 180

WWE World Tag Team Championship 9, 20, 31, 32, 33, 39, 48, 59, 86, 91, 105, 108, 116, 137, 143, 148, 160, 165

Wyatt, Bray 158, 166, 168, 170, 172, 174, 175, 178, 186, 187

The Wyatt Family 158, 160, 161, 164, 166, 168, 174, 175

X

X-Pac 37, 41, 58, 68

Y

Yankem, Isaac 22

Yokozuna 6, 9, 10, 11, 12, 13, 14, 20, 21, 22, 23, 28

Young, Mae 71, 118

Z

Zayn, Sami 182, 183

Ziggler, Dolph 99, 112, 117, 144, 151, 152, 157, 168, 170, 177, 182

Zip 20

Senior Editor Laura Palosuo
Editor Pamela Afram
Senior Designer Nathan Martin
Designer Jaynan Spengler
Pre-Production Producer Marc Staples
Producer Lloyd Robertson
Managing Editor Paula Regan
Managing Art Editor Jo Connor
Art Director Lisa Lanzarini
Publisher Julie Ferris
Publishing Director Simon Beecroft

Global Publishing Manager Steve Pantaleo
Vice President, Consumer Products Sylvia Lee
Executive Vice President, Consumer Products Casey Collins
Photo department Josh Tottenham, Frank Vitucci,
Georgiana Dallas, Jamie Nelson, Melissa Halladay, Mike Moran
Vice President, Intellectual Property Lauren Dienes-Middlen
Senior Vice President, Creative Services Stan Stanski
Creative Director John Jones
Project Manager Sara Vazquez

Dorling Kindersley would also like to thank Helen Peters for the index;
Melanie Scott for the proofread; and Beth Davies, Alastair Dougall,
Hannah Gulliver-Jones, and Joseph Stewart at DK for editorial assistance.

First American Edition, 2018
Published in the United States by DK Publishing
345 Hudson Street, New York, New York 10014

Page design copyright ©2018 Dorling Kindersley Limited
DK, a Division of Penguin Random House LLC
18 19 20 21 22 10 9 8 7 6 5 4 3 2 1
001–308537–May/2018

A catalog record for this book is available from the Library of Congress.

ISBN 978-1-4654-7372-1

DK books are available at special discounts when purchased in bulk for sales
promotions, premiums, fund-raising, or educational use. For details, contact:
DK Publishing Special Markets, 345 Hudson Street, New York, New York 10014
SpecialSales@dk.com

Printed in China

A WORLD OF IDEAS:
SEE ALL THERE IS TO KNOW

www.dk.com
www.wwe.com